D0712374

European Perspectives

A Series in Social Thought and Cultural Criticism

Lawrence D. Kritzman, Editor

European Perspectives presents outstanding books by leading European thinkers. With both classic and contemporary works, the series aims to shape the major intellectual controversies of our day and to facilitate the tasks of historical understanding.

For a complete list of books in the series, visit www.cup.columbia.edu.

White Ink

European Perspectives

843.914
C499w

White Ink

Interviews on Sex, Text and Politics

HÉLÈNE CIXOUS

Edited by Susan Sellers

WITHDRAWN

LIBRARY ST. MARY'S COLLEGE

Columbia University Press
New York

Columbia University Press
Publishers Since 1893
New York

Selection and compilation © 2008 Hélène Cixous and Susan Sellers. For individual pieces see the acknowledgements.

This book is copyright under the Berne Convention.
All rights reserved.

Published simultaneously outside North America by Acumen Publishing Limited.

Library of Congress Cataloging-in-Publication Data

Cixous, Hélène, 1937–
    White ink : interviews on sex, text, and politics / Hélène Cixous;
edited by Susan Sellers.
        p. cm. — (European perspectives)
    Includes bibliographical references and index.
    ISBN 978-0-231-14776-7 (cloth : alk. paper) — ISBN 978-0-231-14777-4
    (pbk. : alk. paper) — ISBN 978-0-231-51971-7 (electronic)
    1. Cixous, Hélène, 1937—Interviews. 2. Authors, French—20th
century—Interviews. I. Sellers, Susan. II. Title.

PQ2663.I9Z46 2009
840.9′0091—dc22

                                                        2008026475

∞

Columbia University Press books are printed on permanent and durable acid-free paper.

Designed by Kate Williams and typeset by Graphicraft Limited, Hong Kong.
Printed by Biddles Ltd, King's Lynn.

c 10 9 8 7 6 5 4 3 2 1
p 10 9 8 7 6 5 4 3 2 1

For Elizabeth Fallaize

Contents

Acknowledgements

I would like to thank Eric Prenowitz, whose vision and knowledge has shaped so much of what is to follow. Eric began this project and played a crucial role in deciding the list of contents, and I would like, here, to pay full tribute to his invaluable contribution. My publishers Steven Gerrard and Tristan Palmer at Acumen have been extraordinarily patient and helpful during the long period of preparation of this volume, responding swiftly to emails and always offering valuable advice. I would like to express gratitude to the Carnegie Trust for the Universities of Scotland, whose award of a travel grant enabled me to undertake research in Paris and to interview Hélène Cixous. The School of English at the University of St Andrews played an essential role in assisting this project, providing support in a variety of ways. Many individuals contributed to this volume and I would like to thank, in particular, the following: Ian Blyth for procuring and copying articles and work on the bibliography; Ian Blyth, Hope Jennings, Elizabeth Lindley, Tristan Palmer, Ravenel Richardson, Abigail Rine and Jeremy Thurlow for helping me think about interview questions; Amaleena Damlé for hours spent trawling electronic bibliographies; Sarah Dillon for checking a Derrida query; Lucy Garnier for many diverse services including braving the bureaucracy of the BN; Jane Goldman for taking the strain on another project as the deadline for this book loomed; Elizabeth Fallaize, Lorna Milne, Judith Still and Emma Wilson for putting me in touch with wonderful translators; Stephanie Amar Flood for responding to emails containing many questions small and large; Andrew Murphy for confirming a Shakespeare query; Marguerite Sandré for chasing down impossible-to-procure articles and making numerous invaluable suggestions; Jim Stewart for transcribing my interview with Hélène Cixous; Ben and Jeremy Thurlow for coping with all the absences and stresses this project entailed; Fabien Troivaux for assisting with the bibliography, permissions and answering a query about *Le Monde*. Finally, I would like to thank my translators, who have given themselves unstintingly to this most difficult of tasks, and above all Hélène Cixous — without whose inspiring work and unfailing generosity this volume would not exist.

The editor and publishers gratefully acknowledge the following copyright holders for permission to reproduce material: Flammarion and Jean-Louis de Rambures for the interview "When I do not write, it is as if I had died", originally published as "Quand je n'écris pas, c'est comme si j'étais morte", in *Comment travaillent les écrivains*, (Paris: Flammarion, 1978), pp. 56–63; *Substance*, Christiane Makward, Beatrice Cameron and Ann Liddle for the interview "My text is written in white and black, in 'milk and night'", in *Substance* **13**, 1976, pp. 19–37, copyright 1976 by the Board of Regents of the University of Wisconsin, reproduced by permission; *Women's Education des femmes*, Kathleen O'Grady and Eric Prenowitz for "Guardian of language", in *Women's Education des femmes* (Canadian Congress for Learning Opportunities) **12**(4), Winter 1996, pp. 8–10; *Politis* and Dominque Lecoq for "Against the emotion of history", originally published as "Les Motions contre l'émotion de l'histoire", in *Politis* 7 July 1988, pp. 46–8; *Fabula* and Henri Quéré for "The novel today", originally published as "Le Roman d'aujourd'hui", in *Fabula* **3**, March 1984, pp. 147–58; Rodopi and Christa Stevens for "The play of fiction", originally published as "Questions à Hélène Cixous", in *(en)jeux de la communication romanesque*, Suzan van Dijk and Christa Stevens (eds), (Amsterdam: Rodopi, 1994), pp. 321–2; René de Ceccatty and *Le Monde* for "Literature suspends death", originally published as "La Littérature suspend la mort" in *Le Monde*, 16 December 2005, "Le Monde des livres", p. 12; *Hors Cadre* for "The author between text and theatre", originally published as "L'auteur entre texte et théâtre" in *Hors Cadre* (Paris: Presses Universitaires de Vincennes), 8: "L'Etat d'auteur", 1990, pp. 33–65; *Genesis* and Mireille Calle-Gruber for "In the beginnings, there were many", originally published as "Aux commencements, il y eut pluriel . . .", *Genesis*, Spring 1997, pp. 131–41; *La Quinzaine Littéraire* and Bertrand Leclair for "Language is the only refuge", originally published as "La langue est le seul refuge", in *La Quinzaine Littéraire* **793**, 1–15 October 2000, pp. 10–12; *Les Nouveaux Cahiers* and Jacqueline Sudaka for "Being a Jewish woman: an ideal position", originally published as "Être femme juive, situation idéale", in *Les Nouveaux Cahiers* **46**, Autumn 1976, pp. 92–5; *Oxford Literary Review* and Martin McQuillan for an extract from "You race towards that secret, which escapes", in Martin McQuillan (ed.), "Reading Cixous Writing", *The Oxford Literary Review*, 24, 2002, pp. 185–201, extract on pp. 192–5; *Cahiers Renaud-Barrault* for "On Marguerite Duras: Michel Foucault and Hélène Cixous", originally published as "'À propos de Marguerite Duras', par Michel Foucault et Hélène Cixous",

Cahiers Renaud-Barrault **89**, 1975, pp. 8–22; Ashley Thompson (trans.), "From the Word of Life: A Dialogue Between Jacques Derrida and Hélène Cixous", *New Literary History* **37**(1), 2006, pp. 1–13, copyright *New Literary History*, University of Virginia, reprinted with permission of Johns Hopkins University Press, originally published as "Du mot à la vie: un dialogue entre Jacques Derrida et Hélène Cixous", *Magazine Littéraire* **430**, April 2004, pp. 22–9; Éditions Galilée and Frédéric-Yves Jeannet for "But the Earth still turns, and not as badly as all that", extract from Hélène Cixous and Frédéric-Yves Jeannet, *Rencontre terrestre: Arcachon, Roosevelt Island, Paris Montsouris, Manhattan, Cuernavaca*, (Paris: Galilée, 2005), pp. 100–102.

Every effort has been made to contact the copyright holders of material reprinted in *White Ink*. However, if anyone has inadvertently been missed we will be pleased to rectify this in any future edition.

Editor's note

Hélène Cixous has given many interviews in the course of her long and distinguished career. In selecting the interviews for this volume, I have kept a number of criteria in mind. I have tried to cover as broad a spectrum of Hélène Cixous's interests as possible, so that while several interviews reflect her primary engagement with the act of writing, there are also those that encompass her work as a critic and teacher, as well as those that prompt her to reflect on topics such as gender, faith, politics, art and the environment. Hélène Cixous's first book was published in 1967, and so another objective has been to select interviews that span all four decades of her writing career. Thus I have chosen to include examples of early discussions — such as the 1976 interview with Jean-Louis de Rambures — as well as more recent exchanges. The collection also contains two new interviews with Hélène Cixous recorded in September 2007.

Hélène Cixous's interviewers have been writers, theorists, scholars, researchers, journalists, and a further consideration in selecting material has been to present something of this diversity. Consequently, the interviews range from dialogues with peers — as in the exchanges with Michel Foucault and Jacques Derrida towards the end of the volume — to media interviews intended for the general public, often coinciding with the appearance of a book or play. Although it has been a deliberate policy to print interviews in their entirety, two exceptions have been made and excerpts have been given from Frédéric-Yves Jeannet's book of recorded oral and written exchanges with Hélène Cixous, *Rencontre terrestre: Arcachon, Roosevelt Island, Paris Montsouris, Manhattan, Cuernavaca*, and from a substantial public interview with Martin McQuillan to which members of the audience were invited to contribute. Finally, wherever a choice presented itself, it has been my conscious intention to privilege interviews that have not been translated into English before, and which appear in hard-to-locate or out-of-print journals rather than in more accessible book form.

Although a few of the interviews collected here were conducted in English, most have been translated — many especially for this volume. Where this has been the case translators have been asked to remain as close to the original French as possible, thereby respecting Hélène Cixous's own insistence on the need for fidelity (see, for example, "You race towards that secret, which escapes" on pp. 145–7). Whenever the inevitable loss the translation process incurs was felt to be too acute, the French has been inserted in parenthesis into the text, or occasionally commented on in a note.

Susan Sellers
University of St Andrews

Preface: On being interviewed

Interview with Susan Sellers.

This interview was conducted in English at Hélène Cixous's home in Paris on 4 September 2007

SS In an early interview with Henri Quéré,[1] you say that for you the spoken word is secondary to the written word. And yet it seems to me that in your interviews — of which you've done many over the course of your career — you often take a great deal of pleasure in the possibilities of the spoken word. There is a sense, in your interviews, that the spoken word can transport in the way you suggest writing transports us in our thinking and understanding. Reading through your interviews, I am also struck that you frequently put things differently to the way you put them in your writing. Do you still feel that the spoken word is secondary to the written word? How do you view your interviews?

CIXOUS I feel I'm not an artist when I write orally, which is obvious because you can't be equivocal — or at least I can't — when you speak. The indirectness, the obliquity of writing, the multiplicity — of layers of signifiers etc. — is almost excluded from the act of writing orally. Why do I say writing orally? Because it is writing. It's simpler, thinner — a threadlike writing. I don't reject the idea of it, but I know it's less illuminated, less inspired. Even the circumstances are less favourable. There's noise around us now. I know you'll tell me that when I write it doesn't work like this, but there is silence around writing. I would like to speak silently.

How do I feel about my interviews? It's not a general feeling because each interview is painted differently, according to the situation of interlocution. Of course, half the situation is signed, created, suggested by the other. So every time it's different. And every time it's differently dangerous, because the responsibility has to be shared — even though the public will attribute the so-called main character (who is not the main character) with full responsibility.

SS You often talk about your writing as being in dialogue with your reader. In an interview, one is immediately and obviously in dialogue — with the interviewer's questions, knowledge, implicit and explicit desires, prejudices and so on. Do you find this dialogue in interview productive? And are you also aware of a dialogue-behind-this-dialogue with the projected reader of the interview? If so, how does this shape and stimulate what you say?

CIXOUS What is interesting when you write is to imagine that your reader is not yet born, so someone writing in say 1824 might think "my idea will be born in 1924". Of course, it's totally poetical; you can imagine what you want, invent the reader. There is excitement and freedom in this dialogue.

Writing is silent, as I've said: you can imagine a kind of music — with pauses etc.; in an interview you don't have this. You can't simply stop and say "now I'm writing mentally for half an hour" as I do when I write, it's impossible. The interview runs uninterrupted: there's always the same rhythm, always a set amount of time. Writing is much subtler than this. It's intimately free. It's the other. When you're in so-called realistic dialogue, you're inhibited from all sides. Of course inhibition can have a productive effect: it compels you to come to the point quickly!

SS Has an interview ever taken you into territory you've not knowingly entered in your writing?

CIXOUS When you write you are always in unknown territory, the same when you speak: but it's true that in the exchange in dialogue, in live dialogue, you may come upon unexpected thoughts. You suddenly realize that the other introduces something vital inside what you're thinking.

SS In your writing you are always careful to go back over what you've written before submitting it for publication. This is almost impossible to do with interviews. How do you feel about this? Have you ever wanted to take back something you have said in an interview?

CIXOUS To tell you the truth I can feel very miserable about this, not because I want to take back something that I've said — but because something has been misheard. This happens all the time, not because the interviewer fails but because you realize that dialogues develop on a moving surface of misunderstanding. It's the ordinary way of exchange: a mixture of guesswork and misunderstanding.

SS What is the best kind of interview?

CIXOUS An interview with a child, because it prompts total innocence. Or with God . . .

SS Are there any questions you dread being asked?

CIXOUS No!

NOTE

1. See pp. 15–25.

Part I: Writing the enigma

1. The play of fiction

Interview with Christa Stevens. Translated by Suzanne Dow.

This interview might also be translated as "The fiction-writing game" or "The stakes of fiction". It originally appeared as "Questions à Hélène Cixous" [Questions for Hélène Cixous], in *(en)jeux de la communication romanesque*, Suzan van Dijk & Christa Stevens (eds), 321–2 (Amsterdam: Rodopi, 1994).

CS Hélène Cixous, you have often described your work as a journey or wandering [*cheminement*] — a journey that has taken you from "the unconscious stage" — that is, from personal and internal texts — to "the History stage", or the major plays you wrote for the *Théâtre du Soleil*. These wanderings take you towards the Other, towards others, be they your historical contemporaries, or, in the exploration of the "I", those others of the I itself. And within that journey lies another that tells the story of the quest of someone making her way in the dark, with her eyes closed, towards the light, in her joys, her suffering, her contradictions, her crimes too. You take great risks along the way, entering territory where you don't know what you'll find. And yet, how can one communicate what is, by definition, outside the field of vision, of naming, of representation? How can one convey this darkness, transmit the untransmissable, the as-yet unknown, or what is likely to go unseen?

CIXOUS A humble word like "wandering" really is the right way to put it, since humble is what is close to the earth — *humus* — and bespeaks the humility of writing. I think that anyone who's writing in a particular direction, who experiences writing as a search, feels like they are on a journey. That word goes back to Rimbaud, to Kafka, to Heidegger's *Holzwege*. It's a drive, a propensity, towards making ground, but not only towards making ground. It's a quest. The word "wandering" conveys the slowness, the step-by-step [*pas à pas*] element, which is really important. For me, it's the only approach that allows one to move towards truth — not to reach it, because it's a long way off, but to go towards it, where step-by-step is the only way to move forward. I'm playing here on all the senses of *pas* in French — namely, "step", "footprint" and the idea of negation — without skipping any either, because inner, psychic or spiritual exploration can only be achieved with patience, or "pas-science" — or knowing how to set your own pace and knowing your limits, your resistances, when to retrace your steps. If you skip anything — be it a step or a barrier, you're repressing. But that doesn't mean you have to go at it at a sprint, or at a snail's pace either: it is possible to go step-by-step, taking each hurdle as it comes, and quickly too. That's exactly how writing makes its way: step-by-step, from hurdle to hurdle, and yet extremely fast. That's its appeal. A sentence, its signifying potential, its signifying energy, can be such that you cover an incredible distance, just like Ariel in *The Tempest*; you close your eyes and you're on the other side of the world, and yet every step of the way it was you who covered all that ground.

When diving into something like that, when going right down into the depths, plumbing the depths of the "I", you're choosing the mouth as the way into the "I". That's your entry point. There is another way, but it's not via one's own self, which in any case, deep down, will take you to that sea-bed of a common humanity. It's *other people*. It's them, they, (wo)men . . . It's possible to begin a quest by entering humanity via other people — namely, the Other Self. But in the end I'd still be entering the same stage — the stage of the heart — with however many characters there are, and with their various roles, functions, destinies. That's what allows you to make observations at various degrees of remove, with microscopes or telescopes. From there you can see something tiny or huge, but always human nature playing itself out.

As for the darkness, it's not that I've got a theory of it. It's just that experience has always shown me domains where there's a shift [*où je me déplace*]. When I start writing, I'm feeling my way in the dark. It's a kind of darkness that's not altogether black — there are a few indicators, lights to guide me, black stars. But the darkness is the one in charge. It's the darkness in which all human beings live. It's there behind the door. As soon as you enter thought, there it is. As a general rule, we don't live behind thought — by which I mean thought that has already been expressed. We don't follow along behind discourse. We are always there in the strip-light or half-light of the already-expressed. But the dark part of ourselves — where psychoanalysis has built its kingdom — is there, all the time, behind our every action, every single day. I sometimes think back to chapters of my life that consisted of years at a stretch when I was myself a character in these kinds of plays, which I didn't view as such at the time, which I couldn't then see as part of the theatre of human life.

To cite a literary equivalent, it's the material that Ibsen or Chekov draw on. What are Ibsen or Chekov doing? They enter a perfectly contemporary, middle-class home. Strindberg as well, but with him there's something else too. You think you're going into a house — the home of Mr or Mrs Gabler — and you find your- self in hell. What's the difference between this hell and Dante's? The difference is that it's a hell veiled by social appearances, kinship structures, etc. The characters are ravaged, wracked, by demons. They're torn apart, tortured, skinned alive, boiled alive, etc., and they can't even say so. They are in the most horrendous pain but they're not supposed to scream at the table. That's precisely why I don't like that kind of theatre because there's to be no screaming, such that the whole thing cannot but end with a gunshot.

We are all walking on a volcanic earth. We all of us have a horde of demons hiding behind the bathroom door, in the corridor. Who are these demons? Ourselves. Our countless terrors that we can all foment. They are those abso- lutely ridiculous things that bind us all, the stuff of comedy. The things that trigger wars are totally absurd details, the stuff of village gossip and taxi-ride chit-chat. And yet they can be enough to kill you. These are the symptoms of the great primitive stage play that none of us got to see, because we were just babes in arms. It's a great primitive massacre scene, the one the Greeks reconstructed in their mythology or cosmology: Cronus eats his own children, Jupiter kills his father, a bloodbath ensues, there's incest, hatred, jealousy and so on. We've got our Judeo-Christian religion rather than this much clearer genealogy that showed us all our childhoods. And yet we've got these Greek genealogies in our cradles. In our cradles there's Cronus, the Titans, or the drives (to put it in Freudian terms), revolts etc. We live alongside our loved ones, our closest friends, our parents, with our children born of the most hideous tragedies, which are tragic love stories. Where there's love there's hatred and fear. What makes all that so hellish is every human being's terror of the fact that in her or his soul, in the soul of the other, are wild animals, knives, arrows, etc. It's totally intolerable, something we can't admit. Which is precisely what our religions, even if we are not religious ourselves, have absolutely forbidden, and which we cannot bring ourselves to deal with. We deal with all that with silence and by blocking it out.

But there's also another kind of obscurity that's there for a different reason. Obscure because too dazzling to behold. It's the lover's adoration, grand romantic passions. It's dazzling because that's where ecstasy and divination are to be found. When dazzled by love we see things: we traverse the body of the other, we see her or him almost entirely ("almost", that is, because we don't see everything), and certain things become utterly transparent. And when you're in that place called love that amazing thing called making love becomes a possibility, and which is really the thing, the time, the moment when human beings are graced with godliness. In moments of grace, of ecstasy, in the dazzling light of seeing the time the place the body the flesh of the passing into the other, the moment of trans is so bright that we cross over onto the other side. As The Book of Revelations says, we see too much: we see a moment in a way that's absolutely incendiary, just like the way we'd see God. But since God is a seer, we don't see God; we pass over to the other side. And in that moment we're in the darkness generated by the excess of light. And yet it's there — at the two extremes, that is — in the darkest and most dazzling of darknesses — all the mysteries that drive us, that govern us, that carry us, that make up our lives and our destinies. So either you ignore all that, and you're born like most people, you live until you die and that's it. You consume and consume yourself and you are finite. Or else you have a genuine passion for creation, genesis, for what we are — creations — and you want to get close to the places from which all this stems and to draw pleasure from them, because these are absolutely inexhaustible, unfathomable treasure troves. But you can only do this under paradoxical conditions, because then you're heading into territory that is by definition beyond us, eludes us. These are good paradoxes to experience, though. Does that mean that we are always falling short of something? Of course not — it's just that there's a gap between what we can perceive in moments of enlightenment, and what we are able to get down on paper. These moments of enlightenment by definition travel faster than we do. A flash of light moves faster than writing. Trying to keep up, not to be definitively held at one remove by the phenomenon of revelation is precisely the conflict that writing has to grapple with [*le drame de l'écriture*], and at the same time the challenge it has to take up. Because there are such things as revelations. Everyone has had that experience. There's a dream, and almost every time the dream gets away from us. A dream is borne along by chariots harnessed to ten thousand horses, and in a flash it's off on the other side of the horizon. But it is possible to capture a dream. It's a technique. The revelations that come along like dreams in fact put us in the same situation as dreams. The dream must be captured, even though it's got ten thousand horses to carry it away. It's not impossible, but you do need a very swift and highly trained team of horses. Writing is also a matter of training: it's not just a gift, but also a physical, linguistic practice. It's a kind of sublime sport and one shouldn't under-estimate how much practice and training is involved in the labour of writing. Writing is something we're given. But it can die if it isn't constantly worked on, begun again, interrogated, nurtured.

CS Your oeuvre now comprises over forty works — you must publish at the rate of a book and a half per year. And you also work in numerous genres: novels, fiction, essays, theatre, interviews, film, translation. Françoise van Rossum-Guyon, in an introduction to your work, links the volume and richness of your writing to the conditions of its production: "for Hélène Cixous, writing emerges from the living, flows from living sources. It's part of an economy of expenditure and gift: the writer does not hold back, be it from within herself or otherwise."[1] Where does this fecundity come from?

CIXOUS Oddly enough, I notice that fecundity is often a cause for reproach. I've always found it extraordinary that fecundity or fertility is often something critics accuse certain people of. It's a real paradox: on the one hand, women are urged to be fertile in reality within society — to have a lot of children, that is — so as to destroy them, to reduce them to baby-making machines; and on the other, they are despised for symbolic procreation of any kind. What to make of this antipathy towards productivity? Your average critic carries on almost as if the real success stories are the people who've only written three books. The less you write the better. This is rationalized by the equation of writing a lot with writing badly, as if when you wrote three books it took you twenty years to get each one out, whereas in actual fact: (1) people who write three books write at exactly the same pace as those who write thirty, except that they have a block between the three; and, (2) each book uses the same time as life as a whole.

Fecundity is the creative person's natural state. The more pertinent question is that of what inhibits it. Why does one get periods of broken productivity? What causes these interruptions? Productivity, it has to be said, has no reason to be broken except through adverse, exterior circumstances. Why any given society's fight against creative people? Because what's at stake is castration. Sterility does everything in its power to block fertility's natural flow. But there are also private accidents, internal dramas, personal tragedies. We could put this to all the writers of the twentieth century, and ask them what it was that made them able, or unable, to write when they had the desire to. The possibility of publication is a major factor. I realize that I'm quite sheltered when it comes to that, given that I have a generous publisher who publishes my work unconditionally. That means that I don't have that suffocating influence on thought that says "what's the point in writing when it won't be published?" I'm privileged. My fictional texts are published regularly. And as for theatre, I've never written anything without there being a stage there asking me to write for it. It's hard to write for your bottom drawer. But we shouldn't think of writing as superhuman, though. Did anyone ever accuse Balzac of fecundity? It was fabulous, how much he could write! Ten times more than me. A staggering amount in a year. It's also a question of how one makes a living. Balzac lived off his books, so he couldn't afford to stop writing. I don't. I've got a professional position that I chose. It's true that my academic salary — which is what I live on — comes from a profession whose forms and applications don't take me far from writing. When I'm giving my seminars I'm not cut off from it, which is very important. If my work took me away from the world of writing I'd write much less because I'd have to come out of exile and back into writing country, which takes quite a while. But I do inhabit the same region where the seeds are sown. When I'm giving my seminars it's not as if I'm writing a book, but still I never leave the territory where a book could be written.

CS I'd like to come back to the origins of writing, but now to the moment where a text itself is born. In your texts, you exploit to the full the start of the text, the moment where, to quote one of your titles, "writing takes to the stage": either you begin with the beginning itself: "In the beginning, I adored" (*La Venue à l'écriture*),[2] or you cut the text off from its fore-text with a decisive: "Have to" (*Portrait du soleil*),[3] or, conversely, you knit them together with an "and" (*Vivre l'orange*).[4] Or else you parody the most classic of opening sentences, namely that of *In Search of Lost Time*:[5] "For years I would close my eyes as he was leaving" (*Le Troisième Corps*).[6] In your seminars you've worked on authors such as Clarice Lispector, Tsvetaeva and Thomas Bernhard, on the "gestation of the text", on early drafts and the material used. What is the status of the final, definitive text in relation to its earlier form?

CIXOUS I never add those things up. I've never thought all of what you've just rightly brought together myself, as such. So now, as I hear the reading speaking back to me, I realize that that's very true. What do I have to say about it? If it stands out it must be because it's very different from the classic, traditional text, or the structure of traditional fiction. I've never produced traditional fiction. Just lately I've been going back over Joyce, and noticing just how traditionally structured his early texts were. He did then go right off to the other extreme, but still. Mine were never the slightest bit traditional. My early texts were already uprooted from the traditional mode. Why and how? I don't know. I think that from the outset, and for lots of reasons that I won't attempt to list here, I was in a transgressive position with respect to the usual obligation, to tradition, to order, because I never thought that was what was important, that it was all those things that made literature. I never felt I had to belong to the old system, such that my texts begin when they're good and ready. And they're ready when I can feel welling up in me the weight, the density, the tear, the fear of a questioning. In fiction I don't write plot-driven novels — I only work on human themes that don't need to pass through narrative to find expression (although, when I'm writing theatre there is very much a narrative). Once I've shaken off the need for narrative structure and once I've located myself somewhere — at sea, say — I'm on course to run into other ships — those of philosophy, say. But philosophy aims to get on board a subject, to go from one port to another, whereas I'm quite happy to drift. To set myself adrift, that is, not like in madness, like someone who's lost her rudder. It's not that. Sometimes philosophy has something to say to the themes that are the living core of my texts, the beating hearts inside them, but not always. Because I don't stick to the side of conceptual reasoning, even if there is a certain capacity for abstraction there. In my text everything remains stubbornly concrete. The material for any text of mine is the raw stuff of everyday life. There are cars and very specific makes of car, saucepans, jam jars, plane tickets — all the accessories of life, both as common objects and as metaphors.

When it comes to the gestation of a text, as I've often said, what I like most about works are the working notes. The notebooks. What I like most in Kafka, and which I never tire of reading, are the letters, the diaries. I'm always very struck by the moments when it all gets started. When I read Stendhal I love *The Charterhouse of Parma* and the other novels, but for me they are texts that have somehow lost their extraordinary power to jump out at you, and which are weaker than the still chaotic autobiographical texts where the form hasn't yet been brought to heel, tamed, tidied up. It's rare for someone to manage to keep within the narrative the spontaneous, frothy quality of the notebooks and diaries. Except Balzac, because he's wonderfully crazy. Some of his texts are very ordered. But whenever the economy of his texts is a bit mad I love it, because he just doesn't care about proportions. *The Girl with the Golden Eyes* is a shell afloat on an ocean. The ocean is because Balzac wants to tell the story of Paris, of sexuality, etc. And once he's in full flow, from time to time, you get "Damn! Where's my narrative gone?" Then all of three words get the narrative back, get the reader back and reassure her, just long enough to calm things down, before the ocean swells and unleashes its visions. What I like about Balzac is his apocalyptic vision. Talk about taking us down a peg or two! The most beautiful, the most free, the least cleaned-up thing we have to say will have been what came before the work. The workshop. And what was it that Joyce did if not find his way back to his own workshop in the end? He starts out from traditional literature, and then it takes him thirty years to get back to his own workshop and it's there that he really breaks free, whereas he started out in chains. I want to see literature break freer still. Which doesn't mean becoming meaningless [*insensée*]. On the contrary, that's where you find the greatest concentration of meaning.

To go back to the question of beginnings, with me, when a text begins, it's quite simply because it's there. And so it starts where it already is. It's much like everything begins in the works for theatre: I hear a character speaking. The character starts speaking, with no particular starting-point, with no particular introduction as it were, because she or he is located somewhere. There's a necessity there. That's how my texts start, out of their own necessity.

CS Your writing presents itself as a speech act, or a spoken word in the act of communication: there's an "I" who speaks, and, implicitly, a "you" as the addressee. In the opening to *Jours de l'an*[7] you make explicit reference to the presence, or the waiting for, this other on whom writing depends in order to begin:

> Enchanted tide alive with silent speech, coursing from town to town, from life to life; a strange legend, inaudible but for an ear to the heart, the story spinning way up high, 'twill unravel you, twill teeming with secrets [...] The air once more filled with voices, whole body become heart. It was the land longed for, the port, the other bank, the unentered house across the way, the sister who would receive the letter and take it in.[8]

In *Beethoven à jamais*,[9] you write: "My thought needs the speech of the person to whom my speech speaks". But who is this addressee? Could it also be the reader?

CIXOUS It's only as you quote me there that I'm reminded that I can't write unless I have faith in the existence of the speech of someone I can speak to in my own act of speech. There's always been a need in me for the other, but for the other-in-writing — of *the other native of writing*. No one can write on that steep, treacherous, disturbing pathway where you feel so alone if there isn't in me, in her or him, in oneself, the presentiment of an other, of a reading or writing other, which is to say someone who speaks that language. It's a question of language. Writing is a highly elaborate language with few native speakers it has to be said, and like all languages it needs to be shared with at least one other witness. I have probably always only been able, been obliged, or wanted to write in the hope or the certainty or the despair as to the existence of the other speaker of that language. Back when this story began I think I must have been in a total mixture of absolute despair and wilderness — no one was speaking to me, or no one that I knew of. The words spoke the languages that I wanted to speak, and there were perhaps people alive who spoke that language, but I didn't know who they were.

To put it even more strongly, I think that in fiction, or in the fiction that I practise, it's God that you're addressing — meaning the being who is infinitely beyond your understanding, who speaks all languages. You try your best to speak the language that speaks the most languages. I don't mean that God speaks back —

He's there to hear. The one you're addressing is the one who gives you their un-divided, unlimited attention.

At the same time, God only exists on earth. God-who-does-not-exist can only exist in the form of a divine fragment, which would exist here on earth. I've gone through periods where I thought that God didn't exist, that there was no fragment on earth, but there was still a fragment of a childhood memory inside me where I did hope that God existed. I got to thinking that there was nothing left for it but to give up hope. Maybe my early texts were just despair and bitterness at God for not existing. But that didn't last because straight away I did come across some divine fragments, right at the point where I was going to give in to despair. When I say "divine fragments", I mean human beings who did speak the language that I had all but given up hope of finding spoken anywhere *in our own time* (because the past is not enough for me, even if it can help sometimes). In our own time, and spoken by someone, living or dead. Clarice Lispector, though dead, is still alive for me. Because she's still writing. She's writing the twentieth century, which is a context that's very much mine. Whatever our texts are, we today are dealing with new philosophical or political questions of which Shakespeare knew nothing. Ancient massacres are taking on new forms that call for new protests and new silences. The problems merge together to make new contradictions, we are tortured in new ways, thrown into impasses that we've never seen before. We are discovering new plagues — diseases, tyrannies, the exiles in their own land of the homeless, persecutions of poets and thinkers across the planet and where Islam is tearing itself apart, oppressions led by invisible international forces (such as debt, or the Mafia), the exponential power-increase of wealth which is extending its poisonous influence into even the best-protected areas, global venalization, crazy carryings on in the field of genetics, ambivalent scientific discoveries with one benevolent face to them, the other quite the opposite. Everything is broken up according to the logics of today. Shakespeare, who does warn us, can't have predicted it all. It's up to us to find the language that will prophesy our age.

And what about reading for someone who writes? I think that the real, realist phenomenon of reading escapes the writer. I don't know how my texts are read. I don't know if they are read. I wouldn't know the first thing about it if someone didn't come along from time to time, without knowing what I'll make of it, to let me in on a fragment of her personal reading. If there were no Christa to come along to perform a reading of a fragment of text in front of me I'd have no idea. It's not when someone says "I like your book" that means it's read. A contem-porary reading, as it were, doesn't exist. But most people who write know that the reading will be a *descendant*. It will only be born just before I die — look at how Stendhal talks about the baby who'll go on to read him.

I'm talking about reading as I understand it. But there's journalistic reading, affective reading, reading that carries you away with it, the satisfaction of reading — all that. It's having an ear for the work that's out of the ordinary. So the writer can't depend on, or work with, reading. Reading does exist, for sure, but it doesn't reach the author, isn't addressed to the author. Except sometimes. I could make out a list of the names of people who have let me know how they have deciphered the notes of my music. There aren't many of them. But when they do that, they're giving me the most precious of gifts. I often think about musicians, composers, about all those who write works that depend upon an orchestra. I often think of them as hearing their works inside their head. Their body needs to hear this silent music from the outside, out loud. That's what I wrote about in *Beethoven à jamais*: there is no imaginable suffering greater than that whose music is entirely within oneself and never reaches one's own ears. And yet that's how it is with writing. There is no orchestra. Perhaps my insistence on reading and being read — that is, on playing the music of the text — bears some relation to that. Writing is my territory, I hear the notes of writing in my head, and I need to hear them out loud.

CS In this language-based music, what kind of human encounter takes place? Because it is, as you say, the author who composes, who makes use of language. People have often alluded to the ways in which you use the rhythm of language, sounds, the allusions that language makes possible. But what is it driving this play of language? Is it the speaker-author, who puts the stamp of her own affect and drives on it? Or is it rather language itself which, with all the wisdom and truth that it can convey, speaks before her, if not better than her?

CIXOUS (It'll be difficult for me to answer here given that it's not for me to describe my own text.) But the kind of text I write corresponds entirely to the Derridean definition of writing that disseminates, works over the signifier, that listens to itself being written and that retraces its own steps, that re-inscribes. All that isn't a craft that I *learnt*. I've already said that there is such a thing as a gift, but it's not hereditary. I wasn't born with writing in my mouth, although I was brought up on it. That's a biographical fact. My tongue was put to work, deployed, caught out by my father in a range of linguistic exercises, but where he had no idea what he was doing. He wasn't training a writer. He was playing.

The other thing is something I want to stress — that we are cultivated beings: our language is an inheritance; on the one hand, to the extent that it's the result of a history that we study in philology, it is itself made up of sediments of a great many languages. I've always been very sensitive to the radical elements of language we all of us experience. We go on unwittingly using a language that speaks much more richly than we ever consciously realize, such that even when we are very primitive in our expression, a well-trained ear can hear in an apparently simple statement layers and layers of resonances, whether or not you can hear the hum of etymology behind it. I've always been very sensitive to that, as if I had always had an ear for each word separately, for its secret, for what it contains and then also for everything to do with syntactical structure. On the other hand there are also expressions, idioms, etc. and a whole cultural background which is constantly being reworked, such that, without our knowing or being conscious of it, we are feeding off ancient discourses. Into our speech, into my discourse, passes that of Plato about which I know nothing, or that of Victor Hugo, into which a hundred other languages overflow. In our Western discourse resonate Western discourses in the plural (I don't know what resonates in Eastern discourse). We've been speaking for six thousand years, and we can be very ancient producers of language, the receptors of the Bible and all the major texts that have come down to us. Yes. We are cultivated, whether we like it or not. In the theatre, the text speaks the author's language, but the author's language speaks a lot of other languages too. An author is all the better for the fact that she has been cultivated like a piece of land, for the fact that her language has been elaborated by a number of other languages since the dawn of time.

I don't know who my language is anymore. Who's speaking? (That should be understood in the plural). There's no counting: it's everything I've ever read. I'm also a very forgetful person, which is a good thing — otherwise I'd never lose my language. I know that my language is very much my language, personal but not proper to me. It comes from my own history, and then it's also shot through with other languages. It's a hybrid, like all real languages. It knows how English and German speak, which I heard when I was a child. It knows how Arabic speaks (I don't, but my language does). My language knows the syntactical and verbal forms of other languages. The linguistic inventions of authors that I've read — be it once or a hundred times — have left their mark on my language. Twentieth-century languages bear the imprint of languages that were current in earlier centuries. The more time passes the more language, in its sedimentation, just like the soil, is on the one hand enriched, fertilized; on the other impoverished, ill-used, polluted, etc. But when I write I always write with all my linguistic finery on, in my number one language, the one that has been the most richly fertilized, even before it began leaving traces on the page. As I'm writing sometimes, who, or what is it I'm responding to? To a phrase that I read three hundred years ago in Milton. He said it and I reply three hundred years later. It's not that I'm quoting him — I'm echoing him. A thought was expressed about a major issue three hundred years ago, and then a reply comes from me today. That's how it goes. There I am trying to think of something that's located on a historical fault-line, some tense, heated historical moment, and then I hear messages from elsewhere, from long ago. These messages come from people who found themselves one day after the flood on top of Mount Ararat. They said such and such a thing at such and such a moment, and, being someone different from them I think differently. But I hear, and I reply — a long time afterwards.

NOTES

1. Françoise van Rossum-Guyon, "Introduction à Hélène Cixous", in *Hélène Cixous, chemins d'une écriture* [Hélène Cixous, Ways of A Writing], Françoise van Rossum-Guyon & Myriam Díaz-Diocaretz (eds), 5 (Amsterdam: Rodopi, 1990).
2. *La Venue à l'écriture* [Coming to Writing], with Madeleine Gagnon & Annie Leclerc (Paris: Union Générale d'Éditions, 1977).
3. *Portrait du soleil* [Portrait of the Sun] (Paris: Denoël, 1973).
4. *Vivre l'orange/To Live the Orange* (Paris: Éditions des femmes, 1979).
5. The reference is to Marcel Proust's *À la recherche du temps perdu* [*In Search of Lost Time*].
6. *Le Troisième Corps* [The Third Body] (Paris: Grasset, 1970).
7. *Jours de l'an* [First Days of the Year] (Paris: Éditions des femmes, 1990).
8. Cours magique plein de mots muets qui coule d'une commune à l'autre, d'une vie à l'autre, l'étrange légende inaudible sinon par le coeur de l'un ou de l'autre, le récit se tissant là-haut, qui te déchiffrera, le tissu palpitant de la clandestinité. [...] A nouveau l'espace est plein de voix, le corps entier est coeur. C'était le pays qui manquait, le port, l'autre rive, et là-bas la maison inconnue, la soeur qui recevrait la lettre et qui l'adopterait. (*Ibid.*: 5).
9. *Beethoven à jamais ou l'existence de Dieu* [Forever Beethoven or the Existence of God] (Paris: Éditions des femmes, 1993).

2. The novel today

Interview with Henri Quéré. Translated by Amaleena Damlé.

This interview is taken from "Le Roman d'aujourd'hui: Entretien: Hélène Cixous" [The Novel Today: Interview: Hélène Cixous] which appeared in *Fabula* **3** (March), 147–58, 1984.

HQ To begin with, I will simply say this: as we all know, you have various activities to your credit. What part does literature play in all of this?

CIXOUS There is this effect of multiplicity which you describe, but, at the heart of it, there is an order, at least a hierarchy of values, and for me, the most essential thing is to write. The other gestures, which are accompaniments, have their roots in writing. For example, I write during the summer and, from what I have written, I bring out what will be the general theme of my seminar.[1] It is the world of writing which is originary, which is the origin of everything I am able to do next; it's the source. Afterwards, it disperses, it channels itself, it scatters forth in secondary gestures which, for me, are still necessary gestures all the same. Well, they are gestures of quick transmission. The very fact that they are quick means that they are also less profound, more shrunken gestures. The difference is situated in the transmission — I will say the mission — from writing to the spoken word; but the one serves the other.

HQ Does that mean that you speak, that you teach, as you write?

CIXOUS I do not think that I speak as I write, exactly. It is the same person who is speaking, so something similar must be maintained. It comes from me, but I do not speak about myself and my texts. In fact, it's a complex gesture. So, this year, I chose to work on poverty and everything relevant to it, wealth, misery, a varied semantic field, contradictory. That is to say that I am also going to work on the poor shape, the poor narrative.[2] Well, or, inversely, how to recount, how to inscribe poverty in writing, given that writing is, by definition, rich, consists of symbolic richness? So, I treat this by measuring the theme, by weighing it — I am intentionally using these metaphors — by means of texts where that happens more or less consciously, more or less explicitly. Where does this theme come from? Well, from my personal experience. Along my personal path of meditation, I encounter such-and-such fundamental question. These are some of the questions which come to me. For example: "To feel rich, in myself, what does that mean?" Such questions, when they come to me, in my history, into my body, produce a written response, a fiction, something poetic. It's mine, this response. But that isn't enough: my response is only a reaction to the encounter. So the general questioning this entails, and which largely exceeds me, remains a sort of immense curiosity that I will carry. It gives me light and I will carry it into the darkness of other texts: I circle with it, interrogating precisely the human experience which has gathered around that point. And it is on this that I will construct my seminar.

HQ What a relationship, then, between you writing and, let's say, everything that surrounds it!

CIXOUS I have always thought in terms of inhabiting two worlds. When one truly writes, one inhabits two worlds. So, one travels, one incessantly passes back and forth from one world to the other, and this entails the possibility of a choice between a principal world and a secondary world. This is a concern which, for me, is absolutely essential. There is always conflict between writing and life, between the act of writing and living. There is a struggle. What interests me is finding out which one wins, or what it is that wins, or which one loses. Literature, works of art, can often be divided up in relation to this question, and this is all too often decided by sexual difference. I think it is something to do with "femininity" or "masculinity" which influences whichever specific side wins within the individual person.

HQ Writing, then, would be the staging of this conflict? As if, by means of transposition, one could say that intertextuality is intra-textual, that it is played out from within.

CIXOUS That's right. I think that writing often serves to bear conflict. To write is a way of ridding oneself of guilt. If you admit to error, if you point it out, you haul it out and you inscribe it outside of yourself. I'm thinking of Kafka, because he is someone who, in the writing/living conflict, honestly said: writing should win, and so I lose my life. It's true that, knowing writing should win, he laid down his life, he paid with his life, with his flesh, with his body, with his lungs, for knowing it. And what I find absolutely admirable and moving, is that when writing won, he wept bitterly. The moment Mephisto came and said to him: "Now, old boy, you must pay," this forty-year-old man began to say, "No, I want to live". He was some-one who, at the very moment he had to pay, said to himself: I got it wrong. Because he was a man who was really full of life. I think that the truth of literature passes through this choice between the value of life and the value of writing. Here we come to the need to write. Why does one write?

HQ Yes, to what end?

CIXOUS I think that most people who write truly vitally, write in relation to death. It's to celebrate life, to produce beauty and it's also — I will say this for me, from my own experience — because I don't have the strength, for example, I don't have the courage to live consuming my life from day-to-day. Every time, I need to bring something, to reinscribe or maybe to accompany for a moment, to re-think it in order to enjoy it. Let's say that I embrace life as tightly as possible. And, at the same time, it's because, at core, I'm rich, I'm not threatened by death, that I do this. If I were threatened by my death, or the death of another, I would immediately let go of the paper. Because it's a screen: it's at once what gathers, what envelops, what protects, but it's separate from the body, it's not skin. And skin is more precious than paper.

HQ Writing as a "diversion" . . . I'm thinking of Virginia Woolf.

CIXOUS Yes, but she is someone who never properly succeeded in living, who wasn't able to do anything else, who truly substituted. I don't think I exist in substitution. I exist in division, perhaps, or in conflict, not in substitution. In a way, I renounce nothing. Writing is not a-part. I de-part from it, I come back to it, but I am never without, never. It's a strength and a weakness, as always.

HQ The detour via Kafka clarified things.

CIXOUS What I don't have the courage to do, either, is only to write. I love life too much. To allow oneself to write is a monstrosity. It's, for example, to think oneself born to write or capable of writing. Well, that, no-one in the world, unless you make yourself a god, can assure you of your capacity, and as such your right, to take back a part of what you owe to society, to humanity, in order to transform that into writing. Only posterity, or I don't know who else, can decide who will have been

17

right or who will have had the right to deprive the world of their embrace and to burden the world with their writings or scraps. Kafka had the right, Genet had the right, and it's for us to say so. They themselves could not be certain they had the right.

HQ Perhaps they didn't see it like that. It depends on the manner in which one conceives of being-in-the-world.

CIXOUS I think Kafka saw it like that.

HQ He saw it, or someone made him see it.

CIXOUS It comes back to the same thing. One is never alone, of course.

HQ One is never alone. Hence my question, on the situation of the novel today: how do you see yourself in relation to what is happening "in the genre"?

CIXOUS I do not see myself in what is happening today. I think that it's part of my singularity not to write within a genre, but precisely in the overflow of genres — I will even go so far as to say in the alliance of genres. And moreover to treat this alliance or this overflow of genres in my texts. It's in relation to the problems of sexual difference. I'm not bringing this back to sexuality. It's the relations between beings which then repeats through histories of sexual difference. I prefer to talk in terms of love. As for this alliance of genres, I'm satisfied when someone says to me, with a hesitation: "After all, what you do is poetry, even so."

HQ After all, and even so!

CIXOUS And I know why there's hesitation. There's a hesitation on the part of the readers because one imagines that poetry is written quickly, that they are poems. I write a text of poetic fiction. It isn't a genre, it's a quality of writing, it's a textual form unspeakable in former codes and which hasn't much currency in our literature either. I would situate myself in a space which tends towards poetry a little and towards philosophy a little: where poetry tends towards the philosophical.

What remains of the novel? The presence of human beings in my texts, of subjects who are no longer treated like those in the novel, although I estimate that one of these days novelistic characters will appear in my texts. But I think they will be set free from the domestic novel or the walls of the novel. Truthfully, little by little, people (characters?) have already returned to my non-genre, and I find that thrilling. I'm not one of those who feels the need to say that the novel is over. Imitation of the novel, yes, reproduction of the novel, yes, because, if one repeats, one does not advance. I consider myself above all as post-Freudian, that is to say as marked by the "banalization" of psychoanalysis. What we can no longer keep hold of in the novel, in my opinion, is that which can be practised at the moment of the novel's flourishing. There used to be a convention, like in the theatre: one opens the book, the curtain lifts, and there we are, the scene is set. Nowadays, one doesn't approach the novel as if one were going to the theatre. If one were to write a novel as during that era, one would have a feeling of excessive theatricality, of special effects.

At core, the genre which suits me the most, and towards which I tend, would be that which dates from before the novel, the narrative, the most simple narration, that which declares itself to be narration, which says I'm going to tell a story and doesn't hide its genre. For better or worse, I've begun to make my texts as territories where I can tell stories. It's the genre of these stories which was perhaps a little strange, because I wanted to write very delicate stories, the ones which are hardly ever told, except when one talks in a space of intimacy. When, in the evening, I feel like recounting what has happened that day, I do not recount a novel, I recount an intimate gesture someone made, or a little drama which might hold great meaning. Besides, that's what makes a poem. It's the little things that hold the greatest meaning. I think we suffer from a general restriction on all of that: we are always asked "to make a spectacle", with grand actions, and grand images . . .

HQ Without the little things . . .

CIXOUS Yes. I don't know why. In the end, yes, I do: it's part of a general economy.

HQ I'm thinking of Beckett, of Beckett's theatre. Making grand gestures from little things; rendering the "insignificant" things tragic.

CIXOUS It's true. But Beckett's regions are not mine: at core, he's a sorry soul, always apart from the rest. I believe that the stone is a diamond, whereas the Beckettian step is to consider the diamond as a stone. What interests me is precisely to enable the celebration of the grain of dust. All of this fundamentally rejoins questions of value, of economy.

Moreover, I think that the question of the novel calls attention to History, not literary (hi)story,[3] but History. Because the great novel of today does exist. There are truly great classical novels, written by Latin Americans, for example. I think there is a direct relation with the fact that their countries are in a state of History.

Whilst we are in a political state. We do not tell (hi)stories because we are governing something. I think people have the impression of living a (hi)story when they live in a History. I think the novel ceased to be in France after the war, when an awareness of living in a History-in-the-making dimmed, as we returned to the State and to the governing of the State.

HQ So, what remains?

CIXOUS I'm going to venture into that. If time no longer exists in the novel, which is our case in France, then where can one turn to in order to find that immense dimension the novel has? I think that at that moment — and it's here that I feel close to Kafka — one would arrive at an almost "religious" space where the question of the death of man would again be posed, which Kafka treated in an allegorical mode, in a fabulous mode. As for me, I would treat it in a poetic mode. These are the questions which are eternal and which change in their encounter with History, with social transformations. These very questions which were in the Bible are posed once again, arise once again with different faces.

HQ Recently an interview appeared in *Le Monde* in which Phillipe Sollers — to summarize — made the opposition between mystification — understanding by that, at core, the spectacle of the world — and "mystical state". And he said something fairly similar: this state as the beyond, as possible excess. Where does writing take us?

CIXOUS Where does writing take us? Do you mean to say who, who is it that writing takes?

HQ My question did not solely treat the destiny of the novel or of fiction, but also bore on the function of writing's discovery, on its heuristic value: writing as exploration, as access to something one would otherwise be unable to reach or happen upon.

CIXOUS That's the very movement of literature. One always writes in darkness. One cannot write . . . there's no sense in writing except in incomprehension, advancing in incomprehension, advancing towards incomprehension. What is understood is summed up, settled, and that's that. It's necessary to leave what is understood. It's necessary to de-understand and to reapply oneself to learning: that's the heroism of writing. That's its only justification.

HQ Isn't it curious that someone who writes, male or female, can say: it's the jump into the unknown, into incomprehension, whilst, on the other hand, it's commonplace to say that the novel, fiction, poetry, is — precisely — that which enables understanding? So, blindness for some is enlightenment for others?

CIXOUS Of course. And it's a blindness in motion. It's apparently a crazy effort to measure oneself to be greater than one is. So, obviously, it's always unmeasured, always panicked. And I would add this: the less one makes of oneself, so much the greater one is.

HQ We're returning to the notion of dust here.

CIXOUS We're returning to not quite the same thing. When I say much greater, it's like saying: "That exceeds me". We always write about what exceeds us. That means that there exists inside us a force that is stronger than us. And it's precisely this which speaks, it's this which launches words. Clarice Lispector compares this to bait. Her metaphor is that she throws out words like bait into the water, to catch what, she doesn't quite know. This is part of this capacity that one has of being more intelligent than oneself. However, most people are loath to be stronger, more intelligent than themselves.

HQ I would like to underline this. On the one hand, then, there is an image of the writer inhabited by what he has to say, a bit like a medium, worked over by something greater than himself. And then, on the other hand, a writing which I will call conscious and organized, in the sense of an engagement, a cause to defend, to illustrate. How does that work between the two simultaneously?

CIXOUS First of all, I don't believe that inspiration comes solely from within. When I say to you: questions have arisen from meeting you, it's true. The answer comes, but it comes after you have been given the helping hand of the question. You have an enigma — of your soul, of the human soul, etc. — and a resolution is demanded of you. At the outset, you don't know anything. But the enigma is there. That's what writing works on. Ten years ago, for example, I set to work on the enigma of the anguish that everyone suffers at some point in their life. One wonders why. In fact, one knows very well that a hidden, huge, determining drama is being played out, which might produce love, or death. I set to work on that, then. And, little by little, the curtains separate, and little answers start to take shape. I perceive that one of the explanations to such-and-such problem is a struggle which is drawn out, even if one does not see it, for example between mothers and children, or fathers and children, or fathers and mothers, etc. I tell myself that what lies behind all this suffering or all this joy, is something, for example, which touches upon political structures. Personally, I have the impression that this happens in my body, in my soul, but in reality the drama is much vaster. And so, on the horizon, an explanation would take shape, among a thousand others, which would be political. So, at that moment, I bring it back to myself, I fix it like a little element, a little bright element. But — to return to your question — I absolutely do not believe in an engagement with writing in the service of a cause. It's true that, at a given moment, in a political space, I will feel close to a certain movement, or a certain formation, or a certain group, but my writing, which continues to do its work, is definitely either in front or behind or to the side of what one might call a "cause".

HQ On the other hand, you have spoken of a feminine writing.

CIXOUS First of all, I do not say feminine writing. I talk of femininity in writing, or I use heaps of quotation marks, I speak of "so-called feminine" writing. In any case, femininity — to define it — also exists in men, it does not necessarily exist in women, and so this should not return to enclose itself in the history of anatomical difference and of sexes. All that is a trap. One cannot speak of it in an exact manner. It's immediately vulgarized in current discourse. It's because, culturally, it is always in question, that I cannot avoid it.

HQ It's awaited from you, in a sense.

CIXOUS I am also waiting, I'm waiting for time to pass. I hope that one day we will have moved away from all this. In reality, it's a certain type of libidinal organization I am talking about. What I call "femininity" I have often read, for example, in Kleist, and not an author whose social and sexual identity would be feminine. If we had another vocabulary . . . one might say — and this would still be inadequate — a certain type of generosity, a certain type of capacity to expend without fear of loss, without calling loss "loss", but rather what is situated in another system of values. For this is what it's all about. To know for example that to lose is not necessarily to lose, that it could be a way of working with life, that defensive rigidity is not perhaps the best defense etc. There are a thousand ways of perceiving this style of behaviour which is in relation to a libidinal economy, that is to say with the conservation of the self, the expenditure of the self, the relation to the other.

HQ Through these references, "libidinal economy" or others, we come to the question of bearings.

CIXOUS I belong to my era. Isn't it perhaps as simple as that? I imagine that lots of people do not belong to their era. I don't feel myself to be marked by influences. But I know that, probably because I have crossed certain fields of writing or knowledge, this must have affected some kinds of outcomes or liberations that I must have profited from after the event. People often ask me about my relation to Joyce. To say that this relation is invalid would be quite a challenge. But that doesn't really interest me, in any case much less than very great works, like those of Shakespeare. It remains that Joyce's writing must have been right from very early on about what resistance might have entailed. Working on signifiers has always seemed an obvious thing to me. Quite late, I realized that it was intolerable for most people, whilst, for me, it was an acquisition from the beginning of the twentieth century or the end of the nineteenth. Rimbaud already was completely free. But perhaps, from that point of view, my era is the era of what poetry has been for all eternity, because it has always turned its nose up at the restrictions on working on the signifier.

HQ That brings us to the situation of the novel, in the context of writing. It's a way of marking out a continuation: to write after Joyce, for example, having read him.

CIXOUS I don't have the sense of writing "afterwards". In fact there is a simultaneity, the general and anachronic contemporary where one can find again and again, in the same space-time, Shakespeare as well as Rimbaud, as well as Kleist, as well as Kafka, as well as Joyce, not taking into account any borders, whatever kind of border it might be. And I feel that I belong to that world. For me, these are the inhabitants of the same universe who have all spoken that same language, in a foreign language, but it's a language which in any case speaks the unconscious precisely. It's here that the question of genres isn't interesting. What I read during my mental or linguistic childhood were, indiscriminately, theatre, poetry and novels. It so happens that the novel or the novels which have been important to me aren't exactly classic novels. For example, Dostoevsky. Why? Because it's not the genre which interests me, it's what happens there, it's what he makes happen there himself. Well, what he makes happen there is "psychical significance". They are stories of the soul. Social stories have never interested me much. Stories of the soul have.

HQ In fact, what you are saying proposes an altogether different typology of texts and of ways of writing. It's a certain relation to language, to the unconscious, to the imaginary, which defines belongings, and not divisions, let's say, of an academic nature.

CIXOUS Absolutely. In fact, I think I have never taken these divisions into account or even realized that they existed. Pasternak, for example, there's someone whom, I imagine, is considered a novelist. In any case, that's what made him famous. But he is a poet. And I think that he belongs to that world, that is to say the world of the freedom of language. And that's the important thing. Then, if it flows into such-and-such mould, for such-and-such reason, this has no importance.

HQ Therefore, instead of genres, this places "families", or rather traditions, tendencies which, like philosophical tendencies, re-emerge here and there and traverse history, genres, forms of writing. In fact, it's a way of circumventing the question of the genre. It's also, prospectively, a way of responding to the question of the becoming of the novel, or writing in general. Have there been, will there always be such families?

CIXOUS The family that I talk about, to which I belong, will always exist. It's universal. It's completely stupid, but that's how it is. And so, these are the same questions which return, elaborated differently. You have a seed which grows upwards and will give you a garden or a tree, or a palm, etc., but it's the same, whether you are in the garden of Rimbaud or Kirkegaard.

HQ There is also this dimension of the narrative that you were talking about yourself. We need stories, undoubtedly.

CIXOUS Indeed, there can be narratives. "A Season in Hell" is a narrative, it's a mad, brief, lightning-flash of a narrative. Again, I have nothing against the narrative. I say that I read Dostoevsky. But I know that what I read there is the same thing as what there is in Rimbaud: the story of a soul in hell.

HQ Yes, but to say that, is once again to imply a sort of literary anthropology which does not conform to the rhetorical classification of genres. And it is also to reintroduce the question of singularities at the heart of families of writers who take the shape of universals.

CIXOUS Singularity exists, obviously. It's because of this that, first of all, these inhabitants of a certain world produce very, very different works. Because they work with their own body, with their own history. And yet, at the origin, there is the same impulse. And so I would like to refrain from attacking the novel, because the novel can also be the space of this type of work. After all, Kafka primarily wrote "fables", but is *The Trial* a novel? One might concur. It is obvious, however, that everyone reads it on its allegorical level. No one doubts that Golding is a novelist. In reality, rather, he wrote a vast collection of allegories. And why not? The novel can serve beyond itself, to something other than itself.

NOTES

1. The reference here is to Cixous's research seminar at the University of Paris VIII, where Cixous holds a Chair in English Literature.
2. The word used is "récit", implying the narrative of the text rather than its story. This distinction occurs throughout the interview.
3. There is ambiguity in this paragraph (and elsewhere in this interview) in the use of the French word "histoire", which can mean both history and story.

3. Literature suspends death

Interview with René de Ceccatty. Translated by Fabien Troivaux.

This interview appeared as "La Littérature suspend la mort", in *Le Monde* (16 December, "Le Monde des Livres"), 12, 2005.

RdC Could you talk about the intimate, about the circulation that happens in your recent texts and in *L'Amour même dans la boîte aux lettres*[1] in particular, between the familiar, the familial, the confidential and a more, shall we say, public reflection?

CIXOUS Nothing more intimate, they say, than love, than where one makes love. But what does one make of love, as a human and animal being? It's a question of life and death, of course, but it's a universal question, the first question. It's the one that subverts, that haunts all the scenes in which we move, which all seem professional, external, "extimate", political, etc. For me, it is always about a questioning of love. Love in turn questions role-playing scenes, in which we play a role, in which we have functions, in which, I could almost say, love would stumble against two kinds of inimical incarnations: on the one hand its opposite, hatred, hostility, war, and on the other hand that which limits everything — and I, personally, cannot accept the existence of this limit — that is, death. Love advances like a sort of vital stream, flanked by powers hostile to love and by powers with which we can have a form of endless dialogue. What I would like to call love is a renunciation of the demands of a self that wants to exert power over the other, a renunciation that would accept, without giving in, so good-heartedly, to deliver itself, to open up, to give rise [*donner lieu*] to the other while respecting them, and that, is love itself. A love that understands it's a case of surrendering, meaning to leave, to take flight, but also to lay down arms, because, alas, all is always measured against war.

RdC In this text, which is not chronological, as you tell the story backwards, you provide dates that go as far back as forty years earlier. How does your memory organize itself when you decide to relate an event in connection with other events of your past?

CIXOUS I am fully aware that, when I inscribe something in a temporality, it is an autobiographical temporality. I completely exclude anything relating to the historical novel. I can't. I could do it metaphorically or by taking a passage from a literary work of the past with a contemporary dimension. But I can't feed into a text like this unless I draw from my memory, from my personal experience which at my age, if I can say so, is rather what has been related to me by the previous generation, that is by my mother. My mother "relates" so much that, when I was little, I had the feeling I was living a double childhood! I never knew if it was my childhood or my mother's. I relived, in a real fairy tale, my mother's childhood as my own. It allowed me to go back, as witness, to the beginning of the twentieth century, being able to refer historically to the way someone lived the First World War, the complete transformation of Europe, the fall of empires (through my grandmother). I need this. Otherwise, I would fabricate, without the concrete elements I need to support my texts, just like my plays. What I keep alive is almost ageless.

RdC Paradoxically, in your case, since orality is very important in your profession — you lecture, comment orally on what you live and read, write plays for the *Théâtre du Soleil* — and in your family, in quite an exceptional way for a writer. Yet your work is a love hymn to the written text.

CIXOUS This could seem paradoxical, but it isn't. When I let others speak or let my mother speak (not enough in my opinion, but I can't do it more), my joy (I don't simply mean earthly joy) is to apply myself to hear the secret of languages. Each of us speaks French, and inside French, their own idiom. Adjectives are forged for writers renowned for their mastery with words, adjectives such as Rimbaldian, Balzacian, Proustian, but for humans beings in general, it isn't done. Yet many of us have our own idiom, and I'm very sensitive to this. That idiom is at the same time vocalized, musicalized and semantic too: each person with some richness of soul has their own garden of words, of phonetics as well. Sometimes, I hear something in the other's tongue, in their idiolect, I perceive their poetic quality. It isn't always easy. It used to be with Derrida and vice versa. When we talked, I could hear the "philosophical poetics". I picked him up on it. It was a game between us.

RdC Your work is filled with very violent events. Have you asked yourself: is there anything so violent that it would prevent writing and life?

CIXOUS But of course, I think about it. But I think the only thing that could paralyse one's writing is a fettering, an arrest of the subject inside themselves. It can happen when one's life force is affected. And I tell myself very humbly that illness, true illness, the body's illness, which introduces a hostile and unfathomable stranger, can steal, strangle the live force of writing. I can bear an unhappy witness to this. When this interruption occurs, writing is put on hold/suffers [*en souffrance*]. But if the illness is ripped out, as one rips out a screw, writing resumes. I am not speaking of moments of impotence, related to psychological distress, to depression. For there are situations in which one cannot write: deportation, all that is "deportation of the self". As soon as there is activity, writing is possible. It's an answer to violence. Even in camps. The process of literature doesn't make one happy, it suspends death — as long as it manifests itself. This is what Blanchot calls the "*arrêt de mort*".[2] It stops death with life. Similarly, when you're dreaming, all pain is suspended. It's waiting for you. Similarly, when you wake up from literature, the pain is waiting for you.

RdC Have you asked yourself these two questions: am I able to write what I want to write, and do I have the right to write what I write?

CIXOUS Yes I do, constantly. The right, constantly. It's an inner and an explicit debate. I can only plead literature, fiction. It is beyond right, if it's fiction. It happens beyond all summons to tell the truth. What is "truth-lies" is displaced by literature. Literature is the displacement itself. It is neither true nor false. No one can prove it. Literature doesn't answer to anyone. I constantly suffer from a need and a desire to confess. I would like to confess certain things, after what I discovered with wonder when I was little, reading Dostoevsky. If only one could confess one's crimes! One realizes that literature hides a trap. Even in confessional literature, the unconfessable is infinite. One cannot lay down the unconfessable in a book. It's the great illusion. When one is sufficiently versed in literature, one knows. One can confess all one wants, the unconfessable remains unconfessed.

RdC You have a political thought that is expressed outside your books. And there, the boundary between good and evil cannot fluctuate.

CIXOUS But it's not clear. One can, trusting to do right, do wrong. As for the political scene, in the end I feel that I belong to no party. I belong to the party of writing. I cannot imagine sticking up for a dogma, it horrifies me. It's the sphere of power struggles. But although I don't have a party, I have principles, very simple ones. Doing the least wrong possible, in the least wrong possible way, in literature as well as in society, in the space of citizenship. I have only one line of conduct, but it's a very difficult one to follow. This is why actions are so uncomfortable to me, because I have to decide between yes and no. Always in binary situations. In politics, that's it. Same thing with sexuality. When I fill in my visa to the USA, they ask me: *male or female*? For god's sake! Luckily in English the word *female* contains the word *male*, both exist at the same time. It's alright, I'll write *female*. I'd hate to write *male*, because I'd be missing the other half. Let's say that, every time such a dichotomy occurs, I am appalled. Like when I must vote. The word election is a deceptive word, because one actually never "elects". One chooses between two possibilities, which has nothing to do with real election, which should be choosing between innumerable possibilities. One is forced to lie, it's a civil obligation. It isn't hypocrisy. I see myself do it and think I can't do otherwise, because I don't want to abstain. This is the aporia of citizen life. I never face this in literature. There is no "binarism". To this question that haunts my texts: "*Are we outside, are we inside*?" I refuse to answer.

RdC How do you see the threat of madness that has affected you?

CIXOUS I hurry and flee when I see it again: there's nothing more terrifying. Madness and terror are the same thing. It's as if I lost sight of the reason for living. Why live? Life then appears to be on the threshold of death. It's a temptation that happens when death, in its endless fight with the angel, gets the better of [*a raison de*] life. Then one drops the key to life. It is a fall, terrifying. It is a hole dug into the self, but which is, in general, caused by an accident. I am not speaking of the madness that condemns one to the asylum, that can't be diagnosed or cured, because the chemical, biological part remains unknown. I am speaking here of what can touch us[3] and resolve itself in attenuated forms, like neuroses. I abandon myself, me abandons I. Frankly, I have no wish to stay in those parts! But when it comes down upon you, you lose control. In general, I don't think I have the keys myself. I sometimes entrust them to others, as with love. Or with the other's death.

NOTES

1. *L'Amour même dans la boîte aux letters* [Love Itself/Even in the Letter Box] (Paris: Galilée, 2005).
2. "Arrêt de mort" means both "death stop" and "death warrant".
3. The word used here is "frôler" which means both "to brush against" and "to be on the edge of".

4. In the beginnings, there were many . . .

Interview with Mireille Calle-Gruber. Translated by Amaleena Damlé.

This interview was published as "Aux commencements, il y eut pluriel …", in *Genesis* (Spring), 131–41, 1997.

MC-G It's the plural to which "beginning" corresponds in the texts you write. And it's in fact precisely a manner of being in the world which expresses itself by this plurality, manner and matter corresponding to the world, corresponding with the world. For *I* does not begin: *I* has/is already begun. *I* is always Beyond — and so it is, for example, just as you call it in *Partie*,[1] BeyondI[2] (but also, since it isn't always obvious, more-than-I):[3] "BeyondI, a character composed of more than a whole, which plays its role at a certain distance from sexual difference."[4] But *I* is also less — just one part of its innumerable parts. And set in motion, then, more or less, *I* is always with: neither One nor All but vibratile, vibrating with correspondences and discords linking it to its surroundings.

So, to say, as your texts do, that one can only begin in the plural, plurally, whichever form that plural might take, masculine or feminine (how should this be written? how might it be heard?),[5] is to say that one is on the side of life. That one has opted for what grows, moves, metamorphoses, and transforms. It's to state that *I* is located, from the beginning, in a tremendous upwards thrust. I is within, in the middle: in the course of time, generations, transmissions. In the beginning pages of *La Fiancée juive*, there is this phrase: "*I sur*-render to the beginnings of the world".[6] With "beginning(s)", in the uncertainty of a plurality which is read but not heard.[7] But there's more. I like, here, the verb "to render" [*rendre/se rendre*], which renders, in effect, all its meaning to beginnings; for this verb, on the one hand, indicates a movement, of will, of energy — it's about reaching the encounter[8] between beginnings like an encounter between lovers. But also, on the other hand, it says: I surrender — in absolute. I give of myself to something, I abandon myself, trustingly — in this situation, in this book entitled *La Fiancée juive*, with an engagement, for an engagement with the unknown, the future-to-come [*l'à-venir*]. It's a response to a call. It's abandoning oneself to what *I* don't know about this plurality of possibles, if it is only availability and faith that are required for this opening out to take place: in order for growth, increase, to have I as its place.

For "the beginnings" in your poetic universe undoubtedly arise from a capacity for welcoming and for permeability. It's a matter of saying yes. Saying yes to difference, to the possibility of being traversed by differences at any moment. With "the beginnings", which take place, take the place of *I*, bring about the subject's epiphany. This assent, which requires what is called a "*blind* trust", you express very well in connection with the *Lectures de la différence sexuelle*[9] where you underline that it isn't a matter of anything either demonstrative, or calculable, or visible: "The growth of the tree cannot be demonstrated". One cannot demonstrate flux, the course of things, becoming. One is there, simply. When your texts call for beginnings, it seems to me then that this all comes together from a philosophy, a certain ontological mode of the subject, and a poetics. It's a task multiplying relationings in the text in every sense, and consequently, inventions; strokes of the pen, which disturb received positions in grammar, which go as far as a-grammaticism. In sum, this poetics stirs up, reflects upon, relaunches the order of creation and representations. Such is the reading that I would sketch of a poetics of beginnings in your work. Could you, from the perspective of the writer, of writing, offer some enlightenment on this knot of pluralities in the text, from which a certain ink unique to you seems to ebb and flow?

CIXOUS It's true: the plural exists at the beginning. I want to say: at the beginning(s) — and already, by saying it out loud, I'm hoist by my own petard![10] — at the beginning(s), there existed many. Or: there were many.[11] There, as well, difference and its play with the phonic and the literal is active in the French of course. Plural is a magnificent signifier, with its ambiguous ending, which until I condense it down in writing, I'm never sure whether it will be masculine or feminine [*pluriel/plurielle*]. And if it is the masculine ending, it would be a divine ending that would phonically echo and include the feminine, as well as the masculine.[12] That certainly refers to the plan of Genesis "properly" speaking. But genesis, for me, repeats or manifests itself every day, in all beginnings. Each day that we re-begin to begin to be. I constantly return to the experience of being, of being born, of not being what I believe to be,[13] everything that weaves life as experience. Not in the banality of the everyday but in the invention, on the other hand, that each day requires us to carry out. I do not have without you and I am not without you; I is not without you, I am born of you,[14] often I am a she and sometime a heshe: for me, it's structural, I do not think otherwise, I have never thought *I* other than in these relations — in its relationality to another close by. *I* think only: to address. In other words, I only think in an address: I only think about address. With address and maladdress. To you: in this place named you; or to that doorway where different people follow, take their seat, are seated, vanish, appear. But all have over me, in some way, a right to life or death. Like me over them. Me who is you.[15] Me who begins through you.

That's to say that, "for me", to be is already to-be-in-the-plural, in that which is Love, War — I don't say Hate: Love is with War, with what Love allows, struggles, clashes, openings, closures. I have always loved — it comes to mind because it's inscribed in me like a motto on the wall of Montaigne's Tower[16] — I have always loved Shakespeare's phrase "Ourselves we do not owe".[17] We do not own ourselves. We do not know ourselves. We are not masters of ourselves. We need to ponder the mystery of this expression of the self which insists, in language, upon the self, in order to redouble oneself (and so, divide oneself), approach oneself, appropriate one's own own, as if I felt that when I am/say "me" I am no longer me, not enough me, not very me, I am as much you as me; we need to listen to the reassembling of the self that seeks to embrace itself, to espouse itself, to record itself: me-self.[18] And more precisely in English: myself; but English slides towards the possessive adjective, "my-self" says the English language, my-own-self, I own my-self. "We do not own 'our-own'", glosses Shakespeare in a powerful paradox. There is an own but who can say: I am the owner of my own? It's all the same! "It's all the same", and there's another one![19] This idiomatic form "belongs" only to the French language. Shakespeare illustrates it, the extent to which we are beings led astray. We might also be misled, or, on the other hand, enlightened beings. It's a grand statement: we cannot even affirm our sexual stability for it's disrupted by experiences of the other such that we flicker. Shakespeare enacts this in his plays, by way of metamorphoses, as in *A Midsummer Night's Dream*, dressings-up, disguises even. That's pushing into the field of extreme visibility a certain type of statement about the instabilities which are our own. Does that mean that I doubt the fact that I am a woman? Of course not. But I think that our human experience, a marvellous, so enriching experience, is alteration. We are altered, we are altered and disaltered beings through the other. If one were able to radiograph the encounter with you, he, she, if one were able — you were talking about spectres — to make the spectre of your encounter appear, one would see incredible instantaneous mutations . . . Except that generally, before or during the encounter, one arms oneself, one becomes tense, one puts down roots violently so as not to be too shaken by the other. But if one doesn't do that, if one *surrenders*, as you quoted from *La Fiancée juive*, if one really wants to surrender to the encounter, then one finds oneself altered. There are surprises. We will be denatured renatured by the other. In the wake of Shakespeare, I would add: I would really like to know myself but I do not know myself, I do not own my-self, I'm even the person who knows me the least well. I do not know my books either. But I do not seek to know my books, and perhaps precisely because there is a mirror there: perhaps I do not seek to know myself.

MC-G The "know thyself" of Greek philosophy, you re-conceive differently then. You re-connect it:[20] to "you", this double redoubled and divided into two. In your books, I is to you, as subject and object,[21] in a literal manner. From whence, undoubtedly, for reading, the delicious impression of familiar foreignness. The duty of analysis, the auto-reflection of the imperative formula thus becomes not a short circuit of the will centring me upon me, but the long course of travel and adventure towards the other. Where "what one is" does not go without what one does; and what one does, does not go without that towards which one is going, towards that which one allows oneself to go. That which allows oneself to go from oneself.

CIXOUS "Know thyself" I don't really know what that means. I understand on the one hand that a person has the duty to examine themself, to weigh and measure themself, I ought to reply as scrupulously as possible with my ready-prepared verbal gestures. And that's what I am trying to do. But on the other hand, I know, from experience, that everything I might be able to say about "myself", my intimate being, my secret fortress of my own, would be nothing but construction, deceptive statements, and hope. I do not seek to "know" myself full-on. Who am I, she whom I think I am because I would like to be this one that one? I am dressed in qualifiers that you will rightly connect to me. Or she whom I would like you to think I am? I "am" also the sum of the ghosts that bear my name in the fantasies of people near or far. We are imagined imaginers. And we endeavour. Perhaps we have this passion I have for theatre characters because they are the only creatures who might *want* and *be able* to be known. Thus we know Bérénice or King Henry V[22] much more intimately than the people around us. What I would like to know is humanity. When one adopts a child, a gesture of extraordinary complexity, without knowing it probably one adopts humanity, not a single child. Perhaps my gesture would be that: a blind gesture. We believe that when we "make" a child we are not blind, but we are. When we adopt a child, we adopt blindly — necessarily. My movement towards the world is that of adopting a child. That's to say: I do not know whom. I choose but I do not know whom. I write: I do not know what. And at the same time: that's it.

I tell you: I don't know myself; that does not mean that I know nothing about myself or that I exist in unawareness. But to claim knowledge, that has no sense to it. I think we must respect this immense territory, the "unknown", which is the most interesting thing about us: what's to come, what's to be realized. What I will perceive and not harness. And then: I don't know you and that's essential. This "I don't know you" one should not understand negatively. At core, what makes for suffering in the relation to the other, and at the same time what makes for exultation, what fosters desire of the other — without which we would not live: life is to desire the other — is precisely the fact that I don't know you, you surprise me, I don't understand you, and yet I exist in a state of desiring to know. This type of analysis about what we are, some of us and others, thus opens out for me onto existence, onto the possibility and the necessity (which does not mean the impoverishment) of *another knowledge*. It's a moving knowledge, mobile, open, capable of accepting that I cannot own the other; that it is what escapes me, that it is the star, the planet that I observe, on which I consistently perceive innumerable signs. To re-write them — that's it, in the end. Which does not mean that I will be able to calculate it precisely, draw lines. Quite the opposite.

All the same, I am this compound of observations, admirations, uncertainties. You were reminded of *Partie* and the BeyondI: it's a shame that we're restricted from using a personal pronoun such as BeyondI; yet, it would be more exact to place Beyond everywhere. BeyondI Beyondyou Beyondus Beyondher . . . We use personal pronouns that bring us back to unity or singularity, which isn't correct. Iyou, Youme: yes. And of course More I . . . less I . . .

So, what are I us? Who am me?[23] I think that we, human beings, we're a mixture, a reality partially perceived in its effects, by others, which returns to us as an echo. We're a mixture of echoes, of narratives, let's say autobiographies and an "ideal self". Certainly, we are social beings, professions, exercises, practices, we are family roles; but each is a totally separate being, the king of a kingdom that's a narrative. Whoever the person, this person is formed for herself and maintained by the narrative she constructs of herself from childhood. This narrative is necessarily a fiction. It is of course formed of real and verifiable elements; but it's sufficient, for example, for me to be with my brother so that, for the same episode we experienced together, we provide narratives that at once agree on true events and entirely diverge on the reading we give of them. We are our own interpreters. We are the interpreters of events. I have always thought that if one were to interview a couple of lovers, let's take Tristan and Yseut[24] at the age of sixty, and if one were to ask them to narrate "Tristan and Yseut", one would have two books: these two books would be fabulously removed from one another, whilst sharing a common heart. That doesn't mean that one would cancel out the other. But Tristan and Yseut would falter, stupefied, saying but how come you were thinking that, on that fine day in the forest? Well, in any account, I think that you think and I only think because I think that you think. Every exchange is an extraordinary tapestry. It creates one braid, and this braid is one. And we hold onto this cord which is a woven silk cord-on(e),[25] so that we don't lose ourselves; concentrating on our movements we go step-by-step because we are walking upon the void: but with deathblows. As you were saying: by *creating* trust — and it is creation — by creating trust, in me, in you.[26] It is a type of wager but not a once-and-for-all wager, like Pascal's.[27] At every moment of life we gamble anew in order to be able to progress into the void.

When I write (I'm not making a theory), I think I write according to this experience. It isn't a knowledge, simply an experience. I write without trying to dispel uncertainty, the undecidable, ambiguity, faltering.

I was speaking about the "Ideal self": on the one hand, we are inventors; I do not cease to invent myself, to invent you, and what's miraculous is that with all these fictions we manage to find each other! And it's through an act of faith. Through an *act*. Through a decision not to take into account all that we suspect, all that we fear to be on the contrary. On the other hand, we are also blind people who run straight ahead, summoned by the Ideal self: that's to say by a figure, over there in front. And this "Ideal self" (what a fine proper noun: it sounds like the name of a racehorse), we don't know *who* it is. It's perhaps someone, perhaps someone else; in any case, it's someone fine, someone grand, whom we imitate, whom we try to imitate, whom we don't catch up with. You were speaking about impulse: this impulse is two-fold, in my opinion. There's an impulse of the living, of life which wants to live, of the body; and that's a miracle in itself. The body is perhaps the part of me which is at once the closest, the most familiar and the most astonishing — this body which wants to live at any cost and which consistently makes us feel life, death pain ecstasy, the beyond. And then there's fantasy, that extraordinary power which creates characters. Everyone has a phantasmatic capacity — let's call it imaginary — without which nobody exists. A person *is* a creation of the phantasm. Not everyone has an equal power to make a creation of the self, a creature. To create oneself is an activity that gives rise to every excess and every refinement. A person is a work of art. From head to toe and from thought to voice.

MC-G Is this a work of creation through/in language?

CIXOUS To conclude, I ought to open a chapter called "Beyond-Language", because what acts, dictates, fore-word, after-word, is my language. "When I write": there's a phrase that seems to me the sphinx itself. Let's imagine a character called *WhenIwrite*. If I grammatically deconstruct it, there is a When, an I, a write, so that precisely when I write (*WhenIwrite*) it's first of all my language writing. WhenIwrite, it permanently produces itself from happy accidents, which I don't turn away. On the contrary, I listen to them, I gather them, an incredible number of events happen to me, inspirations coming from language. I want to say a thing, and then *that is written out*[28] in an unforeseen manner; whilst personally I'd wanted to write some philosophical statement — so it is that my mother-my partner-my girlfriend-my lover-language presents tremendous material. Programmed material but not by a conscious I. There is the mystery itself: how my language speaks and more brilliantly than me. It speaks in its musical range, encouraging phonic elements to intervene I had absolutely not called for; it speaks, weaving the Frenchlanguage, pushing the wheel along at a very fast, very great speed. So the phrase turns so quickly that it scarcely grazes the line in order to uproot it, in the brief and brisk instant of contact, flickers of signifiers, avowals in French, a real abundance of notes born of that ground, giving birth anew from our very substance. Which is a marvel and a catastrophe for it's totally untranslatable. And at the same time, this untranslatability of language is invented by the couple that "I" makes with the Frenchlanguage, it's this that will make the work of art. It's a style. It's not governable. Gods do indeed exist!

MC-G In the woven cord of the narrative that escorts *I* to the present of writing, where everything happens and returns, again, brand new, does the desire of the other, inextinguishable by definition because it nourishes itself from mourning, does this desire of otherness go by "Temptation" as one of its names? It's the name you give as a sub-title to the book *La Fiancée juive*, where you write: "But perhaps in the beginning there was always Temptation".[29] Temptation does not exist without the tension in language that weaves our narratives. The first, in particular, which is the narrative of the first garden, the first tree, the first desire — the other: mineral-animal-plant-human. It's thus that the narrative tends to recount the "miracle of the body" that you were talking about a moment ago: its relation to the range of language, the inextricably interlaced linkages between the human being and the master. Such is the allegory of the Earthly Garden of Paradise that your text has long celebrated. Above all I like the one that appears in *La*,[30] where the miracle of being-beingborn-into-language breathes life into the whole narrative. The title is exemplary: it provides the "*la*"[31] in effect, provides the tone of musicality to be heard; but it's also the mark of the feminine and the article of all beginnings: several more than a thousand and one possible sentences one could start with "*La*". From this:[32] where the feminine and sexual difference are indissociable from the site of writing. From inscription to an emphasis, a vibration, close to textual difference.

I would like to pause on a fragment to create a resonance from what you have just unfurled in the force of your analysis. More precisely, on this passage, the metamorphic passage of *I* which "takes on the manner of water",[33] that is to say not anthropomorphic manners but, more unheard of, manner from matter, from natural elements that give life to the "infinitely body": "I have flowed, become stagnant, festered, I have fallen from above. Mass, rhythmic, in harmony with my millions of drops, *I have rained*. I have been earth with the earths. Foaming, humid, I have slept *a faceless face down*.[34] I have. Had. Lived. Done. Been. *All the words that grow before the tip of the tongue*, before I reach it. I am *a body who has enjoyed creation*."[35] There is here, in the poetic space of the work, what you were saying: this sprouting of language which grows and crossbreeds[36] in every sense, extending beyond the finality of syntax. Thus, according to the terms of rhythmic progression, where a crowd of past participles accumulate, participants of a narrative, which that narrative works to call forth presently, there is the phrase at its acme: *I have rained*.[37] A major accident in language, a case of perfect a-grammaticality. This accident, on the one hand, strongly affirms that the marvellous nourishing the imaginary of our narratives from the beginnings of the world has no place within the norms of grammar. This accident, on the other hand, has, in its poetic stroke, an astonishing effectiveness. There's no mistake here; the "I have rained" is not understood according to the orthodoxy of the French language which should here pick out the verb to please [*plaire*] and not the verb to rain [*pleuvoir*]. Without hesitating, the reader translates, interprets, makes the correct mistake: "I have rained" — "it has rained I, a rainfall of I". Another case of BeyondI: the person grows from what grammatically belongs to the realm of the impersonal (It rained). It's superb, and it's precisely what you were saying: the I-Language couple makes a work of art. Creation and poeticity.

CIXOUS Something happens which can only happen, for me, in this particular case, in the Frenchlanguage. It's an effect of the Frenchlanguage. It's a gift, and then it's lost. I tell myself sometimes that it's human fate. Like in a fairytale, someone gives you infinite wealth, a grace like that, then they take it away from you again. Someone offers you everything — "someone": I was saying "gods" — and straightaway, so that you don't get the wrong idea, they take it away again. Oh you had it? Well, be sure that, in the next-door room, it has no value. It doesn't go. Everything happens then as if someone had given you gold, "someone", language — but this gold has no value except in your home. This makes you humble. This gold is out of circulation except in your circulations.

MC-G In your circulations and even in this passage here which has built up what surrounds it, which makes this "I have rained" obvious in this context. But this coup is unique. Besides, on another page, in another book, you start at the beginning. It's never the same case of textual economy.

CIXOUS That's it too, poetic pain: it's a bursting of wonderful moments and at the same time, in contrast to what is anchored in philosophy, it's ephemeral, it passes by. And so quickly: who will have heard it? When I say "sexual difference, the 'S.D' "[38] passes by, and that's it. There's nothing more beautiful in the world than what "itpassesby", and at the same time it's the most searing because it passes by — and it's lost.

MC-G It's in this that texts give us an irreplaceable experience.

CIXOUS Of mourning.

MC-G Of mourning, but also flashes of light.

CIXOUS Absolutely.

MC-G A poetics of beginnings and interruptions is exactly that. Not stability, linearity but mourning, flashes of light, starriness, crossroads. As for textual-sexual difference, it occurs for example in the displacement, above, of the expression "face down": "a face belonging to somebody down", which makes us read literally "flat".[39]

CIXOUS And at the same time, there is "a face": you no longer know whose. Mine? Yours? If I write "face down", it's mine; if I write "a face down", it could be yours.

MC-G It's the principle of more-pronouns: "Iyou", and the constellations that you write "himorher", "herorhim" where the event can only be glimpsed, in the in-between-letters.

CIXOUS Can only be glimpsed by the person whose soul has the same vibratility, the same organic economy.

MC-G You have often spoken in your books of your need for the books of other writers, those you like and admire. "Without my books, I could not live"; "Without Shakespeare, without Homer, without: the Bible, Kleist, Kafka, Dostoevsky, I would never have been able to live."[40] In other words, at the beginning of your books, there are others-in-writing. One of these texts seems to me to have, perhaps because of the consistency with which you return to it, recurrent citations, diffuse references, a separate place in your work: the Book, the Bible. You draw from this source that seems inexhaustible, brings you to rewritings and displacements. I see several perspectives outlined here. First of all it's the text common to a great number of people who share a certain cultural field, a shared possession; a heritage which you make yield fruit and which allows you, perhaps, to have a more immediate proximity to the reader, who immediately receives an address, an implication. It also seems to me, besides, that you draw very unique effects from it, regarding dream writing in fiction. The dream scene, important in the books you write, takes on an intensity not foreign to that of the biblical dream; has the same foreignness. It's a dream that says "true", which bears a premonitory truth — sign, magic, prophetic vision. It thus constitutes in fiction a sort of primitive power that acts as a medium in the text. It seems to me in the end, and it's not the least of its effects, that your works nourish, through biblical narratives, a vision of the human considered in its at once everyday and ontological fragility: a creature frozen in the silt of the earth and destined to return to dust. As if, by taking on the state of humanity, such as it is painted in the Bible, you consistently put it to the test of a poetic and philosophical questioning which echoes contemporary life. Such that the act of reading is called upon, through the braiding of archaic narratives and their re-writings, to take the initiative in the process of interpretation. Can you talk about your relationship as a writer to these texts that seem to be like the roots of your own?

CIXOUS I will return, first of all, to the "others" present in my writing. The extent to which they are present, these others, in my writing, I do not myself know. It happens sometimes, having to look at my own texts, that I see unsuspected traces of myself. And probably imperceptible, this has been combined, re-worked, shifted, transported, transferred, meditated so much. As for the Bible: I'm not sure that it is more important than other texts . . .

MC-G Not more important: it's the recurring recourse to this book that seems to give it a particular weight, a separate function . . .

CIXOUS That's it, I wouldn't make the presence of the Bible in my texts into a sort of primo-ancestrality, because there are others. But it's true that the Bible has a status . . .

MC-G . . . a status of genesis of your genesis?

CIXOUS It's true, although here again, there would be others. Shakespeare, for me, has the same status. In terms of the Bible, I must say there are many levels in my relationship to this book. First of all, effectively, I must have some sort of phantasm, which I've never formulated, and which would be that books are full of books: that they take their source from books, and that there are some originary books which are ancestors. We are Western human beings. All Western human beings have common ancestors, even if they don't know it. We descend from a certain number of ancestors who are a mixture of Biblical characters and characters belonging to the Homeric tradition. The majority don't know it: the average man doesn't think he's a descendent of Oedipus, and yet he is. I'll clarify: Oedipus the Greek, Sophocles's, not Freud's one. Freud's one is himself a German descendent of the Greek. I add to this: of course we don't descend only from Oedipus, but also from Catopithecus,[41] Moses, the kings of Denmark, Iceland, Jerusalem, etc. I must admit — it's a confession — that my first knowledge of the Bible is from long ago; but, well, it had for me the ranking, grandiose at the time, of legends and fairytales. I did not distinguish the Bible from the myths and legends that have transported me since I was small. The sources were a mixture of children's books, the *Iliad* and the *Odyssey*, which I read very early on, stories by my German grandmother, Omi, who bore, in our fatherless family, the Jewish tradition. (The Bible was passed on by an old woman who spoon-fed us David.) So that, when in my childhood we celebrated Jewish festivals, for me it was always fairytales. The story of the Maccabees, the story of Elijah fed by the ravens, the incredulous Moses, the story of Esther and Assuerus, all this we lived as small children brought up in a certain culture but not in a certain religion. Our family tradition being cut off from a faith, there remained legend and mythology. Here there were very familiar characters, who had absolutely no sacred status. Every one profane and fascinating. My grandmother was born *Jonas*: I have always thought that I was descended from Jonas, there was a whale in my childhood, and I used to remember my travels in the whale's stomach. That was part of my imaginary cradle and it didn't have the grand rank of a Biblical meditation. This was my first Shakespeare — who came later. Before me, there was a superior humanity who had as Other, as partner, as interlocutor, Jehovah known as "Adonai". But this humanity which was superior in its discourse, was not so in its behaviour. I remember having taken part — just as I took part in the *Iliad* and the *Odyssey* and in Shakespeare — in the great quarrels over the course of the story of David for example. To see David enter close to Saul, to be thrilled by the love of David and Jonathan, all that fascinated me, but it was devoid of ethical reflection. It was human. Such that, at heart, the Bible was my first "story-of-France"; it's been a very familiar universe since childhood. The text I read in translations; I have never read it in Hebrew. So there's a linguistic core which totally escapes me, and that I haven't acquired. That says something about my relationship to the Bible: for me it's a theatrical universe. It's my first great theatre. Even later, I read with a definitive emotion the texts "without characters", if I can say that: *Ecclesiastes*, the *Canticle of Canticles*. They have become accompaniments for all time. And in "my" truth, there you have two great sacred texts. I found there a philosophy, at once impassioned and formidable, of existence, beginnings and endings, of the battle between love and death, which for me remains unequal. This philosophy certainly later engendered all the great poetic texts and theatrical fictions. Necessarily.

MC-G What poetics, what theatricality for your texts in particular?

CIXOUS In my texts, it provides me with a partner, partners. When I wrote *L'Indiade*[42] which took place in India and where the characters were not from a Judeo-Christian culture, there was the Bible, just as there would have been Oedipus. Because there is, in the Bible, every family scene, all our scenes which are war-scenes within the family, or wars between families. Let's take the Judgement of Soloman, the primitive love scene: what does it mean but to fight over the body of a child? Who loves? What does it mean to love? To want to take to keep to kill to leave to open out your arms? The judgement of Solomon is particularly beautiful because it's a scene at once private and public. A scene of the bed, the bedroom, the city.

MC-G It's a scene which gives you a structure and which avoids the predetermination of psychological motivation.

CIXOUS And that precedes and engenders philosophy. All philosophy then aims to re-work these scenes which existed as scenes as it were "without commentary". These are scenes which act, which tear into *pieces*, this is precisely the case, in every manner: at once, upon the scene and the human heart.

MC-G You mean that it's also because the Bible calls for commentary, in a certain manner, that it's a text which draws you in? That it's an invitation to interpret, to cross through?

CIXOUS Of course, it's above all because there's no commentary. Each time, it's relaunched, it opens out to all choices. In contrast to a preacher's discourse, which signals, the Bible allows freedom: you can commit another sin, you can be saved, you can choose grace, you can choose love, you can choose crime to infinity. The quality of undecidable ethics that exists in the Bible, like in the *Iliad* and the *Odyssey*, is what renders it precious for me.

MC-G It's not prescriptive, not judged in advance: there is no judgement and the "ways are impenetrable" . . .

CIXOUS There's no judgement. God himself knows infringement. The God in the Bible is a God who makes investments, who takes part, gets angry. He is quick-tempered, jealous surprised so he punishes. He's a sort of SuperGod.

MC-G A SuperGod who is at the same time implicated in human affairs. In this sense, he is rather SuperHuman, the creator of these creatures. And in a permanent relationship of address, of being on first name terms, that is to say of authority but also of familiarity with his human beings.

CIXOUS He's a judge, for at the same time, he settles things ceaselessly. But he's not cold. He's a boiling God; and he worries a lot. In sum, he's an *author*! And as an author, he's furious. Obviously, he becomes a character who's not separable from us. Here's a God who doesn't pardon — there needs to be a Righteousness in order for him to pardon. He pardons, but differently. He's there, furious in front of his creation; delivering it even. The Book of Job is one of the most beautiful things in the world. It's infinite. It's a book in itself, for in the Bible, furthermore, there are *several* books! Personally, I'll never stop reading the Book of Job. It's the work of all works. This dialogue between Job and God and the men is so great, that at core, it's Job who is God. This is unprecedented. "Do you really think that anyone can escape me?" Satan says to God. And God who delivers Job to Satan! Without being sure of the outcome! Finally, here's a human version; if one reflects from a theological plane, one might say that God knew etc. But in the Bible, it isn't stated that God knows what the outcome will be: there's a frightening and magnificent suspense. Job suffers because of God and in opposition to God, he wants to die in opposition to God.

MC-G Is that it, the fight that's replayed, symbolically, at every scene of writing re-begun? Language, daily roles each time explored again? Is it that, in some way, this God-author in the Bible might bring about your own writing, canvassing different points of view, searching for other paths, testing the limits?

CIXOUS I ought to be able to say yes calmly. But as I don't believe in a unique origin, I don't say yes calmly. Probably it's my own theological structure that's in the work; giving me this vision of the world in which I believe in battle, in chance, in intervention. I believe that nothing is simple, that everything is divided from the beginning, intrinsically. Another confession, in this regard; when I was small, I could identify myself . . . it's madness . . . with Samson, without really knowing why. Now, I know. He's a character whom I saw very well how, why, whilst being an upright person, could become twisted having lost everything, by a blindness that precedes blindness.

MC-G The versatile side of destiny touched you?

CIXOUS Yes, but which isn't Greek versatility. With the Greeks, it's an entirely different thing. I've never been moved by the tremendous Greek schemata which is a schemata of heritage. Let's take the Atrids: Oedipus pays for a sin committed generations ago. The same goes for Agamemnon. There's something fearsome, cruel, opaque, terrifying, in the Greeks' transmission of the curse. In the Bible, the role of choice is stronger, and the responsibility begins with me and you. You see then diversions, deviations, the weak man before a Law. An example: Jonas is afraid. He's marked out as a prophet and he puts his fingers in his ears and he hurls himself towards the whale smaller than God this Whale, he's so scared. I find this admirable. It's so true. And Samson who is the man of God, loses everything because, according to God but not according to us, he commits the mistake of loving a woman who's a Philistine, that's to say Palestinian. Samson ahead of God — in — the story. Samson who for not having blindly obeyed God — loses his life. And the Bible allows oblique readings and passes with a light step from the plane of the absolute to the plane of the general and inversely, and the two planes are nevertheless clearly separate. God remains inimitable, incomprehensible, man does what he can, and there will be only one Abraham. The blessed kings rot, the just become annoyed, temptation is everywhere, but also hospitality, there's a crack in every wall, justice doesn't reign, besides there are several — it rises and it falls, the whole Book is made up of a reassuring ferocity: humanity struggles against itself.

MC-G These fluctuations, this opening out to the least logical possibilities, the most improbable of the narrative — sure-and-not-sure, the worst just as much as the best — do they not ally the texts of the Bible to the dream scene? A dream of a particular genre since it is indissociable from creation. And from the Verb. Besides there are dream scenes in the Bible extremely pregnant with meaning, which always tell a truth somewhere — even despite, or because of being part of another order, another kingdom. Do you see some analogy, a filiation between these scenes and the dream's task operating under your pen and which makes an oblique force point out these passages, these crossings — which in fiction abolish all dichotomy between the order of "reality" and the order of "onerism"?

CIXOUS There neither, I'm not sure if the relationship is direct. I am a dreamer, I was born a dreamer. I even remember dreams I had[43] when I was three or four years old. It's true: the status of the dream in the Bible — but you find this again in all the ancient texts, the legend of Gilgamesh[44] for example — makes the dream one of these forces which advance man in the Story. Something unheard of, it's for the light of dreams that Gilgamesh leaves, hero of the Sumerian sword, upon the discovery of the "mortal being", three thousand years BC.

MC-G This is the oracular status of the dream. It makes writing visionary . . .

CIXOUS It could well be, it's a hypothesis, that this has allowed us to consider the dream as not just froth, as they say in German: "Traüme sind Schaüme".[45] Just the contrary.

MC-G In any case, just the contrary in your books, where dream is activity, is the carrier bearing diverse themes which you thus succeed marrying in their heterogeneity. As if it were there [là] the only force strong enough to entail in advance what, without it, might create a blockage.

CIXOUS That's exactly right. Here's an observation: I think that poets are dreamers and that there are, notably, many poems by Rimbaud which are transcriptions of dreams. And moreover, in terms of the dream's rights, or the dream's intelligence: the dream is more intelligent than me, before me, for me, everything that I don't know. Freud developed this at length. Which doesn't prevent the dreamer, even if he has read Freud — even if, then, the Master of dreams told him that there's a task, that the dream's intention makes sense even though it's repressed, that there's space to interpret and that the appearance of the absurd is a mask the dream puts on so it can be performed — even if the dreamer knows this, if *we* know all this, we continue to wake up in the morning saying: I had an idiotic dream! Personally, I need to find someone else in me to intervene, who says: ah you know that when you say that dream is absurd, you should remember that it's this one that's the most interesting and which holds the key to everything. It's a task I carry out all the time: in the morning I am always two in this case. In other words, I am flanked by the interpreter I could be. But the poetic dreamer is always ready to be carried away with the dream.

MC-G In the case of written fiction, you do not offer up interpreted dreams, there's no interpretation. You give the dream life, if I can say that. In its primitive undecipherability, its difficulty of access, its code. You keep its secret and you transcribe it in this way.

CIXOUS It's because the interpreter I am has learned to let the dream speak, in other words to leave it its language. And not to do what one generally does: to reconstruct. The only passage to interlocution, when one recounts a dream, is already to be in translation: in other words very far away at a distance, in the first translation, the second translation, etc. In the ineluctable distortion of the meta-text. One must know that, if I make an effort to let the dream speak in its "own language", which is extremely difficult, what I allow to pass in my text has, all the same, an economy and a necessity. That makes sense. But of course there is no "own language". There is only unbridled language. Uncontained.

MC-G It doesn't speak alone. Language provides an abutment and an edge as well, to thought. That makes the text.

CIXOUS Exactly. I'm not placing in doubt that a text is the eruption of the unconscious. But, what about writers who are able to write the earth's crust, from a cooler perspective? That's a relevant question for me. At that moment, it's repression which is the work's basis. That offers other types of processes, images.

MC-G Meaning that, from the moment one doesn't fix, one doesn't try to tell oneself there is a very clear origin, codified in advance, the explosion of the writing's subject occurs.

CIXOUS For a long time I thought, in a kind of ignorance, innocence, lack of knowledge, that I wasn't the author of my texts but my unconscious was their author — without counting the innumerable other authors of my texts! Observing language's soaring and moving autonomy, I used to tell myself: it's not me who writes this, it's the Night. I was very disturbed. I used to wonder if it weren't a reprehensible act to let go of the reins, to allow oneself to be carried away, and at the end to sign one's name. Well, I hadn't yet measured the extent to which this source, this energy, was present in several other texts. Because dream is textual energy: our personal nuclear energy.

NOTES

1. *Partie* [Part] (Paris: Éditions des femmes, 1976).
2. In French "Plusje". The word "plus" generally connotes a comparative "more than", as in "elle est plus intelligente que moi" (she is more intelligent than I am). Cixous's coinage "plusje" contains plurality in this sense of "more than". However, when employed with a negative, "plus" can also be taken to mean "no longer" or "no more", as in "il ne la voit plus" (he no longer sees her) or "son père n'est plus" (his father is no more [in the sense of having passed away]). I have chosen to translate "Plusje" as "BeyondI" in to order to maintain both the idea of "more than"/plurality and "no longer".
3. In French "mais aussi, lorsque la pronociation ne fait pas entendre le s, plus-de-je". Calle-Gruber here signals the pronunciation of the "s" which is elided in "Plusje" by changing it to "plus-de-je". This pronunciation invokes both the comparative and superlative usages of "plus", with the implication of "more-than-I", or "the-most-of-I", as well as the mathematical sign "plus-I".
4. An extract from *Partie* presented by Hélène Cixous in "Bisexualité et différence des sexes" [Bisexuality and Difference of the Sexes], *Nouvelle Revue de Psychanalyse* 7, Spring 335, 1973. My translation.
5. The English language misses the play with gender here, which is apparent in written French, yet is also veiled in speech ("Or, dire, comment le disent tes texts, qu'on ne peut commencer qu'au pluriel, que plurielle . . .").
6. *La Fiancée juive de la tentation* [The Jewish Fiancée of Temptation] (Paris: Éditions des femmes, 1995). My translation, Gruber's emphasis.
7. Again, the subtlety is missed in English. In the French the plural "s" of "commencement(s)" is not pronounced, which allows this ambiguity.
8. In French "rendez-vous", which re-uses the verb and implies a surrendering of each term to the other as well as the space of an encounter. Of course, its pedestrian usage merely connotes a meeting or appointment.
9. "Contes de la différence sexuelle" [Tales of Sexual Difference], *Lectures de la différence sexuelle* [Readings of Sexual Difference], Mara Negron (ed.), 26 (Paris: Éditions des femmes, 1994). ("Why, I wonder, should I today, in our times, demonstrate that trees grow? Or rather, why should the tree prove that it grows?")
10. In French, "je noie mon poisson!" Cixous here signals the ambiguity of the plural "s" being unpronounced in spoken French.
11. In French, "il y avait pluriel. Ou: il y eut pluriel". Both tenses are translatable as "there were" in English — I have tried to convey the continuity of the imperfect tense in contrast to the suddenness of the past historic by contrasting "there were" with "there existed".
12. In French, "Et s'il est le *el* masculin, ce serait le *el(le)* divin." Cixous plays on the fact that the masculine ending "-el" sounds the same as the feminine pronoun "elle". However if "-el" makes up the first part of "elle", the second part "-le" is the masculine definite article. It could be argued that the masculine both comprises and is incorporated or enveloped by the feminine.
13. In French, "je reviens à l'expérience d'être, de naître, de n'être pas ce que je crois être . . .". Cixous is here playing on the sounds of "naître" (to be born) and "n'être pas" (not to be).
14. In French, "Je n'ai pas sans tu et je ne suis pas sans toi; je n'est pas sans tu, je nais de toi . . .". The assonance is apparent in the French with the repetition of sounds in "n'ai", "n'est", and "nais".
15. The French reads "Moi qui suis toi". The "suis" here might be aurally interpreted as belonging to the verb "suivre", and thus the phrase could be understood as "Me who follows you".
16. The Renaissance philosopher Montaigne retired from public life to his library tower to write in isolation for several years, producing his monumental *Essais*. Upon entry to the tower, he had

a statement of purpose inscribed on the walls, announcing his intention to work and write in tranquillity and freedom away from the world.

17. The quote, which is in English in the original interview, is from Shakespeare's *Twelfth Night*, Act I, Scene V.
18. "Moi-même" in French literally translates as "me-self", as opposed to the more possessive English my-self.
19. In French, "Il y a du propre mais qui peut dire: moi je suis le propriétaire de mon propre? C'est du propre!! 'C'est du propre', en voilà une autre!" The word-play on "propre" (own) in the idiom emphasizes Cixous's point.
20. "Tu le relis donc autrement. Tu le relies . . .". "Relire", meaning "to re-read", and "relier", meaning "to link up" or "to connect", are employed by Gruber for their phonic similarity.
21. In French, "Dans tes livres, Je est à tu et à toi, de façon littérale." The English "you" does not make this distinction.
22. The references are to *Bérénice* by Jean Racine and *King Henry V* by William Shakespeare.
23. In French, "que sont-je nous. Qui suis-me?" The first question echoes another question asked by Cixous "qui sont-je?" (who are I), a homophone of a further question "qui songe?" ("who muses/dreams/contemplates"). Here it is not "qui songe" but "que songe nous", which might be understood as an imperative: "Dream us". The second question "qui suis-me?" could be interpreted as "who am me" or "who follows me", as one might aurally interpret the "suis" as belonging to the verb "suivre" (to follow), rather than "être" (to be).
24. The medieval tale of an adulterous affair between the Cornish Knight, Tristan, and the Irish Princess, Yseut. Like most legends, several versions of the story exist.
25. "Nous tenons à ce fil qui est un fil de soi(e)s tissés . . .". Cixous employs the word "soie" (silk) which sounds the same as "soi" (self), or "sois" (plural selves, or the present subjunctive form of "être" [to be].)
26. In French, "en faisant — et c'est de la fabrication — en faisant confiance . . .".
27. The seventeenth-century philosopher's wager was that, based on the eventual and expected value of the consequences, it is a better proposition to believe that God exists. If one lives one's life according to this and is right in one's belief, one goes to heaven; if incorrect, there is nothing lost. On the other hand, if one does not believe in the existence of God, one arguably has a great deal to lose.
28. In French "ça s'écrit" can also mean "it is spelt".
29. *La Fiancée juive*, 78, my translation.
30. *La* [The (Feminine)/There] (Paris: Gallimard, 1976).
31. In French "la" is the feminine article, as well as the musical note "A".
32. "À partir de là" — the "là" meaning "there" echoes the "la" of the feminine.
33. *Ibid.*, 56, my translation.
34. In French, "à plat ventre jamais membré". The idea is of an impersonal "face down". See also note 39.
35. *Ibid.*, 56–7, my translation.
36. In French there is a play on "croît" (believe) and "croise" (cross).
37. "J'ai plu" draws on the verbs "plaire" (to please) and "pleuvoir" (to rain).
38. The French has "D.S", a homophone of "déesse" (goddess).
39. The French reads, "Quant à la difference textuelle-sexuelle, elle passe par exemple dans le déplacement, ci-dessus, de l'expression 'à plat ventre': 'à plat un ventre membre', ce qui fait lire littéralement 'à plat'."
40. Mireille Calle-Gruber, Hélène Cixous, *Photos de Racine* [Rootprints], 102 and 84, (Paris: Éditions des femmes, 1994). My translation.

41. The name given to the earliest higher primates.
42. *L'Indiade, ou L'Inde de leur rêves* [Indiada, Or the India of Their Dreams] (Paris: Théâtre du Soleil, 1987).
43. In French the phrase is "faire un rêve" which implies a greater sense of creation than the more passive English "to have a dream".
44. Gilgamesh was an ancient Sumerian King of Uruk, in Babylonia. The Gilgamesh epic tells the tale of a part-god, part-human king in his struggle to avoid death. Written on clay tablets by anonymous authors, and conveyed through oral traditions, there exist many versions and translations of these tales.
45. Literally "dreams are froth", the phrase conveys common nineteenth-century and positivist attitudes that dreams have nothing to do with "reality". The notion was called into question by Freud in his work on the unconscious and dreams.

Part II: Writing the feminine

5. When I do not write, it is as if I had died

Interview with Jean-Louis de Rambures. Translated by Elizabeth Lindley.

This interview is translated here from "Hélène Cixous: Quand je n'écris pas, c'est comme si j'étais morte", in *Comment travaillent les écrivains* [How Writers Work], Jean-Louis de Rambures, 56–63 (Paris: Flammarion, 1978). An unrevised version appeared under the same title in *Le Monde* (9 April), 20, 1976. The first two paragraphs are by Hélène Cixous.

A method is a word that means nothing to me. I would not follow one, as my work is analogous to a relationship of love.

The text I write is an object of desire to me. Between it and me, there is an exchange that occurs day and night. It does not matter if this happens on paper or not. In some ways, I live with it constantly. All that would happen within me — continuously fermenting emotions, desires, anxiety — I never cease to recapture and rework in order to return it to this other body in the process of maturing next to me. At root, it is precisely as if I made more than another body with my own body.

J-LdR One point is certain: you are a writer who produces in abundance.

CIXOUS I believe I have much to say on this "abundance". First, from an anecdotal point of view, there is, on the part of the classical editorial houses, a little operation of indirect censorship that consists of leaving manuscripts lying around for two, three, four years. And then suddenly, something unblocks itself. So people are amazed: once again two books by Hélène Cixous coming out at the same time. All the same, the year consists of three hundred and sixty five days. When writing, in that case, wouldn't this only be two pages a day over two hundred days, you do the maths . . . I'd tend to invert your question: how is it that there are moments when a writer doesn't write? For me, writing is the breath, the respiration, it is a necessity as imperious as the need to wake up, to touch, to eat, to kiss, to progress. When I do not write, it is as if I had died.

51

The fact that they emphasize the excessive side of my writing is an effect of the rivalry between the sexes. It never pleases the "economic man" [*éconhomme*] that there is an overflowing feminine. It appears to him incompatible with what I call "God the Old" in which *La*[1] ascribes the woman, like a mythical, imaginary existence. At its extreme, by showing his proper economic restraint, "the old envious man" [*vieux l'envieux*] suspects we are able to produce this "excess" only, moreover, by paying from a "without" — for example, from the sacrifice of our femininity as a potential sensual pleasure: "She writes in abundance, but she doesn't live". Well! I do, quite rightly.

> As long as a woman is possessed and allows herself to be held, body and texts, at the interior of the old, paternal and capitalist structure that reduces and prostitutes her, and as long as a woman subjects herself to the law which recognizes her only as a merchant's object, she is forbidden to think, to progress, to produce the extraordinary, the original, and a life. But we are of an age marked by the birth of a Women's Movement and by its effects of transforming all symbolic structures.
>
> From now on I have this opportunity to publish with the *Éditions des Femmes*[2], a place which straightaway registered outside the scene of castration and its sterilizing economy. A completely different place that realistically gave women the means to transform their practices of writing, and thus to be women in History. At last, writing may cease to be a narcissistic and individualistic gesture. At last, the text may cease to supply a lacking reality, to mask the lack with a utopia, and take its place as a production that thinks of itself without avoiding politics, in a structure that, for the first time, writes, publishes, elaborates new forms of thought and produces — being a woman in desire and reality — all these gestures establishing living relationships with each other. That the stature of writing changed: "*des Femmes*" made this both possible and necessary.[3]

J-LdR You work[4] at Vincennes on feminine writing. What are you planning there?

CIXOUS Careful! I am not trying to create a feminine writing, but to let into writing what has always been forbidden up until now, knowing the effects of femininity. I am still at the research stage.

On the one hand, from a critical reading of the textual productions that make up authority, a reading I endeavour to carry to the level of imaginary structures, where writing, when it avoids contemplating its contradictions and contents itself with the shelter of the real, there, in its house of paper, serves ideology and fabricates prestige more than sense. So much so that in the majority of cases, the "writer" (a worrying, misleading word, that returns to the one whose aim is to be read and who holds the right to be believed, to make law and morals, in the name of some thought, in the name of an image) in fact intensifies the symbolic power I would like women to tackle in writing. On the other hand, from an analysis of the connections that develop between the terms writing — power — women — politics — taking into account the contradictions I myself have to deal with in practice.[5]

For years I have tried to elaborate something, but I sense that I'm now reaching places where this begins to move forward.

To claim writing doesn't brand sexual difference is to consider it like a simple manufactured object. As soon as you admit that it passes through the entire body, you are forced to acknowledge that it inscribes an instinctual economy of entirely different modes of expenditure or sensual pleasure. That women are in a particular proximity to everything of the "interior" order and corporal gesture — of primary structures — is even less surprising than the fact that culturally we find ourselves to have been relegated to the domestic space. The masculine debit is always organized, reserved, held back by the effect of a calculation in relation to an end. Everything takes place as if man had to achieve a precise goal and said to himself: "Here is how I must arrange my weapons, my reserves, my supply, considering the resources at my disposal". On a narcissistic stage, he is always in a position of combat or defence. Woman, in spite of the narcissism that, under the term of coquetry, is assigned to her by popular psychology (one says to her: "If you want to stimulate, be beautiful", then she hastens to make faces), she doesn't have this need of social recognition so determining in the masculine. She is indifferent to calculations. Simultaneously closer to her more agonized unconscious, but also more courageous, she searches to take pleasure in writing in an erotic sense. She genuinely makes love to the text.

I would add that femininity in the text produces effects of continuity far greater than masculinity. What strikes me when I read texts actually written by women is precisely this type of extremely intense process, which lasts [*tient le coup*] a very long time. It's as if they had the ability to subsist in a state of diving, from which they would only surface at very rare intervals to get their breath back. Thus, evidently, for the reader, this makes for a very winding text. But, for me, it is entirely in relation to feminine pleasure that I experience an outpouring, at once without respite and without specific origin.

As strange as this sounds, the writer who, to my knowledge, has been the furthest in this form of continuous and sparsely punctuated writing is James Joyce. Is it because, at core, he was a man jealous of woman and because he could not refrain from continually glueing his ear to her body, her belly? What is certain is that his text (particularly *Finnegans Wake*) lets femininity through in a very powerful way.

> But how? Between obscenity and travesty, Joyce recorded the "stream of consciousness" of his own wife; there, where his text reproduces his wife's lifetime and puts it in book form, all women feel themselves, in an ambiguous way, both heard, but with a dishonest ear, and exploited.[6]

But above all, do not go concluding that Joyce helped me find my voice. I chose *Ulysses*[7] as a thesis subject because being a woman, I knew the resistance of the university to all feminine work, where Joyce is really perceived as a phallus. I said to myself: I will take the most difficult text, the mountain before which smiles draw back (I speak of men). Moreover, it is rather a question of getting beyond the academic stronghold, a terrain studied by texts and where I did not want to encounter censorship.

J-LdR All the same, are there rules you observe in your work?

CIXOUS The only rule I observe is to be implacable and merciless with my unconscious.

In the beginning, I always allow myself to be interrogated by something that affects just my body, let us say my interior life, in the style of a secret and with a particular violence. It's as if there was, in that interior space that psychoanalysts call the unconscious, a strange and unsettling presence which interrogates me: for example, in *La*,[8] why a particular look fascinates me? What keeps me in a face? Or, in the text on which I am presently working (it must be called *Angst*)[9] what is this anguish that has haunted me forever, that means I wake up abruptly as if I were going to die? Of what is it made? Where does this happen? These are the questions I ask myself and that give me the start. Above all, do not ask me where I'm going. I know nothing, or rather I am headed there where I'm afraid.

There is an entire work that consists of watching; not on a trivial level. What people say in the street is surveyed and repressed. I attempt to hear by the silences, the gazes, the manner by which bodies speak. I work solely on the forbidden (it is what renders my texts difficult).

In my work, my luck is to have a writing partner who is none other than the dream. Indeed, as soon as I begin a text, a connection makes itself automatically. I begin to dream in such a way that dream and text endlessly exchange. It is painful and terrifying in a way (when[10] I began *Angst*, in the space of two months I succeeded in having twenty dreams, setting the scene for a certain type of death). But at the same time, it's as if I had a double voice. On the one hand, a conscious voice, which tells me "speak" and to which I am obliged to answer, on the other hand, a nocturnal voice, which doesn't stop pursuing me. The important thing is to note all these dreams at the very moment they flash. And, believe me, it isn't easy. There is always something that tells me "you will remember, you can sleep" or again "what an idiotic dream, without relevance". Fortunately, we know the ruses of the unconscious. So, I use violence. I always have a large notebook close to me and I tear myself from my sleep to write down all my dreams. The text, which is in the process of making itself, re-inscribes others on the text. It's in this way that all circulates between my life, my body, my unconscious, history, my text, and that everything mixes in me, like my own blood.

When I start a text, I surround myself with a dozen other texts (some continuously help me: the Bible in its different versions, Shakespeare, Kafka . . .). Others play a part following the necessity for a type of one-on-one interrogation that I will not stop throughout my work: "And you, how did you survive the tear?" Indeed, I always have the sensation that I'm not alone, but that I write to the other and in the name of others. It's a kind of dialogue with my past selves, those who belong to memory and culture on the one hand and, on the other hand, with those I love in the present and in the future, and with whom I wish to realize a certain joy, a certain pain, a certain strength.

Writing is always a tension in language, a struggle. There is an entire linguistic work that differs according to the texts. During *Neutre*[11] and *Partie*,[12] I endeavoured to play with words and letters endlessly. Because it's a matter of interrogating the subject's relations with the languages he/she speaks and that speak to them. *Angst*, itself, is driven by a very syncopated rhythm. This allows me to use a vocabulary composed of fairly short words. In this way, each text reclaims one or many dictionaries or lexicons appropriated to its movement. One item became very important: silence. Because for me, writing is the decent into hell, and the door is my body. This one must therefore separate itself from a particular exterior, so that this being inside me which is writing can begin the voyage.

For personal reasons of operation, I put myself to work very early, around 5 or 6 in the morning, and I continue until the outside world comes to interrupt me. But then, I am so taken in my vision that everything occurs as if there was nothing else beyond my work. This decent down to hell can last ten hours. I'm no longer hungry, everything outside my work comes to a standstill. Sometimes, when I emerge, I think I have written without pause, even if, in fact, I only covered a single page in writing.

When I came out of my first text, *Le Prénom de Dieu*,[13] it was by crawling, I had neither arms nor legs, only a tongue that moved. At the time of writing the first words of *Angst*, I remained blocked on a page as if a bridge had been broken and I found myself in front of an insurmountable abyss. I began the same sentence again two hundred times in succession, without physically succeeding in moving on to the following.

J-LdR Do you feel relieved when a text finishes?

CIXOUS I do not think at all in those terms. Besides, does one ever rid oneself of anguish? It is content to return with another face. Let us say that I feel pain of a hideous manner when I do not write and of a frightening and menacing manner when I write.

In any case, I do not write with an end in sight, but always for other beginnings.[14]

NOTES

1. The reference here is to Cixous's novel *La* [The (Feminine)/There] (Paris: Gallimard, 1976).
2. The name of a women-only publishing company, started in 1972, by the French Women's Group "Psychanalyse et Politique" [Psychoanalysis and Politics].
3. The inset passage was added in October 1977 by Hélène Cixous [interviewer's note].
4. The text has "travailler" here. This translation has assumed that this is an erroneous setting of "travaillez" (work) which would be the correct form following "vous" (you).
5. The inset passage was added in October 1977 by Hélène Cixous [interviewer's note].
6. The inset passage was added in October 1977 by Hélène Cixous [interviewer's note].
7. Cixous wrote her doctoral thesis on the work of James Joyce, published as *L'Exil de James Joyce ou l'art du remplacement* [The Exile of James Joyce or the Art of Replacement], Publications de la Faculté des lettres et sciences de Paris-Sorbonne (Paris: Grasset, 1968).
8. See note 1, above.
9. *Angst* [Anguish] (Paris: Éditions des femmes, 1977).
10. The French text has "quant" here. This translation has assumed that this is an erroneous setting of "quand" (when).

11. *Neutre* [Neuter/Neutral] (Paris: Grasset, 1972).
12. *Partie* [Part] (Paris: Éditions des femmes, 1976).
13. *Le Prénom de Dieu* [First Name of God] (Paris: Grasset, 1967).
14. The final phrase was added in October 1977 by Hélène Cixous [interviewer's note].

6. My text is written in white and black, in "milk and night"

Interview with Christiane Makward. Translated by Beatrice Cameron and Ann Liddle.

This interview first appeared in *Substance* **13**, 19–37, 1976.

CM I would like to talk about your two principal roles: scholar-essayist and "writer in the feminine" ["*écrivaine*"]. Concerning this word, I saw the defenses go up when I proposed to use it instead of "Women Writers" ["*femmes écrivains*"] at the convention of the International Association of Women Writers in Nice.[1] Do you consider a certain renovation of language to be useful or pointless?

CIXOUS You know, I don't even wonder about such things. I think that in France the language is very rigid. You, in the United States and I, too, in France share this experience: we are well aware that one knows how to fabricate neologisms; when there is a need for them, they come! As for their codification . . . usage decides. Personally, I don't know whether I would like the word "*écrivaine*" at the phonic level. Because of my mania for playing on the signifier, I hear with marked insistence the "*vaine*", *vaine* in the sense of "empty". Therefore I have this immediate reticence: I am not sure it is a good word, a *beautiful* word. But it is obviously quite a problem: I am convinced there is a great deal of work to be done on the lexicon.

CM Would you explain how you happened to found a group for women's studies?

CIXOUS It has to do with a series of steps I have taken over the last few years. It originates simply from the fact that I have been trying to expand my praxis beyond my personal involvement, if you will, by extending it more concretely into the real, the social . . . and I have had quite a few problems. I have been working on feminine writing for four years. At Vincennes I am not accountable to anyone, so I simply set it up!

Theoretically I am an English literature professor: I do go back to texts from English literature but only part of the time. What I do, in fact, no longer has anything to do with English literature and it is at the seminar level, therefore it is limited. At the research level, I must say that it is only in the last two years that I have succeeded in elaborating something structured, which I can be sure of and can communicate. For the first two years I felt my way around: nothing had been elaborated concerning feminine writing. So I explored psychoanalysis, ethnology, philosophy, all the discourses which deal with sexual difference, all of the social sciences. I found nothing except the negative: tableau of a general repression. It took a great deal of time for me to reach a space which now seems sufficiently cleared for me to draw others to it. So for two years now I have recruited an increasingly significant group of students and things are progressing rapidly. A reform in the structures of research was imposed by the Ministry and I decided it was the right time to try and insert something that had never been a part of academic programmes, that was not recognized, that did not exist, had nothing to do with competitive exams. Thus I proposed the creation of a group, something like a "women's studies", officially established and directed toward research.

We organized a group of about twenty women, and a few men, from Vincennes[2] and other universities; the group is also inter-disciplinary. The Ministry approved it on an experimental basis, for three years: this project is quite unique in France. I think we benefited from the fact that the Ministry's position toward Vincennes has always been rather ambiguous . . . so we are starting next fall, without a budget! We always do things for free, you know! It will probably not function too well, for it is new and not funded. At any rate, this will make it possible to have a doctoral programme in women's studies. Symbolically at least it opens some doors: it could be connected with all sorts of practices, with a recycling of women and men at work in the specific area of feminine problematics.

CM Yes, the question of the practicality of degrees in women's studies is also discussed in the United States. In industry, for example, or in labour administration there is already a certain demand for these specialists.

CIXOUS But the same is true in France, I am sure! This is not at all a bad gamble. It is a better gamble than, for instance, the other research group I am involved with, in English literature: there are no opportunities for that except in academia, whereas there are lots of outlets in women's studies.

CM In your teaching of literature, do you tend to use systematically women's texts or do you apply your critical approaches to all sorts of texts?

CIXOUS Of course! In any case, for a long time I did not work on women's writing. I was a literature professor, in other words: I was working on texts that are 99 per cent masculine. On the other hand, I wrote my thesis on Joyce, an author who is capable of reflecting upon the question of woman but who is certainly not a feminist. In my current work — which is, on the contrary, very committed, very militant — the texts to which I draw attention are not necessarily texts by women. Because I am working on femininity, on sexual difference, one of the things I bring out — which are very simple things — is the fact that sexual difference develops out of bisexuality which is the original condition of every individual and is subsequently displaced, transformed by culture.

The fact that bisexuality subsists in a certain number of individuals implies the presence of femininity in men, femininity which is always massively repressed. What it means to be a man, "being-a-man", consists first of all in eradicating femininity. But in writing — particularly in writing, much more so than in any other domains where they can be found — there are men who transmit femininity. And so, I have worked with my students on the texts of men who inscribe femininity, on Genet's works for instance, but there are others. His is an altogether ambiguous world where you have bisexuality, of course, and a very strong maternal dominance as well.

CM We have spoken of women's studies in France, what about the feminist movement in general and your rapport with the "Politics and Psychoanalysis" group and the MLF (*Mouvement de Libération des Femmes*) at large?

CIXOUS The rapport exists in a kind of virtual space . . . Certain writers (of the *Éditions des femmes*) have approached me. Actually, they signed the letter I had written . . .[3]

CM Yes, that is why I assumed that you had rather precise connections with them. There is a certain "rhetoric of the scream and of revolt", according to Catherine Clément,[4] which could describe the most extreme position, the "anarchizing" wing, one might say, of MLF militants. They advocate, in a sense, that women remain on the fringe of any form of power. How do you feel about this position?

CIXOUS It is not at all mine as I indicated in my article in *L'Arc*[5] and on several other occasions. As for the MLF I do not feel obligated to define my position with respect to the MLF. The MLF is a necessity as are other enterprises with varying strategies and means, which crystallize women's struggle. I have never been a part of MLF. Primarily, no doubt, because I did not have a personal need for it. In my own field I have to organize and promote research and collective action: at present there are about a hundred female students who are working — struggling — with me and who are reaching out; there are MLF women among my student comrades.

On the other hand, their problematics — at least the ones defined by the "Politics and Psychoanalysis" group — have always struck me as being encumbered with non-viable contradictions. I have never felt inclined to reproach them for this as I am convinced that a movement which takes its place in History with such a mass of obstacles to contend with, is almost inevitably led to positions of uncertainty, excess or compromise. In other words, the analytical errors or the slip-ups in certain experiences, or again the poor political choices — which are symptoms of an initial stage in the struggle — strike me as inevitable. But all of this keeps me at a distance, in a position of sympathy, certainly, and in keeping with the militant praxis which can be mine where I am and where I can have the efficacy I want.

As for the way they envisage writing at *Éditions des femmes*, I believe it is not yet sufficiently elaborated and that certain partial and idealistic analyses will give only mediocre results. I think it is necessary and I hope they will in the future analyse anew the significance of writing with respect to its "productresses" [*productrices*] and to its political efficacy. I hope they will find positions which will be less detrimental for the "writresses" [*écrivantes*] they support. Positions which will permit them to find for example a new balance in the relationship between writing as a product of the unconscious and the "book" as a manufactured object and commercial product. To avoid being deluded by the individual "source" of energy which comes through in writing and invests reality with a desire issuing from a *non-anonymous* force. To distinguish carefully between the different types of writing: militant discourse which has a prompt and . . . short-lived effect; creative writing which has a delayed but enduring effect.

Finally what bothers me is the strange mixture one finds in their bookstore,[6] all sorts and qualities of texts ranging from bourgeois to petty bourgeois and bordering on the reactionary to subversive texts . . . all of these under the general cover of a woman's name. It is as if the class struggle were nullified, scotomized by the struggle of women. All simplifying positions, which give the appearance of greater strength in a combat, turn very quickly against the very ones who try to maintain them. They are seductive but they disintegrate.

I, for one, am absolutely against marginalization . . . that would amount to going back to this sort of absurd dream: "a man's world/a woman's world". This is not so! This is a world of men *and* women where it is up to women to impose something which is their difference in the equality. This is a battle, and it will be hard but we cannot fight with our backs turned or on one front while the others are somewhere else, that does not make sense!

CM In this issue of *L'Arc* and in your remarkable text which is a pressing appeal for feminine writing, for the free play of sexuality in writing, isn't there also — in the direction you indicate — an entire continent to be brought to the surface which is the representation of man?

CIXOUS Why of course! I must say this is something I don't talk about because I think that the history which is in the making — the history of the awakening of women — is passing through various stages. Now, the current stage is the one which, in my opinion, consists in encouraging women to undertake a work of reflection upon and re-appropriation of femininity, starting precisely with a thorough re-thinking of the body, of sexuality, of the rapports between the sexual and the cultural. They can't take on everything at once — just look at what is happening: it is extremely heavy for women to think *themselves* — I don't believe it is possible for them, at the moment, to think *man*, to re-think him. To begin with, they cannot do it instead of men. At best — and this is part of their reflection about femininity — they can undertake a task which will be very hard, certainly very painful and probably slow, dealing with the significance of being women uneasily [*d'être mal femmes*], of being female awkwardly, uncomfortably. To be woman confronted with man, this is bound to have repercussions for masculinity.

Personally I think this will entail — and I think it is already apparent in the United States but hardly adumbrated in France — such structural upheavals for couples, for marriage and the family that men won't be able to stand pat! Obviously they too will be jolted and moved to ask themselves: "What does it mean to be a man?" a question they haven't even begun to ask in France. But the work on men must be done by men. Then there is work to be done concerning consciousness at the level of representation: "How do you see me?", "How do I see you?", "What do you want from me?" . . . these are the fundamental questions.

CM In your writing you have obviously gone beyond what you see as the general rule since already in *Dedans*[7] you have challenged "from within" the Oedipal conflict, in the dual situation: desire for the father/desire for the mother.

CIXOUS In any case, I cannot and never could identify with the position of sexual opposition. Difference yes, opposition definitely not: to me that seems negative . . . I understand it in women I observe, I regret it. I realize that they are in that space because they have been sentenced to it, but for me it is a space of isolation, of doom, it is hell.

CM You understand it because you have been there — we've all been there — but you came through . . .

CIXOUS . . . because I am a woman. I made war because war was made on me. The death-struggle is not new to me and it goes on of course, only I did not succumb to it: I suffered through it, I was a potential victim of it; then I came out of it. But I see around me women I deeply love who are still so hurt and so vulnerable that when confronted with men they can be truly ferocious. I think it is something one must go through, there is no other way.

CM In *L'Arc* you say: "*writing is the possibility of change itself* . . . the movement which precedes the transformation of social and cultural structures".[8] Does this imply that women's emancipation must necessarily take place through writing, which would amount, outside the Western World, to an admission of impotence and utter pessimism? The vast majority of Third World women — and men — do not have access to writing.

CIXOUS What I wrote in *L'Arc* is not detailed enough — I wanted to say a lot in a limited space. I do not live, if you wish, exclusively at the level of superstructures. In other words, I do not for a moment imagine that the world will be transformed by writing alone. That would be so completely anti-Marxist that it would not reflect my position at all. I believe there is a double movement, a double History . . . there are two currents with two different rhythms. There is one which is really our economic and social history and there, socio-economic structures must change. But even if society changes, in a way that a Marxist or communist might wish, this would not affect the problem of woman's position. Starting with this change — that is the social and economic change — we must completely re-define and re-think the articulation "man/woman".

Just as a change in society is aimed for, similarly and concurrently — and with different rhythms — a reflection must take place upon the liberation of women, upon the feminine revolution, if you like. But I think this can only be efficiently accomplished through a learning process, that is — and I use this word in the strongest possible sense — the woman who does not know *herself*, who has not "thought *herself*", who has not reflected upon *herself*, who remains as she was — ignorant and blind about femininity, because she is alienated — will not be a good militant feminist, will not further her cause, and therefore can always be recuperated by all sorts of political movements: rightist, leftist, anything! I think women must burst the shackles . . . they must cast off the yoke which still really immobilizes them, the yoke of inhibition, of auto-repression. It is absolutely wild to see how women are deprived, obstructed, muzzled!

CM Indeed, there is this blackmail of "giving" which you circumscribe so well in your essay in *L'Arc*.

CIXOUS Why, of course, because it is so easy to make women feel guilty . . . moreover, that's what they want, they have been trained that way! They are made to feel guilty in a different way than men — because men too can be made to feel guilty — but it is not the same at all. What must be attacked is the type of repression which afflicts women. In other words, woman must develop a rapport with her unconscious which is not stereotyped, downtrodden: she must revive herself, recover her vital forces, she must dare *herself*, she must dare to be herself.

I have verified this with my female students in a most astounding manner: in two years I have seen women of all ages being born. It happens almost invariably in the same manner: a veritable explosion. The stories are very different but they have one thing in common which is: "Finally I dare to speak! I speak poorly, it's awful, I say things I should never say, I don't dare . . .". In short, it happens with the greatest embarrassment, with tremendous reserve, but it happens and it is superb: something breaks loose. Furthermore, you know that women's situation in France is quite different from what you have in the United States because their ignorance about sexual matters, for example, is simply unbelievable, a lack of knowledge about their bodies, about the simplest practices of eroticism — which is tragic.

CM When you indicate the necessity of producing new reading — you mention that you would like to do a book which would be more strictly literary criticism[9] — readings which will bring to light the specificity of feminine writing, you do not give as examples either Nathalie Sarraute or Monique Wittig. Can you comment on these omissions?

CIXOUS Yes, I wrote this text a long time ago and . . . I have certain regrets. Not at all for Nathalie Sarraute, I don't consider her writing to be "feminine" in any way whatsoever . . .

CM That is interesting because I have worked on her texts and I think that the fact that meaning comes across, that finally the message can only be inferred through an imagery which is after all rooted in the physiological, in visceral, hormonal reactions: the fact also that it is an example of exploded, atomized writing, all that makes it possible to define her art as "feminine", don't you think?

CIXOUS Something comes through there, yes . . . but this said, it is rather a "paranoid" kind of writing, I mean: a kind of writing which collects, compares, interprets and denounces. She realized it herself: what she does amounts to the writing of "suspicion", the minute identification of signs, an inscription which is very beautiful while neurotic . . .

CM Why, precisely: to the extent that "we are all neurotics . . ."[10]

CIXOUS No, no! I mean it is very special in her case: she happens to be someone who is "obsessive" and I, for one, think there is nothing "feminine" in that; it signifies that for her the feminine is not dominant. In my opinion she is not a writer who transmits femininity. Why didn't I mention Monique Wittig? For lots of reasons: first of all, I don't know her well . . . at least, when I wrote that text I was hardly familiar with her work. But *she*, most definitely, is on the side of feminine writing. With her, undoubtedly, the body is there! But it is a disturbed body, a body intoxicated with words because she is trying to conjure up the flesh, to evoke it with words: this body, in fact, is very absent. And her anxiety about it is truly the anxiety of hysteria. It is indeed: "Where are they, where are my organs?" That's what her question is, and it is quite typical. But I think that the most powerful writing is that of Marguerite Duras.

CM Yes, there is a consensus on that point: I have heard it said in MLF circles and you do mention her expressly in your essay. Since you are directing a new collection for 10/18, "The Feminine Future", do you see in the research which comes to your attention a trend toward psychoanalytical criticism: this trend, compared to what is happening in the United States, seems to largely dominate feminist criticism?

CIXOUS Yes, because, obviously there is much to do in this area, but it is not exclusive. We are coming out with something on that. Psychoanalysis, however, has reached an impasse, it is tightly boxed in, hampered . . . to the extent that it remains tied to its ponderous patriarchal origins and also because it is still heavily dependent upon the domineering masculine personalities which oppress it in France. Therefore, although some women analysts are beginning to emerge, they are still rare and are gaining little ground. So there is much to do with regard to the reading of feminine practices. There is a man who is going to write about the plastic representation of women; femininity is manifest in this man.

CM Do you mean the representation of the female body?

CIXOUS No, representation in the works of female painters and sculptors.

CM At the level of literary criticism, do you think such concepts as the relationship of the body to space, to natural cycles, to matter have a special significance, in the feminist perspective?

CIXOUS Yes, of course: I believe that anything having to do with the body should be explored, from the functional to the libidinal, to the imaginary; and then how all of this is articulated at the symbolic level. It is beyond doubt that femininity derives from the body, from the anatomical, the biological difference, from a whole system of drives which are radically different for women than for men. But none of this exists in a pure state: it is always, immediately "already spoken", caught in representation, produced culturally. This does not prevent the libidinal economy of woman from functioning in a specific manner which modifies her rapport with reality.

CM I would have liked to take a motif which occurs in Tombe[11] — that of the squirrel. It is one of the major motifs of the text and its connections are too complex to be set forth now, but can one say that one of its main meanings is the ascending movement, freedom in relation to space?

CIXOUS Probably . . . I really can't answer you about *Tombe*. First I would have to reread it, undertake an action which I do not normally do . . .

CM I hoped to get you to recall how this motif came under your pen. With certain motifs it is visible enough, they originated from other words which you exploit, dissect, play with . . . The squirrel is at once an image which is extremely welcome, extremely gratifying; there is a whole work of integration on the level of typography, especially, which is altogether fascinating. The fact remains that the motif itself seems rather incongruous when it appears.

CIXOUS One could go on and on about it . . . If you want to talk about space and elevation, yes, for me that works.

CM Is it to be set in relation with the fantasy of flying which is present in all your books?

CIXOUS Not all, but I must tell you that that squirrel has a history. It goes back to something very complex, which, as an exception, is caught in a certain reality. I say an exception because, most of the time, what I inscribe is of the nature of fantasy, of the unconscious, of the dream, and then this is reworked by an operation which I perform on the signifier. Much of what I do begins in the unconscious; of course the squirrel exists in my unconscious but as it happens I did see the squirrel, I recognized it. It is a squirrel which I saw and which remained with me. Why did it remain with me like that? Because a mass of associations formed around its body.

CM About this example of the squirrel, I wanted to ask you whether, in the critical commentary such as you envision it, it is necessary to go further, that is to go beyond the level of the structures of the text and the immanent reading, to the psychoanalytic level. Without that, is criticism truncated, void?

CIXOUS Not at all! And then, one must first define the psychoanalytic level.

CM Yes, since in the case of the usual literary critic, I mean the male psychocritic, that would mean a phallocentric reduction, because of the nature of the concepts currently in use.

CIXOUS True, if you are alluding to the psychoanalytic praxis of the classical literature, which is an interpretation and which refers one to certain massive symbols; in that case of course you would say: the squirrel is a phallus . . . But that isn't how it works! I mean, the phallus, the vagina, one can find them everywhere, and it's always the same thing!

CM Exactly, so therefore it isn't necessary, in your opinion?

CIXOUS No, it isn't interesting. What *is* important, however, is what functions in the unconscious of the text and inscribes itself in the work on the signifier. There, with the squirrel, it is very complex because first of all there is a structure, a scenario, which is a real vision, and that is a fantasy; and so behind that comes something from the body, very powerfully. And then there is the whole work on the signifier which I don't remember, I would have to reread it. But it is certain that the squirrel scratched something into me, through the medium of the French signifier [*écureuil*]: through "*oeil*" (eye), through "cure", the "*cure-oeil*" (eye-pick), but also the eater of acorns [*glands*] . . . things like that, certainly, like you do when you dream. And that, of course, is a question of listening, it is not just the word.

CM For a number of new critics there is great taboo which is the "reduction of texts" to a few clearly defined ideas, to certain procedures, a reduction which starts with the application of a pre-determined grid. Would it be better, in your opinion, to limit oneself to a reading at the level of the textual structures and not reduce them to precise conclusions?

CIXOUS Frankly, I'm not at all certain that the one excludes the other. I think that there are some university teachers who, for reasons which have to do with their own unconscious, frequently make a choice, have a real repugnance to noticing the unconscious; for this reason they go in the direction of, for example, structures, linguistic study, analysis of genres, to the complete exclusion of the unconscious. They don't perceive it, in other words they don't involve their bodies, they don't involve their ears, their skin, their eyes. In that case there's nothing you can do, it's insurmountable!

This year we have been working on Genet, whose text is difficult and at first gives a sort of vertigo, because I have them work on his writing at the level of the *signifier*. What do I do, in general? Because I am a writer, for me reading is an operation which makes writing possible. For this reason what matters to me is to make a text live, really, a living text in its totality. I always start in the same manner, in practice: I give back to the text what it is in reality, that is its musical composition, its formal esthetic organization, its surface. I get my students to feel it, I fling it in their faces, their eyes, their ears.

So instead of having a text with its discourse, its keys, its organization, one has to begin with a system of effects which strike the body and from then on I point out the figures. I reorganize both on the graphic and phonic level, make them isolate the figures which by means of metaphors are going to introduce continuities into the text, continuities which already transmit meaning at the level of significance. And then — and I insist a great deal on this — once we have done that, I return to the signified because I pose the question: "What does that mean?", but only afterwards. And when I say "afterwards": it is because if you begin with "What does that mean?" that bars the way to the "How does that touch me?" That always institutes a censorship, and so I proceed in this fashion.

CM There is a passage in "James Joyce ou la ruse de l'écriture" (which was published in *Poétique*)[12] and which I suppose comes more or less from your thesis on Joyce . . . No? It is a totally new text?

CIXOUS Yes, yes! Anyway it is a text which is already obsolete, I reworked all that in *Prénoms de personne*.[13] There I was working almost on the level of the signifier.

CM . . . It's about reading: you propose a sort of theory of the reading of Joyce which leads one to believe that this is perhaps the way you would like your own texts to be read. You speak of "renunciation of all conclusions" and of imagining "a reading which would accept 'discouragement' not at all in the hope of 'recovering' it by taking it as a metaphor for the Joycian occult . . . but seeing in this ambush by which signification is confiscated the sign of a deliberate imposture which traverses and betrays the whole of Joyce's work . . . Nothing will have been signified but the enigma . . .".[14] Do you think that form of reading is desirable for your texts?

CIXOUS That aims at Joyce because Joyce is precisely someone who has a very profound relation of annulment toward the act of making sense. There is a very negative side to him, a mocking side which is a settling of accounts with dogma, with truth. So what I have written there is suitable for him. Now, the first part of the quotation, that is that it is non-conclusive, that concerns every text. Actually I don't know if that would be suitable for my texts because I think that on the contrary I insist — at least I try to — on some strong points which I hold to, which I am trying, precisely, not to eliminate. Joyce — he ends up logically with *Finnegans Wake* where nothing holds, where the same thing annuls itself right at the level of the insignificant, in a polysemic work by which he says "white" and "black" at the same time. In other words, nothing is posited. But I, no, I don't do that, I insist on positing certain things, precisely because I engage myself, even politically, and that is very important to me.

CM Is that why you attach importance to writing the little notices on the covers of your books, yourself?

CIXOUS No, that's because no one wants to do them! When I arrive at the publisher's they all throw up their hands and say, "It's too difficult, *you* do it!"

CM Is it important, necessary to reread the feminine literature of the past? That is a question which preoccupies educators because it could seem more urgent to concentrate on the present, from the point of view of the political significance which writing can take on.

CIXOUS Personally, I read very little in the past because I do not have the time. If I had the time I would do it but it is evident that what interests me is what is happening now. I do however have the intention of returning to some texts which I have completely forgotten, for example *The Princess of Cleves*. I am convinced that that text is very positively feminine, in the manner of Marguerite Duras. On the other hand I have worked a great deal, this year, on Saint Teresa — not on the sanctity, on the writing!

CM Did you consciously choose your form of writing, which has evolved, obviously, but not in such a spectacular manner as that of Marguerite Duras; or did you find your basic manner at the first trial, as happened with Nathalie Sarraute?

CIXOUS Frankly, one is very ignorant of oneself. What I can tell you is that I haven't chosen . . . I have never chosen a way of writing, I have always started on impulse. The only choices which I have made were almost exterior. For example, from one text to another I do not stay in the same place and I search for just that place which is always determined for me by a problematics. In other words, I am like a philosopher and I start out, after all, from certain questions. And it is these questions which lead me to write in a certain style — which is mine, if you wish — but really it is *that* which determines.

CM But after all, it is more than a "style", it is your whole attitude in relation to meaning, the established meaning . . . in a way it is the question of legibility which I am posing to you.

CIXOUS Yes, but then I did not even pose that question for myself when I began to write. I mean that I have never had any relation of obligation to the law of legibility.

CM But you didn't write your papers that way, when you were a student?

CIXOUS I wonder if that wasn't just it, at that period, because I had, actually, considerable problems. I didn't write my papers as *writing*, first of all that would never have occurred to me; but certainly, in order to get to the point of writing a paper, I had to combat the writing in me. Obviously, what I was doing was not academic, I could not bend myself to that sort of work ordered in a certain manner; I already had to do something very explosive. You know, I invested very little in the academic type of production, it was very constraining . . . I don't have good memories of it.

CM We have already touched on the subject but perhaps you might elaborate: does your writing involve a form of automatic writing? Do you use the material of dreams in a concerted fashion: are you one of those people who wake up in the middle of the night when they have an interesting dream, in order to take notes? Or do you trust your memory without worrying about censorship?

CIXOUS On the contrary, I mistrust it a good deal. Indeed I am a person who writes down her dreams as swiftly as possible. Because I know that what is precious in the dream is the signifier; that if I wait, that is what is extinguished very quickly. But I must say that I am bothered by that term "automatic writing" — I'm not even sure what it means! It is obvious that as soon as I begin to write it up, I *elaborate*, and I know by experience that the more I wait, the more I elaborate.

CM And also, things happen when one writes which one can consider as arising from mechanisms . . .

CIXOUS Certainly, but the more you take it on the level of the pre-conscious, the closer it still is to the period of production in the unconscious, the lighter the censorship is, that's certain. Censorship is a very clear-cut thing, it's like a bar: it comes down, like that, and then — bang! it falls! Really, an hour afterward it's there, well at that moment I am already writing.

CM The "Eye-man", for example, in *Révolutions pour plus d'un Faust*,[15] does that come from a nightmare inspired by Bataille?

CIXOUS It's really a dream, like thousands of others that I've had. My relation to the dream is a relation of intense curiosity which is more and more rewarding. For a long time I was afraid and ashamed, because in my naivete I said to myself that it wasn't quite proper to watch myself dreaming like that. But certainly in the future I intend to go much further in that domain.

CM Do you think that as you make yourself more and more receptive to that material the passage from the unconscious to the conscious opens out? You recover it better and better?

CIXOUS I think it's that way for everyone. Freud noted it already and it's true: when one begins to be interested in one's dreams the unconscious knows it and gives you great gifts. The more you listen to your unconscious, the more you dream.

CM In *Révolutions pour plus d'un Faust* which has just been published by Éditions du Seuil, I noticed that the *"je"* is not feminized as in *Portrait du soleil*[16] and other texts. Did that pose a problem for you?

CIXOUS Oh yes! That's part of my enterprises: as I told you, my standpoint changes from one text to another, and it changes in relation to certain questions which I want to pose. The question I pose in *Révolutions pour plus d'un Faust* is very complex: what is the relation between thought and action, between the intellectual that I am — which we are, and which is therefore neuter — and History. That's why the "I" is neutralized, that is, I went back to a well-known cultural figure, a myth . . . a myth, precisely, of investigation, interrogation, the myth of Faust. And that posed some problems for me because I held that text at a very great distance from myself, whereas there are some texts, on the other hand, where the scene is myself, and in such cases I enjoy it infinitely more. When I hold it at a distance from myself, it is something entirely different, it is a sort of violence which I do to myself and which has led me to a different kind of form, a theatrical form. Apart from this, the text is four years old, in the meantime I have written three other texts which are, on the contrary, extremely subjective.

CM So that decision you made for *Faust* implies that the specifically feminine is annulled at a certain level of activity?

CIXOUS Yes, of course, moreover I do sometimes neutralize but it is rare with me and it is getting harder and harder. However there are places where the real annuls me as a woman: in certain circumstances the sexual difference is suspended. History makes itself: they don't ask you whether you're a man or a woman. And then it can also happen that it is masculinity which is transmitted . . .

CM You say "the real annuls me as a woman", but it seems to me that the fundamental problem of women is precisely that they are identified as women *a priori*, before any other judgement.

CIXOUS No, no, no! There I find that there are circumstances where the world annuls me as a woman and recovers me as a neutral being, especially circumstances where women play the role of political agent. When you are in a demonstration, no one asks you if you are a man or a woman . . .

CM The opposite was experienced by Simone de Beauvoir, that was precisely what led her to become a militant feminist.

CIXOUS Don't misunderstand me, it's something I also speak of in *La Jeune Née* which is to appear in October.[17] I have also been determined, with respect to feminism, by that experience. Apart from that, the demonstrations which have taken place — it's like literature. They were demonstrations in which the masculine note dominated; either you participate and you are not a woman, that is the woman is annulled in you; or else you do not participate. I have always chosen to participate, at the expense of my femininity. I have gone to all the demonstrations up till now, often not as the woman I am, which always annoyed me terribly and led me to much more aggressive positions. But, that's the way it is. That's what reality is like! I've got myself clubbed, I've got myself beaten over the head, and it really wasn't as a woman, I assure you. It was as a militant. I hate it and at the same time it is an experience of reality, that is undeniable. That's what I'm fighting against.

But at the time I wrote *Révolutions pour plus d'un Faust* I was posing a question which for me was of the utmost importance, at that time (as I say, it was already four years ago). I did not pose it like that, to myself as a person, but precisely as a person engaged in a struggle: "How do I conceive of History"; that was a necessary phase.

At the present time feminism, in which I am profoundly implicated, seems to me to be threatened by certain internal contradictions which are badly thought out or not recognized. That worries me and I know that is what I am going to struggle against in the years to come. It is threatened by something excessive. I would not want anything to do with a feminism which lost sight of the dialectic articulation with other struggles, and that seems to me to be happening even with students, even with the women who write, who paint . . . I am afraid that, in the indispensable phase of interiorization and exteriorization of femininity, part of reality, of its complexity, might get lost. Do you see what I mean?

CM Very much so, and I share your apprehensions because, in spite of the sympathy, the understanding which one may have for everything which tends toward separatism, extremism, that can only be conceived as a kind of apostolate without much hold on reality.

CIXOUS That does frighten me!

CM Personally, of course, I see the situation in France from a fairly great distance: Nice was my first contact with those women who are still represented as regular hags, not in the physical sense of course, but as terrorists, mouths full of curses, and so forth . . . That wasn't at all what I observed, so I am reassured, with deeper sympathy.

But once more on the subject of *Faust*, there is a passage which seems like a description of intrauterine space — at least I read it that way — with the suggestions of the process of menstrual nidification, and notations referring to red, words like "filament", "a heart", "a full mane of flames and threads", "brilliantly-coloured . . . cloth", "carpeted", and so forth. Well, once more, it's a subjective reading . . .

CIXOUS No, no, I believe you, but you would have to show me where.

CM It's in the first quarter of the book and your "I" is led into that space by the "fool". Without any kind of penetration, by the way, the uterine space builds itself up around them; it is in a way the beginning of life which is replayed there. What I want to ask you is this: since it is a neutralized *"je"*, do you think that this kind of fantastic imagery arises from a specifically feminine imagination? Do you think one can find such a description, such a fantasy, in a masculine text?

CIXOUS In all honesty, I would be surprised if anyone found that . . .

CM It does imply a very positive relation, a relation of interiority and intimacy, to the feminine body?

CIXOUS Certainly! When I say that, in that book, I went in the direction of the "neuter", I mean that I did not particularly bring out, expose, highlight the femininity in that text, a locus of enunciation anchored in my tongue, my unconscious.

CM There are still two points which I should like to incite you to comment on. This next text which as you have indicated to me is called "Souffles"[18] — does it represent still another very different form of writing?

CIXOUS Yes, very different. First of all, it is no longer called "Souffles", at present it is called "Vol/e".[19] There is a little extract which has just come out in *La Nouvelle Critique*, called "La Noire vole".[20] You know: that issue on women, with an interview by Luce Irigaray. In any case it is a piece of writing with a completely different continuity, a continuity which is infinitely less disseminated and which in fact is much more powerfully elaborated at the level of fantasy.

CM Is this new text ready to come out soon?

CIXOUS I think it is going to be published next year by Seuil.[21] It is a rather architectural text which carries . . . which transmits a sort of meditation on "blood", "breast", "milk", on the relation between the text and the "milk", between the text and the "breath", that is, something touching the very production of the text, which passes through the feminine body, and which produces, advances (something I have never done before) a narrative. But they are false narratives, they are pseudo-stories which simply follow a course. It is a passage through a night, if you like, but really it is the passage through a body.

CM Do you take the trouble of de-constructing those stories, or do you simply leave us in suspense? Do you leave us our lectorial illusions?

CIXOUS It is finally a false narrative: it is narrating itself in the narrative tense, so there are some imperfect tenses . . . but it ends, of course, the way I end a lot of things: in something endless. It starts out with an uneasiness, an uncertainty, it starts out with a bed, an awakening, and it ends with all possible kinds of births. But it also poses the question of the relation between the body of the loved person, a man, and the body of the mother: these bodies are completely interchangeable. So there is an entering and an exit from a man's body which is at the same time the body of a mother.

And then it is also an exploration of the feminine body which I have begun and which I am continuing at this time. There is a part of this text which touches finally upon homosexuality, that is, the other as man and the other as woman. Globally, if you like, it is a text which is for me as erotic as possible, which also poses the question, "What is eroticism?", "Where does that touch us?" And then also, it treats of the black continent, of the entrance of woman into the (her) body. The end of the text is: how to re-enter the body, the continuity.

CM Can you indicate the origin of this metaphor of the "black continent?"

CIXOUS Yes, it's Freud who uses it.

CM Does it go back to the Bible?

CIXOUS Ah, I don't know.

CM I thought there might be for you a relation with Genet's *The Blacks*, or at least there seems to be.

CIXOUS In any case one of the characters in the text is Genet himself: it's a fictional Genet but still, he's there. The most important thing is that he is there *as* Genet.

CM So then there would be an extension toward the problem of racism?

CIXOUS Yes, definitely! My text is written in white and black, in "milk" and "night", in fact, and not at all as Mallarmé said: one writes in black ink on white. No, one writes in white, it is white ink, the white ink which is also the ink of the black woman: this text is called "La Noire vole". For me it really does come through the Bible: "I am black but beautiful". In Freud, I don't think so. I think that it is a metaphor which comes quite naturally, which belongs to a kind of pseudo-colonialist imagery.

CM Last question: what happened at the recent meeting of PEN in Paris, where you were supposed to speak, according to *Le Monde*, on "woman as creator of values".[22]

CIXOUS Oh, that — I created quite a furor! I didn't know what it was: I came back from there sick! I had set some political conditions and I had been told that Gisèle Halimi[23] would be there and so I said to myself: at least there'll be a limit. But when I saw the audience, I almost walked out! It was taped, so these things are recoverable, you will find them in my printed texts. I spoke very anarchically, it wasn't what I had outlined, not what I intended to do.

CM But surely it is important all the same, since you are one of the few people who are engaged in trying to define and promote feminine values, to give them once and for all a reasonable basis, so there is nothing shocking in your having given an improvization centred on yourself . . .

CIXOUS I did it as a political act, at that moment. Otherwise, I would have done something theoretical, but when I realized the situation, I attacked. I did something that I never do: I did something biographical, explaining how I became a feminist. But it was rooted in a very, very ancient opposition, which goes back to the first woman. It was an anti-colonialism, all the fiercer because I was born in a colonial country. So I described this colonial, and the slavery. In the end the experiences cross and re-cross to infinity. I was born in a violent parturition and since then my rage has transferred itself from place to place until the moment when I said to myself, "But as a woman?"

CM In conclusion, and only half in jest: I remain flabbergasted before the abundance of your works and I wonder what iron discipline you must impose upon yourself: have you found a way of doing without sleep?

CIXOUS Perhaps it is something like that! At this moment I am in a period of uneasiness because I have to rethink my existence: I have too many demands placed on me and I feel threatened. Really, next year, I am going to try to withdraw a bit but now I am getting into a system of contradictions which is painful for me: the fact, for example, that I receive letters from women every day: I feel extremely guilty not to answer as I should, and at the same time . . .

NOTES

1. The Nice Book Fair took place in May 1975 and the Convention, sponsored by the French government, was held on the same site (*Palais des Expositions* — Exhibition Centre). Several prominent French feminist writers attended but a number of others declined, including Marguerite Duras and Hélène Cixous.
2. Hélène Cixous holds a Chair at the Université of Paris VIII at Vincennes.
3. An extract from this letter was published in *Le Monde*, 3 May 1975, 19, signed by a number of French women writers. It explains the refusal to participate in a government-organized conference of women's writing [editor's note].
4. Catherine Clément, "Enclave Esclave" [Enclave Enslave] in *L'Arc* 61, *Simone de Beauvoir et les femmes en lutte* [Simone de Beauvoir and Women in Conflict], May 1975, 13–17.
5. Cixous's article, "Le Rire de la Méduse", appeared on pages 39–54 of this issue of *L'Arc* (see note 4). It appeared in English as "The Laugh of the Medusa", translated by Keith Cohen and Paula Cohen, *Signs* 1(4), Summer 1976, 875–93 [original note amended by editor].
6. The "Librairie des Femmes", 68 Rue des Saints-Pères, 75007, Paris. [The bookshop can now be found at 35 Rue Jacob, 75006, Paris, editor's note.]
7. *Dedans* [Inside] (Paris: Grasset, 1969).
8. "Le Rire de la Méduse", 42.
9. *Ibid.*, note 3.
10. A contemporary feminist slogan.
11. *Tombe* [Tomb] (Paris: Seuil, 1973), 17, 30, 78 and *passim*.
12. "James Joyce ou la ruse de l'écriture" [James Joyce or the Ruse of Writing], *Poétique* 4, 1970, 419–32.
13. *Prénoms de personne* [First Names of No One] (Paris: Seuil, 1974).
14. "James Joyce ou la ruse de l'écriture", 424.
15. *Révolutions pour plus d'un Faust* [Revolutions For More Than One Faust] (Paris: Seuil, 1975), 16.
16. *Portrait du soleil* [Portrait of the Sun] (Paris: Denoël, 1973).
17. *La Jeune Née* [The Newly Born Woman], with Catherine Clément (Paris: Union Générale d'Éditions), Collection 10/18, 1975.
18. *Souffles* [Breaths] (Paris: Éditions des femmes, 1975).
19. Flight/theft [feminine].
20. "La Noire vole" [The Black Woman Flies/Steals], *La Nouvelle Critique* 82, March 1975, 47–53.

21. See note 18 above.
22. *Le Monde*, 16 May 1975, 20.
23. A lawyer and feminist, Gisèle Halimi founded the "Choisir" (Choose) league for the legalization of abortion. Her book, *La Cause des femmes* [The Women's Cause] (Paris: Grasset, 1973), shows that she was strongly opposed by some MLF members at the time of the Bobigny trials on the question of *anonymous* militancy. (Halimi acted as counsel in the 1972 Bobigny abortion trial [editor's note].)

Part III: Writing and politics

7. Guardian of language

Interview with Kathleen O'Grady. Translated by Eric Prenowitz.

This interview was published in *Women's Education des femmes* (Canadian Congress for Learning Opportunities for Women) **12**(4) (Winter), 8–10, 1996. It was preceded by a brief introduction to Cixous's work and an extract from the interview in the original French, both of which have been omitted here. All notes have been added by the editor.

KO'G In the 1970s, through both fiction and theory, you constructed a Derridean inspired concept of *écriture féminine*. Texts like *La Jeune Née* with Catherine Clément[1] and "Le Rire de la Méduse"[2] develop a theory of writing based on the libidinal economy of the feminine and call for a re-examination of bisexuality. The subsequent "Extreme Fidelity"[3] continued to augment and clarify this concept by locating sexual difference within a cultural domain. How does this theory inspire your own philosophico-poetic texts? Does it provide an ethical and political framework in addition to its aesthetic dimensions?

CIXOUS For me, theory does not come before, to inspire, it does not precede, does not dictate, but rather it is a consequence of my text, which is at its origin philosophico-poetical, and it is a consequence in the form of compromise or urgent necessity. Each time I have written or that I write a so-called "theoretical" text — in quotations because in reality my theoretical texts are also carried off by a poetic rhythm — it has been to respond to a moment of tension in cultural current events, where the ambient state of discourse — academic discourse, for example, or journalistic or political discourse — has pushed me to go back over things, to stop my journey and take the time to emphasize, to display in a didactic manner the thinking movement which for me was indissociable from my poetic movement, but which seemed to me to be entirely misunderstood, forgotten or repressed indeed by the topical scene. So all that is called "theoretical" in my work is in reality simply a kind of halt in the movement that I execute in order to underline in a broad way what I have written or what has been possible to read for a long time in my fictional texts. Never has a theory inspired my poetic texts. It is my poetic text that sits down from time to time on a bench or else at a café table — that's what I am in the process of doing at this moment by the way — to make itself heard in univocal, more immediately audible terms. In other words, it is always a last resort for me. So no, it does not provide an additional ethico-political structure; it is the concession a poet makes in accepting pedagogic responsibility.

KO'G Though you praise the works of Colette, Duras, Genet, Joyce and Shakespeare throughout much of your work, it is the voice of Clarice Lispector which permeates your fictional texts. *Vivre l'orange*,[4] "Extreme Fidelity", *Reading with Clarice Lispector*[5] and *Three Steps on the Ladder of Writing*[6] constitute an honorary identification and exchange with the texts of Lispector. In what way do her words stimulate the mythical quality that infuses your writing? Does Lispector in any way motivate the incessant return to divinity perceptible in your fiction?

CIXOUS First, it is true that Clarice Lispector has an absolutely exceptional place in my space of references, and that she is unique for me. I compare her with no one. With no one among our contemporaries. Another person also has a unique and exceptional place, it is Jacques Derrida, and in a certain way, I could say — it is a simplification — that each of them occupies a sort of ideal place of writing for me, taking sexual difference into account, he occupying the space of a certain masculinity capable of femininity, and she occupying the space of a femininity capable of masculinity.

As for the relation I have with her: I began to read her in 1977, and I only really began to know her text, to be able to respond to it, two years later; let us say that I worked for two years to really understand her thought. I began publishing in 1967; in 1977, I had already written twelve or thirteen books of fiction, four or five volumes of theoretical essays, which continue to be points of reference like *La Jeune Née*, *Prénoms de personne*,[7] several plays. That is the person who encountered Clarice Lispector, which is to say someone who had a rather long literary, poetic and political experience, and I had the good fortune to recognize in Clarice Lispector a companion and a contemporary woman. The presence in my texts of what you call the "mythical quality" or else of inscriptions of a system of allusions to God, in quotes, is originary for me. My first collection of short stories, from 1967, was called *Le Prénom de Dieu* (First Name of God). I have always played with God. For me, the signifier *Dieu*, as I have always said, is the synonym of what goes beyond us, of our own projection toward the future, toward infinity.

What I must say also is that clearly, like all writers who invoke *Dieu* the word and the word *Dieu* in their texts, I am religiously atheistic, but literarily deistic, that's it. Ultimately I think that no one can write without the aid of God (but what is it, God?), without the aid of writing, God-as-Writing.

KO'G   In addition to being an acclaimed novelist and theorist, you are also a successful playwright. *L'Histoire terrible mais inachevée de Norodom Sihanouk, roi du Cambodge*[8] and *L'Indiade, ou l'Inde de leurs rêves*[9] have been attended by large audiences in France. Your plays indicate a discernible shift in your writing, from introspective prosody to an examination of historical characters and events. In your essay, "Le Lieu du Crime, Le Lieu du Pardon"[10] you indicate that this shift is an ethical one. What subjective force can theatrical performance provide that a prose text cannot? And in what way does this amplify your earlier concepts?

CIXOUS   There is no decisive "shift" between theatre and fiction, in any case relative to an *engagement*, something that is on the order of a responsibility of writing. What happens with theatre is what theatre allows an author and which the fictional text does not allow, that is to say a direct relation with the audience, and thus clearly an intensity, a greater, more immediate density of the ethicopolitical message. That is clearly the difference in "responsibility" between the theatre and the fictional text: it's more immediate. It is a staging or a putting on the stage, it's the effect of the *mise en scène*.

I ought to say, once and for all, a certain number of banalities or truisms: there was an issue of *L'Observateur* quite recently, with a long interview of Jacques Derrida entitled "Yes, my texts are political", which is to say that the journalistic attitude or superficial reading oblige him to repeat something that is absolutely obvious, it's that his philosophical writing is a writing that is always political, that always has political effects — and it is the same thing for me. It's as if a certain audience only used the term "political" for that which has as its object or as its centre a reference to historico-political events properly speaking, events that could find a place precisely in the newspapers and the history books. Yet the political — this is a triviality, I am ashamed to have to say it — does not stem simply from the political scene, from the political events reported by the media; it begins obviously by the discourse of the speaking subject on him- or herself, which is to say that all that makes the political scene — relations of power, of oppression, enslaving, exploitation — all of this begins within me: first of all in the family and in the interior of myself. Tyrants, despots, dictators, capitalism, all that forms the visible political space for us is only the visible and theatrical, photographable projection of the Self-with-against-the-other. I suggest we add the preposition "withagainst" to the English language. The equivalent in French being: "*contre*". I cannot even imagine how one could think otherwise. So when I write texts of fiction, and when in these texts of fiction I deal with problematics either that touch on the definition of the subject, or a human subject, or when I put family scenes, questions of exile, into metaphor and into poetic narrative — my first narrative which was called *Dedans*[11] reads in fact as an oblique ethico-political treatise on the conscious and unconscious situation in Algeria between the 1940s and the 1960s — one is not obliged to read it in that way, but that is what it is. There is *always* a political reflection and engagement running through it. It is thus simply a different form of the same fundamental scene that is the scene in which Shakespeare, or Kafka, portray their characters. It has exactly the same dimension. One cannot divide, for example, human destiny between the introspective, which would be non-political, and then a sort of exterior which would be political. It makes no sense, no more than if one were to consider the Greek tragedians. A human subject has a destiny in so far as it is a human being citizen. It cannot be separated. In this way I could say that there is not a single one of my fictional texts that does not resonate with echoes of world history. I was born political, in a sense, and it was even for political reasons that I began to write *poetry* as a response to the political tragedy.

And in the same way, as I have very often said, there is not only the question of the representation or the inscription of an ethico-political problematic, there is also the question of *action*. I know that here too it is thought that action — that is, what is called action — is an action that ought to be visible in the field, in the field of war or in the field of the political scene, properly speaking, of the parliament, etc. And I am uncomfortable saying that literary actions are actions that have a force of transformation, a force of political affirmation, and a *revolutionary* force that no person who has been in a situation of distress has ever denied, quite to the contrary. The Algerian exiles, the Algerian intellectuals who are exiled, that is who are threatened with death, those who survive the massacres, are the proof: the first ones to be killed and massacred are those who make gestures of writing. Another proof: among them, I have many friends for whom it is essential to come into a text to text relation or communication with people like us. Finally, and what is more, in France there is a tradition of a relationship between the literary text or the writer and public opinion. Poets, novelists, philosophers, etc. have always thought of their gestures of writing as a political gesture, and they have carried it out also in this manner. When Zola goes from the work of art to the combat for Dreyfus,[12] he takes only one step. And so I am not going to enumerate the gestures I make in this domain, but they exist.

And I will add that, in a manner that is strictly specific and reserved to writing, I think — I have always said it, I am reaffirming it — that the writers who are conscious are guardians, not only of the *res publica*, the commonwealth, which is only one aspect of their work, but above all — it is their role, it is their mission — they are the *guardians of language*, that is to say of the richness of language, of its freedom, of its strangeness, strangerness. Language is a country in which scenes comparable to what is happening, for example, at this moment in France, in the domain of the opening or the closing of borders, are played out in the linguistic and poetic mode. There are ways of writing French that are ways of writing "good" or proper French in setting up its borders and defending at all costs French nationalism and nationality. There are, on the contrary, ways of degrammaticalizing or of agrammaticalizing French, of working in syntax for it to be an open, receptive, stretchable, tolerant, intelligent language, capable of hearing the voices of the other in its own body. And this is a great revolutionary tradition of French poetry — in this sense I feel myself to be in the lineage of someone like Rimbaud — a certain breach of the limit, a certain unfurling of language, above all, a certain work on the signifier and, of course a necessary political attitude. One could well imagine that power could be taken over by "good French" in Academia and the media, and in that situation there would no longer be freedom of thought, quite simply.

KO'G In 1974 you founded the Centre d'Etudes Féminines at the University of Paris VIII. Recently the government threatened this, the only academic women's studies doctoral programme and resource centre in Paris, with closure. What events led to the creation of the programme in the 1970s and what about the 1990s brought about its threatened demise?

CIXOUS I created the Centre d'Études Féminines in 1974 for two reasons. One of them, which was fundamental, was that I was professor of English literature, and I felt I was hemmed in, since I had become an academic, in a definition of which the referent is national. For me, a literature cannot be a literature enclosed within borders. That is the first thing. *Literature* is a transnational country. The authors we read have always been the citizens of the other world, border-crossers and outlaws. And they have always strangered their own language. And the second thing is that literature — like all discourses — is in its great majority masculine. And so I was someone who taught, with passion by the way, a restricted literature, that is to say English and masculine literature. I'm very happy to do it, on the condition that there is not an exclusion. So I tried to get out of the enclosure of the unisex, unilanguage, etc., and I made use of a reorganization of the university structures, of the doctoral structures in France, and of the need, for French research, to create new doctorates, to propose a doctorate that had never existed in France, and which was women's studies. And in 1974 it was accepted. It was a doctorate that was interdisciplinary and, of course, inter-cultural, interlinguistic, etc., that knocked down the absurd partitions between literature and philosophy, and between languages, and on the other hand, from the moment it sheltered other discourses than strictly literary ones, and when one could also hear a historical voice, a sociological voice, a psychoanalytic voice, etc., it allowed me to introduce the theme that was dear to me, the theme of sexual difference. Very quickly I began to work with a general thematic: *the poetics of sexual difference*, which had never happened before in France. But it is for exactly the same reason that this programme was threatened with suppression, and has just recently been threatened again, because the new authority in research in France, who dates from the Balladur Government,[13] asked why we had any need for women's studies in France when there are no men's studies, there you have it, it's very simple! This speaks to the ideological backwardness of France. France is fifteenth in Europe with respect to all the problematics concerning women, and fifteenth also with respect to the development of the equality and the recognition of women in society, equally placed with Greece.

KO'G And finally, Iris Murdoch once wrote that it is "always significant to ask of any philosopher, what he is afraid of". So I ask you, what is your greatest fear? And in asking this, I wonder if I am not submitting to you the other, unspoken side of your own recurring question: "Que sont-je quand je songe?"[14]

CIXOUS I would say that I am so afraid of being afraid that I am not afraid. Now clearly, if I wanted to stay in the domain of austerity and humility, I would say that, like all human beings, I fear seeing the people I love die. But I do not think this is a great fear, I think that it is being human, it is living, that's all, it is not a fear. Living — we do not live without fearing the death of the other: I am alive, thus I am contracted with terror at the idea that one of those close to me could be killed, could suffer. But I cannot say that it is what one calls fear. All the rest, for me, is anger; I am angry at the spirit of betrayal that dominates individuals and society.

NOTES

1. *La Jeune Née* [The Newly Born Woman] (Paris: Union Générale d'Éditions) Collection 10/18, 1975.

2. "Le Rire de la Méduse" [The Laugh of the Medusa], *L'Arc* **61**, 1975, 39–54.

3. "Extreme Fidelity", Ann Liddle & Susan Sellers (trans), in *Writing Differences: Readings from the Seminar of Hélène Cixous*, Susan Sellers (ed.), 9–36 (New York: St Martin's Press, 1988).

4. *Vivre l'orange* [To Live the Orange] (Paris: Éditions des femmes, 1979).

5. *Reading with Clarice Lispector*, Verena Andermatt Conley (ed. & trans.) (Minneapolis, MN: University of Minnesota Press, 1990).

6. *Three Steps on the Ladder of Writing*, Sarah Cornell & Susan Sellers (trans) (New York: Columbia University Press, 1993).

7. *Prénoms de personne* [First Names of No One] (Paris: Seuil, 1974).

8. *L'Histoire terrible mais inachevée de Norodom Sihanouk, roi du Cambodge* [The Terrible But Unfinished Story of Norodom Sihanouk, King of Cambodia] (Paris: Théâtre du Soleil, 1985).

9. *L'Indiade, ou l'Inde de leurs rêves, et quelques écrits sur le théâtre* [Indiada, Or the India of Their Dreams] (Paris: Théâtre du Soleil, 1987).

10. "Le Lieu du Crime, le Lieu du Pardon" [The Place of Crime, the Place of Forgiveness], published in *L'Indiade, ou l'Inde de leurs rêves, et quelques écrits sur le théâtre*, 253–9 (Paris: Théâtre du Soleil, 1987).

11. *Dedans* [Inside] (Paris: Grasset, 1969).

12. This refers to the famous case of Alfred Dreyfus, tried and convicted for treason in 1894. Zola wrote an article entitled "J'accuse" [I accuse] which had the effect of exposing the cover-up that had led to Dreyfus's conviction.

13. Edouard Balladur, a right-wing politician, was Prime Minister in France from 1993 to 1995.

14. Literally, "who are I when I dream"?

8. Against the emotion of history

Interview with Dominique Lecoq. Translated by Jessica Benson.

This interview originally appeared as "Les Motions contre l'émotion de l'histoire", in *Politis* (7 July), 46–8, 1988.[1]

DL Why have so many writers this century been seduced by the call to political action and the temptation of power?

CIXOUS Action and power are two different things. Who are you thinking of?

DL Of André Malraux, for example. Jawaharlal Nehru, on meeting him again, exclaimed, "So now you're a minister!"[2] The fascination with power has never been without consequences . . .

CIXOUS Far be it from me to speak of Malraux. Perhaps, towards the end of his life, he wished to tread the boards of a stage which he thought had been transformed. If a writer is drawn to power it is because he is not, or is no longer, in love with writing. The only thing left to do is to become a minister. Poetry and power are estranged nations: it is impossible to hold both nationalities.

DL Perhaps this rift is the locus of what I would call the disappointment of the text? The writer has difficulty coping with the apparent lack of social acceptance of his chosen career, along with the simultaneous extremes of humility and pride which it demands . . .

CIXOUS In my opinion no true poet exists in whom a desire for power has been awakened by the realization, one day, that his book has not changed society.

The poet (by this I mean the writer for whom the literary text is a question of life and death) knows very well that the influence of a text is always postponed: but it does exist. The text is active, but later, and in a different way to action. Poetic gestures transform other aspects of both the soul and of human life beyond those which are modified by political action.

This is the origin of the familiar and poignant image of the poem as a message in a bottle, floating through the centuries as it awaits its reader; an image which has been expressed in different ways by Mandelstam, Celan, Akhmatova,[3] and all the great visionaries of our century. We know that a book will reach its audience in fifty, or even in a hundred years. It is an agonizing destiny, but one which is not without its secret happiness.

Friendship and recognition will be posthumous. Our "contemporaries" have not yet been born. This is a beautiful thought, as long as one has the strength to bear it.

DL Nonetheless, there are poets in certain countries who are conscious that their work has a political effect which runs counter to the governing power.

CIXOUS Yes; there are two scenarios in which writing takes on a political significance that is not inherent to the act of writing. In revolutionary eras, when both civilization and culture are fragmenting from misery and pain, then the poet is the voice of the people. Here though, the question is not one of power, but of liberty; of speaking out across the silence. Then again, there are countries in which the act of writing itself is divided, such as the USSR. Suddenly, in the midst of our terrible century, art became regimented, and the majority of artists flocked to the safety of the established order. To write from outside the protection of this boundary — outside the protection of the state — thus becomes itself a kind of historical gesture. I have a passionate admiration for the three or four Russian poets — Mandelstam, Tsvetaeva[4] and Akhmatova, for example — who remained outlaws from the Union of Writers, and who, despite pressure, insults, and repression, changed nothing in their writing. The signs of the rootless alien, of exclusion, and of mourning are inscribed into the fabric of their texts, but they have not been enslaved: stubbornly, without straying, they have kept to their path. And thus, in our eyes, their works take on the value of immense, invisible flags. They are banished, unedited in their lifetime, and condemned to anonymity: deported because of a poem, they become citizens of the nation of poetry.

DL Whilst working on the collectively written book *Pour Nelson Mandela*,[5] I felt as though the name "Mandela" unlocked a kind of liberty, thanks to the symbolic power accorded to it, and to the singular life which it evokes. But in the France of today, is it conceivable that a poet should be able to articulate the "voice of the people", as you suggested earlier?

CIXOUS Modern-day France is neither in a critical nor a tragic crisis. And so the French nation is remarkably unworried about the plight of the Mandela family, as though our country lacked nothing spiritual, as though it had no need of the lesson of uncompromising nobility brought to humanity by the Mandelas. The tragedy is played out in the distance, and our indifference only increases.

The name "Mandela" is precisely what the French people should be hearing today: and on hearing it, we should tremble with horror.

Nor must we forget that any nation with indifference in its soul, which allows its moral standards to slip, has the potential to become as vile as apartheid Africa. It has already happened to us. Today, as in the past, a writer can say that memory is horribly fragile, that we must continually resuscitate it, teach the same story and the same lessons to every generation, even year by year. We always need memory, and a mirror to reflect it back to us.

We always need to listen to the other, whether he is a close or a distant neighbour. When I reflect morally and poetically I feel the terrible pain of South Africa behind my right shoulder: if my body were a map I would feel pain in the south of my body. And as for the hostages! For three years I identified with them, carried them painfully in my imagination. My identification was hesitant with regards to the prisoners though, for I did not know where they were, I did not know under which sky they lay sleepless; my mental images of them crumbled, and thus suffering itself became difficult for me. I thought especially of their waiting wives, however, and sympathy with their plight allowed me, here, in this very room in Paris, to get closer to them, to imagine suffering.

When they were liberated, television journalists interviewed passers-by on the streets, surprising them with the news. Politically speaking, people responded with rationalizing caution, rejecting the idea that the event could be electorally motivated. Poetically speaking, their reaction was even less engaged: "It's a good thing", they replied. No trembling. They did not laugh, cry, or flinch: they had not spread their wings in the realm of the imagination, and that upset me.

From time to time people ask me how I can justify writing about people such as the Mandelas, or about places such as Cambodia, given that I am neither black, nor Cambodian, nor in exile. What annoys me though, is that people do *not* write about these things. It is such a small thing to do, not necessarily to write about, but, with one's skin, with one's heart, each according to their means, to approach another's suffering, not to ignore it, and to do one's best to bear witness to it.

To write poetically is to come close to others precisely where they are the most alive, most mortal, closest to death.

For me, a text has no urgency unless it is agonizing. Unless it rips open the heart. Unless it pushes us beyond ourselves. These days pain is elsewhere. We should feel it as our own, even if it's not French.

DL But why not, then, broach France itself?

CIXOUS That, for me, is the most difficult thing of all: to "broach" one's own country. It is impossible to work theatrically without finding distance, without a stage. To write about France would mean divesting oneself of one's nationality, uprooting something from one's imagination. Cambodia shows me a foreign face, with which I must familiarize myself: to achieve such a distance from France, to find the metaphorical dimension within which one can create, I would have to become foreign to myself.

DL Wouldn't this be possible with the Barbie affair?[6] How could generations who neither lived through the Second World War, nor through its aftermath, imagine monstrosity from the image of that little old man?

CIXOUS The coverage of the Barbie affair lacked the violence of the poetic gaze. Television cannot conjure up the magic of Dante's breath: only a poet has the power to plunge into the depths of the human soul. In the Barbie affair we saw much more of the mysterious executioner — who is mysterious precisely because he appears so human — than we did of the victims, who, being simultaneously sacred and taboo, remain dangerously veiled. In the magnificent afterword to *If This is a Man* Primo Levi studies the mystery of evil, and the necessity of re-establishing our own, and humanity's limits. This is, in my opinion, a fundamental question. Many poets have tackled it, but each time humanity drifts back off to sleep; nothing seems to work as an example, our collective memory is erased, and all is to begin again.

DL Our society is becoming more and more administrative, privileging the object, quantification, and the real. The possibility of writers being read, or poets being heard must then surely be either postponed, if not, indeed, cancelled altogether.

CIXOUS And yet we have creative resources. France is a country which is steeped in history. The mythical humus of creation, a secular universe; first-hand experience of greatness, grief, shame, humiliation, the sum of all disasters: we have all the necessary materials to make a work of art. My own writing draws on the experience which History so violently thrust upon me: the confrontation, before I was even three years old, with anti-Semitism and colonialism. Negative experiences are gateways onto discovery. In France there is nothing abstract about hell, and whoever is ignorant of hell must necessarily be ignorant of paradise. But herein lies the risk of cultural impoverishment: the appreciation of literary works is threatened by the global world of mass media, whose foundations lie in money-fuelled programming and narcissistic over-investment. Celebrity culture, the emblem of the power of the soulless image, is the enemy of art, and this is what has encroached upon the territory of appreciation. Creators who are not affiliated or easily assimilated to the system are pushed into ever-shrinking corners. The reading public, those who love poetry, the text, the theatre, are cut off from the sources of creation by walls of silence and secrecy.

But the reader and the author are inseparable partners. They cry out to one another through the walls. They are compelled to find a way round them, dig under them, even travel the world in order to find each other again. The search becomes an ordeal, but one which it is imperative to undergo.

DL Nelson Mandela is, without doubt, one of the most morally significant of our contemporaries, but this significance is in no way linked to the ruling power. It stems, rather, from the acknowledgment of his people: this kind of strength, it seems to me, has something of a poetic or sacred function about it.

CIXOUS As far as power goes, I don't quite agree. Mandela's greatness resides in his personal merit, his courage, his capacity to live the unliveable. This man, whose life has been stolen and replaced with a living death, succeeds in overcoming his sentence and daily transforms his death into life. Ever since his childhood in the tribe, however, Mandela has been accustomed to immense power: from the beginning he was a king, and has the bearing of a leader of people, a royal shepherd. Steve Biko[7] never wielded a sceptre like Mandela's. If Mandela does not yet have institutional power, he will one day, and he already has symbolic power. He knows that he reigns over all the dreams of his people. Although imprisoned, he knows that in the outside world he is kept alive throughout his entire country. He has at his disposal a great power which has genuine effects in reality. Added to this, he is nourished, supported, kept alive by Winnie Mandela, who provides him with half of his strength. Without her, living and breathing for him on the other side of the prison walls, he would be dead. She is the reality, the embodiment of each day.

Together they work, they make love across the walls, and build Africa hand in hand. This is what is most incredible in their story.

DL I was struck by the royal character in your play *L'Histoire terrible mais inachevée de Norodom Sihanouk, roi du Cambodge*,[8] as the king seems to have both a comic and a tragic side to his character.

CIXOUS It was, in fact, the actual prince, Sihanouk himself, who invented the character. He is a statesman who knows very well that "all the world's a stage", and, knowing its tricks and its laws so well, it is on this stage that he embodies his own persona. This intuitive theatricality was my inspiration. He is the product of his own creation. This capacity to act out his own character, the fictionality of his existence, has been, in part, the saving grace of his country.

DL But only the sovereign, or, rather, the sovereign figure, can embody poetically those connections which ensure the coherence of History; and it is this which justifies his power.

CIXOUS Not every king has the same power to dazzle the imagination. In order to exercise a magical power, one must be able to embody a myth, to enchant one's public — one's subjects. One must recreate the Narcissus-myth around oneself.

Saying that, "royalty" should not be the preserve of kings. For me, the poet who confronts power is the true embodiment of royalty.

NOTES

1. The interview was prefaced with the following:

> The newspaper *Le Monde* has recently revived the issue of the absence of intellectuals from contemporary debate. At the same time, writers such as Marguerite Duras are appearing on television in order to take a stand against the timid mediocrity of today's discussions, and are daring to speak the truth. Duras's surprise at the violence with which many of her articles on current affairs have been received is a pertinent reminder that literature retains its ability to scandalize. Some, however, consider that it is the silence of many writers which is scandalous, and that there is something risible in the call to bear witness to the historical era coming from some of the same figures who, not so long ago, joined their colleagues in mocking woolly-minded humanitarianism. To write or to take a stand: such is the dilemma with which we have attempted to straitjacket our authors. This dilemma gives rise to a certain silence, stemming not only from the encroachment of ever more global techniques of communication, but also from alarm in the face of a world which

is becoming uniform in its radical otherness. Is this to say that the representation of our history has become impossible, or that it can only be achieved through the blinding flash of the visual and its brutal immersion of the subject into the horrors of reality? Perhaps not. Indeed, the very failure of literature is, at the same time, its opportunity to come of age once more; under the condition that, in the words of Georges Bataille, the writer "does not trail behind the masses, and that he knows how to die in solitude". The following interview with Hélène Cixous will thus be a matter of singular observations on our collective history.

2. Jawaharlal Nehru (1889–1964), a disciple of Gandhi, was leader of the Indian National Congress Party and the first prime minister of independent India. He and André Malraux, who served as Minister of Information in De Gaulle's post-war government, then as Minister of Culture from 1960–69, met several times between the 1930s and 1960s.

3. Anna Akhmatova (1889–1966) and Ossip Mandelstam (1891–1938) were both stigmatized in Soviet Russia: publication of the former's work was banned, while the latter eventually died in a Siberian gulag. Paul Celan's (1920–70) work is, on the other hand, profoundly marked by his first-hand experience of the treatment of Jews at the hands of the Nazis: both his parents were killed in the holocaust, and Celan himself spent a year in a concentration camp in Moldova before being liberated by the Russians in 1944.

4. Marina Tsvetaeva (1892–1941) spent seventeen years in exile from Soviet Russia from 1922 to 1939, her return being swiftly followed by her suicide in 1941.

5. Jacques Derrida, Nadine Gordimer, Jorge Amado *et al.*, *Pour Nelson Mandela* [For Nelson Mandela] (Paris: Gallimard, 1986).

6. Klaus Barbie (1913–91) was a notorious figure throughout the German occupation of France. Known as "le boucher de Lyon" (the Lyon butcher), he sent thousands of French Jews to their deaths at Auschwitz. He fled France following the Liberation, living first in Germany, then in Bolivia under an assumed name. He was extradited to France in 1983 where he was imprisoned for crimes against humanity. He died in prison in Lyon in 1991.

7. Steve Biko (1946–77) is widely seen as one of the greatest martyrs of the anti-apartheid movement in South Africa. He died of head wounds in police custody, although the police claimed both at the time, and during the Truth Commission hearings in 1997, that his death was accidental.

8. Hélène Cixous, *L'Histoire terrible mais inachevée de Norodom Sihanouk, roi du Cambodge* [The Terrible But Unfinished Story of Norodom Sihanouk, King of Cambodia] (Paris: Théâtre du Soleil, 1985).

Part IV: Writing and theatre

9. The author between text and theatre

Interview with *Hors Cadre.* Translated by Lucy Garnier.

This interview first appeared as "L'auteur entre texte et théâtre", in *Hors Cadre*, vol. 8, "L'Etat d'auteur" [State of the Author], 33–65, 1990.

CIXOUS It's best if I attempt something like an account of (my) theatrical writing.

An account, because I won't be theorizing, except where certain aspects that I'll be talking to you about are concerned; for example, the question of the characters, which I think is essential.

The fact is that writing remains a solitary process. When I write for the theatre, I write in my corner, like for fiction, but positioning myself differently in relation to the text that emerges from the *Théâtre du Soleil*.[1] Here I'm referring specifically to my relationship with the *Théâtre du Soleil*, not to my relationship with theatre more generally. For example, this year I wrote a play intended for X. In that instance, I was the one giving the orders; it was my fantasy, my desire, and didn't come from anyone other than myself. It was a play for five women. With the *Théâtre du Soleil*, it's completely different because there's a commission and I'm the one taking orders.

The commission already dictates certain characteristics; not of the writing itself, but of the economy of the play. For example — a certain length, a certain breadth, a certain scope and a certain quantity. There are twenty-five or thirty actors in the *Théâtre du Soleil*. I don't write *in order* for them to be employed, but I *know* that there has to be a lot of space for play and players, because twenty-five isn't just twenty-five, it's twenty-five multiplied by how ever many, and obviously that affects everything I want to do. At first this was a challenge for me (and I think it still is). For me, stretching my imagination to such dimensions is the most difficult exercise. You realize that a brain that imagines things is just like a womb, there's a limit to the amount it can bear — it's only human. I can manage to conceive a work with five or six creatures but I stop there. For *L'Indiade*,[2] for example, I had a lot of trouble because I had to conceive scenes with twenty or twenty-five. I never managed to do it in one go, I mean in a way that remains corporeal and creative. There was no artifice, but a mechanism. I knew that at a given moment I needed a scene that would bring twenty people on stage. I couldn't fit twenty people into my head, into my body. So I had to keep coming back to this scene, repeatedly putting its genesis back into play. I was forced to relive the scene bit by bit. This brings another problem, which is that the creative moment is no longer the same. I need twenty days, but at the same time I need at least four pregnancies. There's a problem with the maturing process, and a disparity between characters that should actually be twins.

HC Does this kind of fragmentation, this going back in time, lead to changes and to creative variants?

CIXOUS That's what I have to watch out for. There are different types of maturing, there are different states in fact. I am not in the same state at one or two weeks' interval and this requires an extra creative effort. I have to get back in touch with a previous state in order to bring it back to the present. I'm describing this simply as a difficulty that has nothing to do with the writing as such. It's the state being called into question, not the language, nor the writing hand.

HC It's the state, or condition, of the author.

CIXOUS That's exactly what I should say. Because I think that the terms and metaphors of pregnancy are totally appropriate in this case. To come back to what I was saying initially, when I am writing, when I'm elaborating, I am alone. But with the *Théâtre du Soleil* there's an initial contract, an agreement between Ariane and myself on the subject. On a non-specific subject, the general nature of the subject, not, obviously, on the story itself. For example, at the moment I'm writing about the Resistance. The subject we agreed on was the Resistance in France. Then it has to be specified because the Resistance in France is a thousand different subjects, a thousand different possibilities. And the way in which it will be told — the choice and definition of the plot, the characters — that's up to me, in the same way as it was with *L'Indiade*. I work from that, with these constraints of space and number that come from the other. I say "constraint", but it's actually also a form of freedom. For an overflowing, prodigious imagination it would be an unlimited "licence to unlimit". The *Théâtre du Soleil* has no theatrical "limits", so to speak. However, for me this "freedom" requires an extra effort. While I have no difficulty writing a play for five or six characters, I do have difficulty with twenty-five, thirty or fifty characters. Someone dynamic could produce a scene with twenty-five characters in one go, but I can't.

So I work in my corner for quite a while (not that "quite a while" is quantifiable). Then comes the moment of relay; the moment when the troupe starts to rehearse. There's a text, a story, characters — and then come the adventures. And they vary a great deal. I'm giving you a very simple account here; the chronicle of creation on a basic level. Afterwards, I'll complicate this account somewhat. What happens when the Company begins to work? Firstly, the writing is never changed. There are two dimensions, two working registers — what I call the writing, I mean the style, the language, and none of that is ever changed, nor touched upon by the world of the Company. I'm not saying, of course, that there aren't interventions on an unconscious level. It's not impossible that, unconsciously, I write in a particular way precisely because I know the destination of the text, but that's something I can't really account for. It's not impossible that what I know about the *Théâtre du Soleil*, about its memory, changes something of my own writing project. The interlocutor always intervenes. In the same way that when I give a seminar I speak-to . . . and in a particular language. That becomes interesting when you think about the nature of a fictional text. When I write fiction, who is my interlocutor? Who am I addressing? I can't name the instance which works upon the unconscious of my language. It must be a mixture of myself, of God, the absolute, etc. since the public has neither face nor presence. There's an element of censorship, too, of which I'm aware. I've felt over the years that I was being threatened internally by the effects of censorship.

HC Which stem from the theatre?

CIXOUS No, in fictional texts. Obviously, I resist as hard as I can, but I know that when I started writing, I didn't know anything about the drama of reception. I was in a sort of completely unbridled freedom. Afterwards, the world — never academic work, but everything to do with the mass media — reflected an image of the forbidden back at me and I rejected, and rewrote, that image. I feel I am vibrant and that sometimes I write a protest against the forbidden into my own texts.

HC What sort of forbidden?

CIXOUS Always the same accusation — of being hermetic, unreadable, incomprehensible, difficult. This "critical vocabulary" has resounded for twenty-five years; I hear it all the time. Sometimes even without hostility, with connotations of intimidation.

HC Did the move to theatre represent a concern for being more perceptible, more readable; a concern for more direct reception? Was this part of a new constraint? You spoke about constraints of space and number, leaving the faces of the audience in the dark, but with regard to this question of being unreadable that you've flagged up, do the demands of theatre not require — and this is nothing to do with censorship — that something be more directly perceptible?

CIXOUS Yes, it's unavoidable.

HC So these demands alter the writing?

CIXOUS Absolutely. But I don't perceive it as a constraint. It's another pact. And that's why I mentioned my seminar.[3] In the seminar, I have another language; my seminar language, which is very free, but which is obviously linear. It's oral so the effects of writing are necessarily reduced. And yet it's a fairly elaborate language that I "speak-to-myself", one that I don't speak, for example, if I give a lecture abroad, because I bring my language down a level, and I displace it. It's true that where the theatre is concerned, it's also a certain language that isn't even already determined by the audience, but by the characters themselves. I don't see how my characters could speak *my* language, one of my languages . . . no. I try and hear their other languages. So obviously there's a mixture; their other languages mixed with my language — there's an incredible displacement.

So it starts there. For *L'Indiade*, I had a problem that I resolved in extremis. At one point I even thought "I won't write this play". It was the musical score, if I can call it that, of the peoples that escaped me. I didn't know how ordinary Indian people spoke, and I was incapable of imagining. As for how I could know how the higher castes spoke, well, they left their mark. There are a great number of texts by Gandhi, Nehru and other famous individuals. And I've read them. So although I don't try to imitate Nehru or Gandhi's language, I can get a feeling for something of the imaginary, something of the mythical world of these characters; a secret ground in which I plant and graft something. A note that I tune into — it's basically a reading.[4] And from my reading, which includes the effects of the unconscious, I can move towards the creation of a language that resembles, or at least I hope resembles, what their own bodies could produce. Of course, it's not intellectual; it's emotional. But with the ordinary people, there are no sources! I had to take a second trip to India, I finally had to find the mediations to allow me to understand how a village woman or a craftsman feels, cries, trembles, is stirred . . . so as to be able to enter into the daunting adventure of generating idiolects, because it can be pure betrayal. And if I hadn't been able to find the mediations through a second trip, the play wouldn't have existed. So this is the first step in this displacement of language, it's the character.

HC Not the public, but the character. You construct characters in a dialogue, as if you were conversing with them. . . .

CIXOUS I identify with the character. It's really an organ transplant. A heart transplant. I say heart, because that's where it takes place, and if I can't manage to graft this second heart, nothing happens. I don't always manage this equally well. Sometimes the transplant is rejected. When I find someone profoundly *unpleasant*, I can find it difficult. I have to manage to find the heart of a traitor, I mean to feel the heart of a traitor, within myself. But it's very interesting, because traitors have their reasons. It's up to me to find the right pitch to the passion, its sincerity, which means its suffering. That said, there are traitors I could never bring to the stage, I've always known that.

HC It must be a problem for the Resistance.

CIXOUS It's a problem for Hitler. But I'm not trying. I thought about it a lot. It's difficult and it leans towards the repugnant but, after all, maybe it's a lesson too. I don't think I have the nature of a traitor, but there's certainly a point where, on a human level, deep down in my very marrow, it's possible to understand the traitor.

HC If I've understood correctly, the task of writing numerous characters allows you to become yourself again (you speak of sympathizing, of the need for a transplant, the need to identify) but through a process of alteration. The demands of characters provoke a plurality of voices and force you to listen on multiple levels thus imposing an intellectual task, which you carry out like a systematic project. Within this, there's a play on alteration that I find very interesting.

CIXOUS Alteration is vital. When I'm working, I'm not an intellectual at all. I'm not developing anything, theorizing anything or thinking anything. But, afterwards, because I do have this role myself (of intellectual, academic, etc.), afterwards, it's true, I do start to question myself about some of the effects. So yes, alteration; it's essential to allow yourself to be altered. But how and by whom? For example, if I had to write Pétain (I haven't tried, so I'm a clean slate) in this case, just like you, I'm faced with Pétain and in fact we're in a situation of very limited inter-subjectivity. There's no interiorization — actually, we reject him, and we give in to the pleasures of disgust.

HC With the only difference being that we sang "Maréchal, nous voilà!"[5]

CIXOUS Me too. At the age of two, I sang it and I've never forgotten it. It's very important because it makes us experience a Pétain who has become inconceivable to someone who never sang, "Maréchal, nous voilà!". But that's the Pétain effect. But what if I had to cross over to the other side, to the side of the person producing this effect? Who was Pétain? I don't know if I'll try, but it's incredibly difficult for me, because he is strange to me (it's not that he's a stranger to me, but that he's strange to me). If I had to give life to Pétain and make him speak, where would that come from? Where do all those words I now know by heart come from? Where are they produced? What's his base, his true land? Not his psychological base, because that exists too. I don't have the key, and I have to find it.[6] Whereas with de Gaulle, I'd have a different problem. He's not strange to me, on the contrary I sympathize with de Gaulle, or I'm able to, so these affects are affects that I could have — the problem of identification is reduced.

HC Don't you think you would write a better Pétain, precisely because of this strangeness that you speak of?

CIXOUS Not necessarily, because I'd have to find Pétain's truth. For the moment, I don't know Pétain's truth. Maybe, if I put myself to it, I'll end up finding it. But that's actually very mysterious. Let's not talk about Pétain and de Gaulle, which are extreme cases. There are characters that come to me, that are accessible to me, very quickly, or rather relatively quickly, compared with the difficulty I have with other characters. Probably because there are similarities, a system of emotions I perceive very quickly and affects that are familiar to me. I probably find myself in a loving place, the place where you love someone. I wouldn't say it's about narcissism because that would be oversimplifying it, but it's something positive, something good, something that does no harm; there's an element of an Ideal-self present. There are characters that I search for. It takes an incredible amount of time, I fail to find them and it's as if I were failing to reach a certain level. I feel them pass me by, and in the end maybe they remain on the level of insignificant or indifferent meetings; the level we have with most people we meet. It's neither real nor fake; there's no depth. What's missing is the very element that will be the source of a whole life, a whole destiny. So because what I'm writing is flat, I realize I haven't found the element that will create the warmth and depth of a text. The thing that in writing, you realize, is expressed through metaphor. And I haven't found the source of the metaphor — I mean the translation of the soul, the body, etc. into metaphors. That's a warning sign. In that case, I look a little further.

HC Can we develop that further? This kind of very plural movement is extremely important. Basically, you're saying that when you can't sympathize, if sympathy and empathy aren't possible, then the writing has no source, but that it's the metaphor which is the source of this writing because it puts into play a displacement. Again, we have here a certain movement back-and-forth, a passing-on. And, to a certain extent, a rejection, a process of taking up and taking up again. And all this is multiple in itself, don't you think?

CIXOUS Quite.

HC What is the role of the metaphor? It's not just a sign of the writing. What does the metaphor pass into the body of the other, the character, through you?

CIXOUS That's the theatre or the theatrical. It's obviously — I won't say "the other scene" — what makes a character become, *be*, worthy of the theatre. For me, the ultimate example is Shakespeare. All Shakespeare's characters are like that already. Each one is their own little theatre; each one steps onto their own stage. Each of Shakespeare's characters has their own little kingdom, their micro-kingdom. We could say that each of Shakespeare's inhabitants (let's not say characters) is exceptional. They're rich, they touch us, we're fascinated by them; they're not the kingdomless characters we can meet in the street. There are lots of people without a kingdom. And if you put them on stage, the theatre fades away. At least, the theatre as I imagine it, the theatre that I like, because there's also flat theatre. There are fake stages, like those of television for example, so a lot of the characters that we see don't bring us anything, because they have no inner universe and they don't produce any signs. And yet on television there can suddenly, extraordinarily, be someone worthy of the theatre. It's never a presenter. There was one person who overwhelmed me. I saw her once two years ago, this person who happens to be a cook, a woman who's a chef, and who was explaining how she cooks. She had such a wealth of language . . . she delved into the very roots of the human being. What she was saying was worth any book of psychoanalysis, but much richer, much more substantial; it was magnificent. If you put that woman on stage, it's all ready. Why? She has substance. She knows everything about life. And she knows how to speak that knowledge on the stage of language.

So when I write for the *Théâtre du Soleil* with a set of specifications, my chances aren't equal where the characters are concerned. Because (up until now, at any rate) it's been a question of stories putting into play characters that are (partly) real and inescapable — there are a certain number of historical figures that I can't get around; they were historical agents.

HC It's impossible to invent a phantasmagorical de Gaulle?

CIXOUS De Gaulle is very, very rich. There are characters of the Resistance who were incredibly important; that doesn't mean they are personalities worthy of the theatre. And it's sometimes hard for me to lift them on to the inner stage; they must already have their own inner stage before they can reach the real stage. Not everyone has an inner universe, not everyone has a poetic dimension and not everyone can be poeticized — some people resist that. Because I'm not entirely free, because reality — particularly French reality — prevents me from being totally free to invent and, because too many things can be checked, sometimes I can't dramatize. I had less difficulty with a more distant reality. I had less difficulty with Cambodia because for us, the French, it was further away and without any trace. With Cambodia, for example, I had no trouble inventing a ghost King. When an author is under the scrutiny of contemporary history (by that, I don't mean censorship) and has to answer to the views of their contemporaries, it's much harder to transport characters.

HC So here the censorship doesn't come from the theatre, it comes from a relationship to a known reality. Would it be the same thing for a fictional piece, a novel, or even an essay?

CIXOUS I don't think so. I'm not sure, because I've never asked myself the question. An essay — no. An essay gives total freedom. But for a novel, I don't think I should answer, because I wouldn't be able to write a novel about this kind of thing. That would touch upon my relationship with the text, and what I can and can't do in a fictional text. For example, something I've never tried to do in a fictional text, because I don't think I'd be capable of it, is precisely bring to the text someone I dislike. Why? Because the fictional text is much closer to me than the theatrical text where, once I've written the character, it can go its own way. That's a mystery. I can't tell you how it happens, it's very strange, but once I've drawn it out of me, I can let it loose to go off and make mischief on its own. It no longer feeds off me.

Whereas a text is never separated from me until it's finished, and so I literally wouldn't be able to bear it.

HC This supposes the theatrical text has an autonomy the essay and fictional text don't have?

CIXOUS At a certain moment, yes. For me, as things stand, my greatest progress in this domain is my latest book, called *Manne*,[7] where for the first time I brought real people to the text; something which, in fact, I was only able to do effectively after having been through the theatrical experience. But I have to say, they are people whom I admire, who I like, and with whom I don't have an unpleasant relationship. There's no way I can imagine lending myself to Pétain in a fictional text.

HC Nonetheless, despite all the contracts and constraints that you're describing, all the multiplicity and resistance of the theatre compared to fiction, you're writing theatre, and you crossed over to the theatre as if there were a necessity, or a desire, for plurality.

CIXOUS My move to the theatre? It was overdetermined. First of all, I have to say it wasn't a decision on my part. I accepted it, which was maybe part of the decision. But everything I've written for the theatre has always been commissioned. I didn't go looking for the theatre, if only because I don't know how you could. Incidentally, I've never considered myself to be a playwright. Theatre's such a particular genre, which presupposes the adjunction of so many material conditions etc. that it seems difficult to me for someone to label themselves as a theatrical writer.

HC Does theatre intervene in the authorial experience? Could it be equated to a certain moment of that experience?

CIXOUS Exactly. It's something which happened for me, but without it being totally conscious. That's to say that my first play — which was *Portrait de Dora*[8] — wasn't written as such. It emerged without my having planned it from *Portrait du soleil*,[9] a fictional text within which the play was hidden without my knowing it. When I first read my writing, I thought I could see hints of scenes. I said to myself: "Oh look, there are scenes in there", it was very bizarre. And then there was a stroke of luck. At that point, I met a woman who was a director, who read my texts and who said: "You should write for the theatre"; that's how it happened, through Simone Benmussa's encouragement. I didn't even know what writing for the theatre was. So, under Simone Benmussa's professional eye, I cut out and stitched back together pieces of text. I don't consider that to be a theatrical experience *as such*, but rather a certain kind of oblique coming to the theatre. It didn't give me the impression of being a playwright. I had the impression of doing it obliquely, illegitimately. A naive impression, because that obliqueness is, in itself, theatre.

HC So in such a case the characters aren't created in the same way.

CIXOUS Not at all. But it has to be said, it was very unusual. It was a staging of the unconscious. A character didn't have to be created. And *Portrait de Dora* is a very short play, with few characters. The parameters are completely different. I experienced this three times because I wrote three short plays, and it's a very different thing. It's one scene. I'd say you could almost establish sub-genres. For example, the one-act play. And it's true that it's a single writing act, on all levels. In time . . .

HC . . . in space, and in number.

CIXOUS Yes, on all levels.

HC The experience you are describing with the *Théâtre du Soleil* is something quite different.

CIXOUS Yes.

HC I asked myself a question yesterday whilst reading a few of your texts . . . I was struck by the difference between the texts written in 1976 and those written in 1983, which correspond roughly to the moment when the theatrical experience took shape. In the texts from 1976 the insistence of the subject — the passiveness of the subject, because you say that language, languages, pass through you — is very strong. Whereas what struck me in the texts from 1983, particularly those approaching the aim of writing-painting, was the search for the third person and the move from "I" to "he/she".[10] Did the theatre not play a role in accelerating this shift, with the "he/she" becoming a "they"?

CIXOUS Yes, that's completely true. It doesn't mean abandoning my originary writing because this remains the writing that carries everything, even if I distance myself from it sometimes, I am that writing. It's in that writing that I recognize myself, it's that writing which reassures me, it's my base.[11] Without that writing, I wouldn't take risks. At the same time, that very writing is already an adventure in itself.

HC The breath? The thing that pushes you, that passes through you?

CIXOUS Yes. And, at any rate, definitely a certain passiveness. I'd say that passiveness is the greatest strength. Let's say that when it writes itself, it's a relief, it's what I'm most sure of. I definitely need to be carried forward in that particular way.

Now, about this other, theatrical, writing — yes, it separates me from myself. I need myself, so therefore I need this originary writing, in order to start conceiving. Afterwards, that writing separates from me, because there are all these others. And that's when drama, as it were, begins. Not the theatre: drama.

HC The drama of the author?

CIXOUS Yes.

HC You wouldn't use the metaphor of pregnancy for a text?

CIXOUS No, I think that separation takes place when the text is finished. That's a total and definitive separation. It's absolute. I'm talking about this strangely quantifiable time of bringing to life characters from which I will be able to detach myself at a certain point, as they are able to detach themselves from me. It's true that it's a relief. At first I'm the one writing, working furiously, and then there's a blessed moment where the characters take their leave. So much so that sometimes I think, oh look, I didn't write this scene, they did it, it's their business and that pleases me. That means they are structured enough, strong and dynamic enough, so that when I give the signal: "This scene has to be done", they come in and do it.

HC But this happens through listening to the voices you were talking about.

CIXOUS But I had to reach that point. At that point, I come back to a sort of passiveness. They do their work. But this comes quite late. (At the moment, on the contrary, I'm right in the most difficult phase.)

Shakespeare is always my point of reference. I say to myself, to think that, for him, his characters come on stage and there you have it, it's done, they're there. But sometimes, to console myself, I say to myself: "How do you know Shakespeare didn't have the same problems as you?" But it's just an attempt at consolation. I have the feeling that this state of total freedom that I reach very late on, he must have reached immediately.

But to come back to what we were saying, about the time when the Company starts to work — the Company is the first audience. The characters and the Company — that's the audience. Then lots of unpredictable things happen. There are notebooks containing all of this, kept by Ariane's assistant Sophie, a remarkable person, who records all the work, including the countless shifts in the staging and the work of the actors. One scene is rehearsed umpteen times. I don't think that we, as readers and spectators, really understand the work of the theatre. I don't think we know, unless we've been on the ground, what a rehearsal actually is. I write "Enter so and so" but there are a thousand ways of coming on stage. And it changes everything. That alone is already an incredible amount of theatrical work. In come the characters, in come the actors. They come in from the front, from the back, from the side, on all fours, upright . . . they run. And it changes everything. So unpredictable things happen concerning the scenes. I don't know the mysterious rules — because they do exist — which mean that a scene is more or less performable, or finds its bearings on stage immediately or not. Sometimes I'm happy, I think: "This scene is beautiful" but during the rehearsal there'll maybe be a jam, something will jam, and we won't know what. Or else Ariane reads a scene and says to me: "No problem". And then there's every possible problem. The actors can't get it, and, conversely, when I think there will be problems, there aren't.

HC But when there's a problem, you rewrite?

CIXOUS This is what happens. It starts with the work of the actors. We don't know who is responsible for the jam. Is it an actor who can't get it? Is it all the actors, all of *this* group of actors, who can't get it, because we can change that? In this case we check, anyway, because the troupe is incredibly mobile and Ariane's work is open, i.e. the parts aren't assigned permanently until the last minute. (It's also essential to know that. For two to three months, the troupe rehearses without any set casting, which means all the actors who want to try a role do so.) So we'll have three, four, five or six versions of the scene.

HC Always recorded?

CIXOUS Written down by Sophie, and in Ariane's memory. And it's worked on a lot. Sometimes a different actor will take over — what one person can't do, another can. Sometimes it's a mysterious question of staging that Ariane will discover at some point or other. It can perhaps be something in the writing, in the dynamics of the scene, which is miscalculated. I'm still a student in the matter; I've learnt things, but miniscule things. I'm not a very good student where this is concerned because I keep forgetting the lessons all the time. Let's say that because I am, originally, who I am, the text is where I'm most proficient. What I'm not so good at is the technique of staging. Not staging as in direction, but the things that make a scene theatrical. For example, the entrances, the exits, the arrival of a character, the use of space; obviously all of that isn't in the direction, it's in the text. What I have to watch out for is the very interiorized relationship I have with the text as a verbal world. Sometimes I can write a scene that isn't sufficiently theatrical, that doesn't immediately carry the actors into a space. But sometimes it's something else. Sometimes there's definitely something that certain actors can't *live*, because an actor can't do absolutely everything. Death, for example. Acting death. So I rewrite a scene.

HC So you rewrite it according to the space?

CIXOUS Not necessarily. I put another version out there. The content of the scene, what the scene has to bring to the action and the way it moves the story forward, remain. Because the scene is governed by a necessity of plot. I try and transform the way it works. And that can be in a thousand different ways. Because it's a question of an *economy of dialogue*. So, I can decide that instead of all the characters coming on stage, only one comes on, etc. There are a thousand ways of rewriting a scene. It's incalculable. And it's terrible, precisely because you don't know. Everyone plunges into darkness and so I've sometimes written ten versions of one scene.

HC How far can this variation go?

CIXOUS In *L'Indiade*, I published four versions of one scene as an example.

HC But how do you see it? How far can variation go?

CIXOUS Until the scene disappears. Until it's cancelled. So when it doesn't disappear, it means that it's an indispensable scene. There are scenes which disappeared because they couldn't be acted. There are scenes which disappeared despite having been rehearsed. Because we realized that we could do without them, overall, and things have to be cut, all the time.

HC Can there be changes in the meaning, the direction?

CIXOUS Of the story?

HC Of the scene. The type of relationship, the type of conflict, which are pretty important in theatrical practice, the interpretation of the characters . . .

CIXOUS Not really. Maybe I'm wrong in saying that, because I could be having a moment of amnesia. It's very hard to explain — I think that, in theatrical writing, there can be specific mistakes. I can have failed to reach the stage, failed to reach the imaginary stage on which everything must be written, and done something which falls into the area of fiction. That, yes. That happens to me, and it's the problem I come up against incessantly. I can allow myself to give in to something which would be closer to an ethico-philosophical exchange than to theatre. And there, the clue to the problem is that it's abstract. Whereas the theatre is concrete — let's say that what I can fail to capture is the *present* of theatre, and I can stray to the side of the eternity of reflection. But once it's being rehearsed, I think it's a question of the dynamics. Sometimes, because there's something to tell, something to bring across, what I can't find is the right footing, the rhythm to the action — I can't manage to weave the threads together fast enough. I know that with *L'Indiade*, we had a general breakdown with one of the scenes — I've got countless versions of that scene — and no-one ever managed to understand why we couldn't reach a point of satisfaction with it. For *Sihanouk*, we had that as well, but I think it was because I hadn't managed to feel sympathy or antipathy for the Americans, or Kissinger I suppose; I'd become dispassionate.

HC And yet it's such a strong scene, the Kissinger scene.

CIXOUS For Ariane it remains "the blemish",[12] I don't know how to say that in French, the stain of *Sihanouk*, the scene which failed.

HC The Kissinger scene? But it stuck in my memory, maybe in a slightly different register, more Brechtian.

CIXOUS I don't relate to Brecht, but I accept what you're saying. But now we're entering into the realm of measuring, of evaluating — critical realms. I can't reply because, that, I don't know.

HC What's becoming apparent here, in a very interesting way, is the question of heterogeneity.

CIXOUS I find it interesting that you should say that. But I can't say anything, I'm impartial.

HC For Ariane Mnouchkine, apparently, it breaks with the homogeneity. And for me, it stayed in my memory, because, at that moment, maybe another avenue opened up.

CIXOUS The adjective that you used, and which I never use because I don't frequent Brecht, clarifies things for me. I wasn't used to that scene. There was an estranging effect for everyone.

HC If I remember the scene correctly, it really carried the actor. The Brechtian effect was much more visible.

CIXOUS I'm realizing that's exactly what it's about. My failures — what I call my failures — that's what they are, they're moments of dissatisfaction because my libidinal economy is "anti-Brechtian". That's why, where Pétain's concerned, I wouldn't trust myself as far as I could write him, because for the moment I'd do something "Brechtian". And that's what I don't like — it doesn't convince me; it requires a performance of actors rather than blood and tears. Sometimes I feel I'm reduced to that because I can't do any better — I can't manage to reach right inside, into the body of the character which makes the actor's body appear.

In practice, I discovered there's an incredibly surprising relay between my work and the actor's work. (And what I discovered with a different sort of surprise was that I had no relationship with the staging.) On the other hand, I'm in direct communication with the actor's work, without that passing through any theoretical elaboration. We're treading the same boards.

What happens, then, is that until I manage to curb this distance, until I'm able to do my work successfully, able to read what I call the body or the imaginary of a character, I feel as if I've stooped too low. For want of humanity. For want of sympathy, warmth, inspiration, etc.

HC And at that moment, in a way, you disavow yourself in your capacity as the author, as the figure of your authorial status, but it's also another authorial state . . .

CIXOUS As a theatrical author, in that particular space. It's very specific. It's not the writing that fails me, I don't lack writing. But I can lack the right state, like an actor.

HC You can lack the right state and that's what you're highlighting in the case of the Kissinger scene.

CIXOUS That's very interesting, and you've taught me something. So there's a problem (it's very specific) which is the collective work that means the actors of the *Théâtre du Soleil* have learnt — because the *Théâtre du Soleil* is their school too — to be this way inclined, to tend towards this state. And they only feel carried away, and at ease, if they are able to relive and reconnect with this particular state, which is totally draining, but at the same time completely reassuring. They know they've got there. And if they haven't, they're lost. But the actor you're talking about, who played Kissinger (and this, too, is very specific) is someone who, at that time anyway, had in him that capacity for separation, for distance and representation.

HC And so, in a sense, the actor took over here . . .

CIXOUS But it was by chance.

HC But that's part of the theatrical writing process.

CIXOUS Oh yes, absolutely. So what still changes during the work of the re-hearsals? There's an immense amount of work, different kinds of work. Firstly, this is due to the fact that I don't know how to tailor a scene accurately; but then no-one can do that. For example, *L'Indiade* has just been filmed by Sobel. The proportions have totally changed and there's something which just can't be calculated — the dimensions of the stage. There's a space which has to be crossed, and this space therefore takes up time. That time is eliminated in the cinema. And so a scene that lasted, say, ten minutes in the theatre, will take six minutes in the cinema etc.

HC The play is no longer there, the rush of the characters . . .

CIXOUS There's something else. It's been replaced by something totally differ-ent. So these measurements, what is given to the *Théâtre du Soleil*, to fit the specific rhythm of the *Théâtre du Soleil*, I only cut it to measure at the end of rehearsals.

At the end of rehearsals, if we're going to have a performance that will last four and a quarter hours, four and a half hours maximum, we'll have about seven or eight hours. That means two things. First, that I will tighten things up; secondly that they will speed things up. We rehearse slowly. So the measurements, the alterations to the material, the cut . . . these are all last-minute things. And that's hard because as the process has been so unpredictable, there are two different texts, in fact, and there's a huge disparity between the text we start off with, and the one we end up with.

HC This changes the relationship between the spectator and the text. The spectator only sees the final rhythm, but . . .

CIXOUS But that's good, because what happens at the end is perhaps better, at any rate it's the best it can be for the *Théâtre du Soleil* — there's the right rhythm. Ariane strives for speed, but at the same time for something structured, for something that can be heard, understood, as much as possible. There's a struggle (that we, as spectators, cannot imagine) as far as the actor's body is concerned. There are actors who have an incredible relationship with movement, an immediately flexible and delightful relationship, which fulfils the spectator's desire. It's a completely physical relationship that you can sense immediately. And then there are some who, on the contrary, don't have this gift of relating easily to space and communicating meaning through the body, and that's where the work lies. That's Ariane's job, enabling the actors to grow in all fields — in terms of diction, use of space, etc. And above all, there's a question of harmonization afterwards. Everyone has to master their own role, which has to be as elaborate as possible, but then there's also the question of being in tune with the others.

HC But there's also what you've just said, and what Ariane Mnouchkine has to do. You say: "I have to tighten things up; they will speed things up". So what does tightening it up actually mean? Is it making cuts in the content of the text, or in fragments of the text? And also, what is the relationship between the tightening up and the speeding up?

CIXOUS The speeding up is their problem. But there's also the staging of the voice. It's completely impossible to speak the way I'm speaking now, for instance.

HC The delivery, the textual race, speeds up?

CIXOUS Yes, but not in the sense "speak faster, go faster". It's a question of economy, finding the right gesture. These are actors who have to speak at great distance. You realize a voice which has to rise in that way unfolds more, and therefore takes longer than a voice which is going to be recorded for cinema, for example.

HC But do these constraints modify the text?

CIXOUS What happens is that there's a moment when it has to fit into a given time-frame. At that point, there's a part that comes back to me and I cut it. I realize that I can economize, that I can remove the last three lines. Sometimes I trim it down, whittle it down, to a word.

HC So it goes right to the body of the sentences, that's what I wanted to know.

CIXOUS It can be a word. I can have used an unnecessary qualifier, that can happen. In general, I try and find the unnecessary sentence in the lines. It's always a problem — I'm the only one who can do that, because by now everyone's clinging on to the text. No-one can manage to let go of it; it's their very sustenance. The actors look the other way; they don't want to know . . . In the end, I'm still the one who manages best to sacrifice things (because it's often a question of small sacrifices) as I took pleasure in writing what I wrote and once it's written it can disappear.

But we mustn't be under any illusions — when I write a fictional text, like with *Manne*, for example, I cut forty pages at the end. I hadn't calculated because for the first time I'd had it typed up on a computer, and that's very deceptive. When it was printed, it was twice as long as I'd imagined. I made choices.

These are complete reconstructions of scenes. First, when a scene is completely dropped, which does happen, this gives a new continuity between two scenes, and that can require reconstruction. Because unfortunately, or perhaps fortunately, this is the name of the game with theatre — the entrances and exits of the actors are also calculated in what I wrote. I can't have a scene with both "Exit de Gaulle" and "Enter de Gaulle": it's impossible. Obviously, in fiction, there's no problem. In other words, when I write, I have to weave the entrances and exits, the alternation and minimum time necessary, in my mind's eye; you mustn't forget that the same actor could be playing two different roles and that he'll need his requisite five minutes to change. These are things that happen all the time. You can even have the problem of the same actor playing two roles in the same scene. In that case, everything has to be changed. And so the text that is finally published is tailor-made. Which means that another director putting on the play with another troupe will have the same difficulties. And what will he do? He'll unpick the text.

HC So the text is tailor-made for Mnouchkine and the *Théâtre du Soleil*.

CIXOUS For that particular production. *Sihanouk* was staged by two different German producers. What would have had to have been done? I'd have had to have been there to do the same work that I do with Ariane, to rewrite scenes that were right for them, for their actors. So as I'm not there . . .

HC But surely they can't rewrite it instead of you . . .

CIXOUS They cut it. They transform it.

HC They take it apart? Put it back together again?

CIXOUS I can't tell you exactly what they do, but at any rate they have an impact upon the text. Shakespeare's plays in general . . .

HC . . . they're very often badly treated.

CIXOUS Well, they're nearly always cut, anyway. There are scenes which are dropped, things which are moved, etc. When I write with the *Théâtre du Soleil*, I do these alterations, these cuts, etc. myself. But afterwards, I'm no longer there.

HC So some of the theatrical writing is done with Ariane?

CIXOUS I'm there. So, up until the last minute . . .

The conditions are ideal, because right up until the end the text can come back. When I'm not there, that's what happens anyway; the director does it because it's necessary, the author has no control.

HC So that's what will happen afterwards then.

CIXOUS Always. It has already happened. It happened in Germany.

HC And, later, when your plays are shown in a hundred years, it will happen in the same way as with Shakespeare later.

CIXOUS Always. So let's talk now about the state of the author once the play is finished. What happens when it takes place without me (which is nearly always the case)? It's perfectly true, I try not to be there afterwards.

HC When there are performances with an audience?

CIXOUS I try not to be there. Because I have to be totally absent.

HC You don't alter it according to the audience's reaction?

CIXOUS Oh no. Not at all.

HC It's completed. The text is definitive, the scene is definitive?

CIXOUS Absolutely. It's absolutely definitive. And I can tell you that whilst at the beginning there's an extraordinary freedom and lots of time, given that we rehearse for a very, very long time — six or seven months at least, which is a lot — at the end, everything is absolutely set. There's not a single thing that isn't set. Especially since you mustn't forget that there's music. But the music is set. And the actors are set to the music. The musicians are tuned to the actors; they can't fall out of step. There's actually a very funny and moving relationship between the actor and the musician — an actor can't fall out of step, he can neither let himself go nor be absent, without a stroke of music reminding him.

HC So, if you cut your text, that can pose problems when you rewrite while rehearsals are going on?

CIXOUS No. They only learn the text at the last minute. They always work with the text to hand. In fact, they don't ever learn it, because in the end they've been acting it, living it, in such a way that they've actually lived through it. The time to learn never comes.

HC There's a moment where they fix it, though?

CIXOUS But it's already fixed. I can't remember having ever seen an actor having to learn his lines. They have them to hand until very late in the day.

HC It's a bit like someone who starts off sight-reading a piano piece and who ends up having the piece at their fingertips.

CIXOUS Exactly, that's exactly how it is. Musicians have the same problems.
Sometimes we got stuck. I didn't know, Ariane didn't know, the actors didn't know . . . until it unravelled itself. When that happens, there's a moment

of hindsight. You say to yourself: "Ah, yes, of course, it's obvious, that's what it was".

HC We've spoken a lot about the relationship with the actors, about incorporation, but little about the relationship with Mnouchkine. You spoke about Mnouchkine commissioning a particular subject, but you didn't say anything — but maybe there's nothing to say — about the extent to which she accompanies — or doesn't accompany — the writing process.

CIXOUS Well, I can't establish a fixed rule or a general law about this — it varies a lot. What can I say? It's a question of different types of evolution. For example, I don't exchange anything with her as far as the staging is concerned — I don't even know when she begins to imagine it, or what she does. We don't speak about that. There'll be a moment when I've written a certain number of scenes, and I'd like to show them to her. That particular moment varies a lot. I mean the moments aren't planned; they depend upon what she's doing, on when it's possible for me to tell her something, and there are moments when it's not possible. Obviously, I show her something quite advanced before she begins rehearsals — the material is there. Even if I've not finished. Each time, the rehearsals have begun before I've finished working. I carry on during the rehearsals.

HC So there are rehearsals which accompany . . .

CIXOUS The problem isn't artistic, it's financial. It just so happens that all three times — because this is the third time I work with the *Théâtre du Soleil* — the troupe has been out of work. So there's a question of the practical concerns of living; the time they go back to work is determined solely by financial constraints. It can only be drawn out so long. Work has to start again at a given moment, because the actors have to live. It takes a long time. If this weren't the case, if they could wait for me, I'd have finished before.

HC But the fact that rehearsing has begun doesn't have an impact, or place constraints, upon the completion of the writing process?

CIXOUS It does actually, because while they're rehearsing, they can get stuck with a scene which they then give back to me and which I take on board . . .

HC And that is changed immediately. That's the question I'm asking. I've understood that scenes are changed, but . . .

CIXOUS It doesn't alter what comes afterwards, not necessarily. Because I do have the narrative in mind. I start writing with an unfinished narrative. Generally it's the ending that remains the surprise, just like with a fictional text. Nonetheless, I already have most of the narrative, the way it will unfold, within me, otherwise I wouldn't be able to write — I can't move forward blindly. It's me that changes, as I continue to write. I'll have told myself that there'll be this scene and that scene, like chapters in a narrative. And then sometimes I will change this programme myself, because it turns out that when one scene is written, it actually accomplishes the work of three scenes. I mean that one scene I've already written contains the two scenes I thought would follow. But this narrative economy is dictated by the narrative itself. That's where it happens, above all, on the side of an economy that is actually beneficial.

HC But that happens during your personal writing?

CIXOUS Yes, not during rehearsals.

HC What role does the performance play? What I'm asking about here is how the stage and the staging intervene in the writing act. Does it then move forward in a consciously theatrical way? I'm wondering whether, actually, this figure of theatre that you describe acts like a mirror for the writing during the writing process.

CIXOUS Unconsciously. What happens is that I realize afterwards that theatrical writing condenses things a lot more, it's not calculated. I imagine that I'm going to have to do a much longer and far more detailed development of events than the theatre allows for. In fact, you could say the theatre draws things together. It's almost a question of poetics: it would be the literal translation of something that I take a lot longer to think through, something that discourse takes far longer to show.

HC The theatre is an accelerator; it speeds up the writing.

CIXOUS Absolutely. And that's very strange. I sometimes replace a scene with something that is played out between two lines, by an allusion; that can be enough. It will be deciphered, filled out, by the audience, by the actor. I don't need to comment upon it.

I do want to come back to the question of working with Ariane, though, because I'm trying to think it through. There are three cases. Firstly, what I said to you, that she'll tell me "this scene won't work, but I don't know, this scene will work, but I don't know". She still doesn't know. There's also the case where, from the outset, she says "You're not in the theatre here — this is a text, it's not theatre". If she's completely sure, I rewrite it immediately, it doesn't even go to rehearsal. I trust her because, firstly, it's not something that can be checked, and, above all, I never know what I'm doing. What I'm doing is very deceptive, very strange, and I don't have any critical instinct with regard to the theatre, to theatrical writing.

HC But you do for fiction?

CIXOUS I think I have more, but perhaps I don't have any. At any rate, I don't have the same feeling of uncertainty as I do with the theatre. Really, I don't trust myself at all when I write for the theatre. Perhaps because it's less linked to me. Because I've been known to have moments of intense satisfaction with a scene that, in the end, just couldn't be acted. It's the naughty goblin hidden in the writing that can lead me astray. I can have moments of satisfaction that are actually to do with writing, and which act as a screen. I can have got the wrong stage, the wrong writing, the wrong genre . . .

HC So this can bring about another sort of writing. In what you're saying, there's an alteration of writing. But would you go so far as to say that there are variable moments of theatrical writing, so far as to recognize or accept this heterogeneity, this plurality? We've touched upon it a few times. There's a sort of fragmentation in the theatre.

CIXOUS Certainly, yes. Being an author for the theatre is a fascinating experience, but pretty painful. I'm not even ashamed to say it — I think at the beginning of these experiences I was a bit embarrassed because I didn't recognize myself. Personally I find that it un-structures me, my self, my very being; it splits me apart in a very violent manner. When I write, I always tell the people who are close to me that they have to leave me alone that evening. It's as if I were mad. I'm lost. I don't sit down in front of my paper and say "right, now you have to lose yourself", but this act of identification makes me stop identifying with myself, and it's so violent that I'm completely beside myself when night falls.

HC It's an ordeal?

CIXOUS It's an ordeal because of having to fit back into a social setting. What would be right would be that I simply go to bed and there would be time for it to pass, for me to return. The problem is when you have to talk to someone. And

119

you're just not there. Hence why I take precautions — the days when I'm writing for the theatre, I stop everything else and make sure I don't have any engagements whatsoever in the evening, because I won't be there.

HC And writing fiction, or an essay, doesn't have the same effect?

CIXOUS Not to the same extent, no. The effect is one of madness. Firstly, I'm haunted by others. I'm all the others, but I'm not myself. It causes real fainting fits. The first time it happened to me, I was scared. Now I'm used to it. It doesn't bother me; I understand it. You're so much in someone else's space that it's a total disappropriation of the self.

And that's why I don't have any critical judgement. Because it's really not me . . . With the text, I'm in a state of permanent tension — I'm on a journey . . . but it's still me taking the journey. Part of me is still present in there. How can I describe the pain, the terror, that I can feel at the moment because, with the Resistance — for the moment, anyway — I'm in so many different worlds? In fact, it's the story of the Resistance that is like that. The worlds were completely detached. And when I'm in a world, I live it completely, so I lose myself, and not only do I lose myself, but I lose all the other worlds. So, to use a metaphor, it's as if I were so deep down in the well of France that England, the US, China, etc., all of that, didn't exist. It's destructive; it radiates destruction. And that's terrible, because it causes amnesia. The universe around is obliterated.

HC Is the return to the text a sort of refuge?

CIXOUS I know I couldn't live without text. I know that I could never just be a playwright, that these two acts which are so different are complementary, and that that complementarity is always enriching for me. Difference, the differential, is obviously enriching.

HC But you maintain the difference.

CIXOUS Oh yes. There's a difference, on almost every level, between the writing postures, the relationships at play. With the text, I don't have the kind of torment that I have with the theatre. But then, the text doesn't bring me the same sort of intense pleasure as the theatre does (afterwards, of course). I'm going to say something very banal — the text is written alone, and is read alone. Which means that the response is so delayed, it's so . . . there's no response from the text. The author has no response. The text is read, we know that it is read, but this reading never responds. Even our closest and most attentive readers don't come back to us. The text remains silent. And an author is perfectly used to that. With the theatrical experience, everything is different, it's something that is shared with the audience and thus made to resonate. It's true that the theatrical ceremony is one of the most beautiful things in the world. And it's part of something I believe I belong to: a great struggle for culture. There's something very necessary and gratifying in that meeting with the audience. I believe we're part of a small army defending a certain number of values, and being able to confirm that really does create a certain sense of joy; it's valuable on so many levels.

There's also the shared experience of this extraordinary sort of ship constituted by a theatre, with the entire troupe working together. But that's also specific to the *Théâtre du Soleil*; it's something joyful, it could be different. It's a collective adventure, and that's something which is rare. It's also a metaphor because this universe where sixty people work contains everything. Sixty people is already a society with everything that can happen in a society — love, war, a cause to defend, etc. The metaphor I use to describe it is that of an army of knights fighting for a certain cause, something totally noble, so in itself it represents more than just the theatre.

The reward of writing for the theatre is in this moment when a whole community begins to work together.

HC It's a collective object, but the author doesn't feel dispossessed.

CIXOUS I don't, at any rate.

HC But what about the disappropriation you spoke about when you're writing.

CIXOUS That's something I accept, because it's the proof that it's theatre, it's an extreme experience. The extreme suits me — it allows me to discover new things. I go through an emotional suffering that just doesn't exist with a fictional text and it's precisely because there's this expectation on the other side. I have a much stronger feeling that something isn't good enough with the theatre than I do with a text. Why? Because I'm no doubt far less consistent as a result of being divided between various characters.

The return to theatre in the text is what happened with *Manne*. Bit by bit I ventured into introducing characters to the text, something I never did before i.e. bringing in the third-person. Now there are five of them. It's still in my particular register; it's not a traditional fictional narrative, but now there is the presence of the third-person. It's not a third-person that is disconnected from me, like with the theatre — there's still the thread linking us; there's still "me", the cord, as it were . . . And here we come back to this problem that I don't have in the theatre, which is that of the body. In the theatre, I don't have anything to do with sexual difference, something which is very important to me. In the theatre, sexual difference is taken on board by theatre itself. I've always said that, in my fictional texts, I write with the body of a woman and I can't put myself in the place of a man's body. I can only deal with a *jouissance* that I know myself and I can't deal with male *jouissance* in the first-person. And yet that's the only way I write; through *jouissance*. With theatre, on the other hand, I don't have that problem. I can put men in my theatre because the actor lends his body to the play, the body's there. It's the actor who performs the link, through his sexed body, so it's not my problem. But with a text, it is my problem and I came up against it again, when writing *Manne*, because I don't have an actor's body — my body has to stand in for all the bodies, and here I come up against my limitations. I can go as far as possible in this identification with the other, including a male other, except when it's about *jouissance* or sexuality. I've done what I could, gone as far as possible, in writing the male body — or its exchanges, because there is a sexual exchange. I've done what I can with what I can perceive of male sexuality in my capacity as a woman, and with what I can perceive of what male sexuality can perceive of female sexuality, again, in my capacity as a woman who has that relationship towards female sexuality. Any further and it's beyond me. And I think that it's something unsurpassable, something insurmountable. When writing *Manne*, I managed to make my third-person feed off my first-person up until a certain point. Until it became a lie. I began to stray too far from myself and it became something I dislike, how can I put it . . . ? I no longer had any guarantees. What I was writing hadn't been lived. It's as if, to reassure myself in writing, I had this cover, this absolute point of reference which is my own body, not just a sexed body, but a body with affects. If I don't feel any affect, it's that there's a lie, it's over. It's true that by going too far with the third-person, you become disaffected. And that's when I stop. I'll end up philosophizing, or I don't know what else, but it won't be a text.

NOTES

1. A Parisian theatre company founded as a collective by Ariane Mnouchkine in 1964. It is based at the Cartoucherie in Vincennes.
2. *L'Indiade, ou l'Inde de leurs rêves, et quelques écrits sur le théâtre* [*Indiada, Or the India of Their Dreams*] (Paris: Théâtre du Soleil, 1987).
3. Cixous's reference is to the fortnightly research seminar she holds throughout the academic year for the *Centre d'Etudes Féminines* [Centre for Feminine Studies] at the University of Paris VIII where she holds a Chair in English Literature [editor's note].

4. "Un sol secret à partir duquel moi, je plante et rebranche quelque chose. Je me branche, c'est une lecture, tout simplement." The French plays on the dual meanings of the term "sol" ("ground" and the musical note "so"). The use of the verb "se brancher" (translated here as "tune into") maintains both lexical fields by recalling the word "branche" (branch).

5. "Marshal, here we are!" — a song in honour of the Maréchal Pétain which became the unofficial hymn of Vichy France.

6. "C'est quoi son sol, son vrai sol; pas son sol mental, parce qu'il y en a un aussi; non. Je n'ai pas la clé, et il fait que je la trouve." Once again, there is a play on the word "sol" here. Alongside the musical metaphor concerning the necessity of "hearing" a character's voice (reinforced by the reference to the "clé" or "key"), the word "sol" — understood as "ground" or "home" — evokes connotations of "le sol français" (the French territory) when used in association with Pétain. In the song "Maréchal, nous voilà!", reference is made to the "sol natal" (native land).

7. *Manne aux Mandelstams aux Mandelas* [Manna for the Mandelstams for the Mandelas], (Paris: Éditions des femmes, 1988).

8. *Portrait de Dora* [Portrait of Dora] (Paris: Éditions des femmes, 1976).

9. *Portrait du soleil* [Portrait of the Sun] (Paris: Denoël, 1973).

10. The French has the grammatically correct masculine subject pronoun only here.

11. The word "sol" is used again here, bringing across both the idea of grounding and of homeland, as well as allowing the musical metaphor to resonate.

12. In English in the original.

Part V: Writing roots

10. Language is the only refuge

Interview with Bertrand Leclair. Translated by Carol Gilogley.

This interview appeared as "La Langue est le seul refuge", in *La Quinzaine Littéraire* **793** (1–15 October), 10–12, 2000.[1]

BL I would like to start with a multi-sided question, and let you choose on which you would like to settle. After reading *Le Jour où je n'étais pas là*, I initially thought of the purloined letter, or the hidden letter, and then of the hidden self, including you yourself, in all your books.[2] For example, I am reminded of that recurrent wordplay on "pregsaintcy"[3] in your previous texts, and if I may say so, since that is what you call the dead child, the saintly finds a place in this book. Or again, I think of those extraordinary pages in which you evoke a complex relationship with your nose, making the most tragic moments in History spring forth from the most personal of stories,[4] all without losing for a moment the constant slippage which carries "a nose borne" into "born", to "an un-born", to this "inexact child" — when I remember that twenty-five years ago you published a book entitled *La Jeune Née* . . .[5]

CIXOUS That is immense . . . I'm going to start with the most straightforward, if I may call it that: with the perspective of personal history and what is called History. I have always had that perspective. No matter from how far I have viewed myself, I have always seen myself in this double scene — the most personal scene and the scene that is the most universal, historic. As if one were reading the other, helping me to read the other, as if I could only read the intimate scene when it's superimposed onto the world's great stage and vice versa. It's essential one scene be reflexive of the other. This isn't theory: I can't think otherwise. I don't think I have ever written a book which is, shall we say, unscathed by this perspective and which is also heart-rending, always tragic, even if the comic merges with the tragic. If that isn't history, then it's an equivalent, transposed into what accompanies it: literature. That said, my writing comes from the innermost reaches of myself, and what you probably feel in my most recent books is that this inside, this intimacy, I delve down into it more and more as time passes. It leaves me no choice.

So . . . the purloined self — that corresponds exactly to what I do: letting the French language bloom in all its glory, in its written glory, phonic, in its syntactic theatricality etc., that suits me perfectly. It also touches on the subject matter of some of my recent texts, although this has nothing to do with the purloined letter of Poe or Lacan, but the one that haunts me, about which I feel you are right to say that its twin is the purloined self. I question myself about the books that come to me, that have come to me, and I'm aware that I'm always watching out for the ghost: that is, the purloined book, the one I don't know, or whose face I know but which escapes me, and which is at the same time, in some way, forbidden me.

BL The theme of the forbidden book, which was very present in this book, already featured strongly in *Osnabrück*.[6]

CIXOUS Indeed, and in *Or* which came before it, where, in fact, I talk about the 600 letters from my father, from which the last is missing.[7] This struck me retrospectively as a metaphor for my own work. I said to myself, there will be 600 books, figuratively speaking of course, and I'll miss this notorious letter. I think, moreover, that this is how the writing process works. We have to be pushed to the limit, impelled by the call of that unknown letter, which escapes, which we hope to receive before dying, but without any certainty. My whole life will have been this kind of prayer, this waiting or struggle to pursue this letter, this book. All my books seem to me to be like descendants, or ascendants, books already written and books I am yet to write, and which only the larger movement of writing can deliver, bring into the world. For example, I always tried to say something about this child, long before *Le Jour où je n'étais pas là*. There's a book that's very difficult to read, of which I'm very fond, but which was really difficult, for myself above all — that I wrote in 1971 — called *Neutre*,[8] which deals just with that, but in an extremely encoded way, for the simple reason that this story was still too close: I couldn't write it. And at the same time, it made me write.

BL What, in my eyes, has become clear in your most recent books, since *Or*, is that you have allowed yourself to approach the mother without being consumed by her: in three books, you have reinvented your mother, or a mother, to allow the maternal voice to speak down through you, a mother burdened with all the memories of *Osnabrück*, but also with the memories of that child.

CIXOUS I write what comes. I'm very trusting in that respect: I rely on something which is at the root of the mystery of writing itself. One work which was shattering, for example, was *Or*. I was absolutely not expecting that. I don't even remember what new project I was involved with when the door opened and my brother came in with a box containing these letters from my father. A true accident — an absolute real event, to be more precise — when I've always tried to distance reality, because I've never wanted to enter into realism which I hate. It caused such a *fracas*, something so unexpected, that I wanted to turn and run. I argued with myself. I said to myself, oh no, you have already written about your father, you're not going to start again. I rebelled against myself. And that created a book, obviously, because I saw, heard myself: I sit myself down in the circle and I watch the stage, myself spectator-analyst of my own scene, to which I don't know the ending. I saw myself arguing with all these voices, this chorus. I said to myself, but why, what is the law, the rule, the forbidden? What is it that determines I must not? The deeper I delved, the more I saw enormous issues unravelling, telling me, it's not that simple, it's not that I don't want to write a book about my father, it's rather that I'm afraid my father might be an other. But this is an absolutely vital subject for me, the "writing about": I could expand on this forever. Writing is an extraordinary violence, of which I am very conscious. I don't write novels, I write what I call fictions, I transpose, I transfigure from the living, I nourish myself on the flesh and blood of those around me. I always say: I'm a "carnivore of souls", which is, for me, an ineluctable tragedy. I have a feeling, which does not go as far as guilt, but of intense anxiety. I have always thought that I should not write about my mother, and I even risked, blindly, saying as much during a talk in 1991. But as soon as "I will never write" is said, the mind has already been touched by the possibility of writing, by the risk, the imminence. And some years later, I did it, not without hesitation and not without tears. It's just that the time when I said to myself that I would never write about my mother had been overtaken by a time in which I asked myself if it wasn't a mistake not to do it. Moreover, she too was asking herself the same questions, in a way diametrically opposed to me, evoking — with her serious way of speaking in her own language, which is the image of her and which I attempt to transpose in my books — all those people who are dead, and who will disappear with her. I saw it in the way she treated the disappearances all around her. How she stored them away, but, on the other hand, how the dead come back, how she incessantly brings them back to life in anecdotes, stories. Little by little, this work is passed on from pure memory to the archives of writing.

On the other hand, I was terrified. I knew that I would translate her, therefore I would betray her.[9] I sought the lesser evil. I began to write, trembling, in a position of new responsibility.

BL You used to say — and perhaps you still say — *"Je suis là où ça parle"* [I am there where it speaks], and today you write that it is the book which speaks, which guides. Like the transition from a scene of the individual unconscious to a scene of the collective unconscious, or, at least, shared.

CIXOUS It's a matter of emphasis: I continue to be there where it speaks. I'm in touch with the unconscious at all times. I'm very aware that the energy or the power of writing comes from there. There are always dreams in my texts, these are very powerful motor forces, that's a given. The outpouring of language is gifted to me by the unconscious. But I realize — and you're right to point it out — that I take the book more and more into consideration, which has now come to be known as a familiar character in all my texts. This brings us back to the reflexivity I was talking about a moment ago — I'm a person who writes a book, and something always takes place between the book and me. On the one hand, one side of the book is turned towards the book's reading, and on the other, it is more and more present in my texts, because I too am inhabited by the consciousness that I'm writing a book. What I eliminate in the gesture of writing, is, in fact, the fiction of fiction. The act of acting "as if writing a book that is not a book". But what I'm talking about here is writing, that is to say about that art which isn't recognized in the world of publishing. Because it is an art. I think, and I work constantly, recalculating over and over the incalculables of what a text needs to produce as a work of art. It is an art that speaks, the only one, and therefore it carries immense responsibility.

BL About one of your pronouncements, this "century stitched of camps",[10] all your work tends to show that it is always the person who is open to the other, who goes beyond the boundaries, who is struck. This brings us back to one of the themes of *Le Jour où je n'étais pas là*. The inexact child is also that other who transcends boundaries, who cannot be fixed by a definition.

CIXOUS I think now — although it might be that I'm only telling myself a story, but that's all there is, nothing but the stories we tell ourselves — I think that, in fact, this child brought about my initiation. I knew, already, because my childhood had been lacerated by the suffering of the other — lacerated, because I myself was protected by cheerfulness, by the poetic side, innocent about my parents, until the age of ten, until my father's death. I was in a place that came into contact with the war (1940s Algeria),[11] which certainly felt terrible reverberations, but which was never directly threatened. On the other hand, that allowed me to suffer for the other. I couldn't bear the humiliation, the dehumanization to which the Arabs were being submitted. It made me ill. I was born of that. So, I knew exclusion, persecution — my entire childhood I was treated as a dirty Jew — but I had some defence against the discourse of hate. Then, all at once, this incredible experience presented itself, if I may put it this way, to become a mongol. I would rather say that, because, fundamentally, that's what happened. I was, philosophically, deeply naive. I was so young: I expected death, but not that; to be tied, body and soul, to an indefinable being. The waters of the world had broken, and I had come out on the other side: I realized that until that moment, I had used words without being fully aware: I would use the word "human" . . . without even having noticed the enclosure which that represented in language itself, in thought itself. The experience has left me forever uprooted, destabilized, and it's a blessing. Of course, it was awful too, but I owe everything to this birth which happened without my knowledge. This revolution had created all kinds of mutation, and I responded to it in the same way as my mother, that is, by getting back on with life, as fast as possible. I put down my pen, I began to become what I never thought I would become: a mother. All of that happened without my knowledge once again, and when this new structure gave way because this child died, what was completely unexpected was . . . writing returned with tremendous force. It is he, in a way, who will have presided over my birth as a writer. It is unheard of, and a million times more complicated than this linear account of events. I must say that it was a secret to me.

BL Do you know the extent to which you have made it difficult to gain access to your new book? The first thirty pages, which are very beautiful, conjure up the image of a gate at the entrance of an abandoned park, which has to be pushed open, and creaks.

CIXOUS Because the text is performative. I made it a rule of mine, precisely, in fact, that I would let the text find its own way along its winding and metaphorical path, not because of the modesty that once pervaded me, but because of my continuing fear that this story, which I consider to be extraordinarily delicate, should not be threatened with too much exposure.

BL It seems to me that form is no longer something which overly concerns you. Formal invention remains essential, but the question of form is secondary, even if it is a form — and this ties in to what has just been said — such as that which can create a reader, create in the reader the ability to listen.

CIXOUS I understand [*j'entends*] perfectly. What matters most to me, in fact, would perhaps be voice, or voices. What I think about constantly is the sentence, the page, I could say the paragraph, all that is arranged in parataxis or in hypotaxis. These are forms, and I would even say, for me, these are the fundamental forms. I think that it's between these that sentences speak, speak amongst themselves, say to themselves, gainsay each other, cut each other off, start up again, and it's this dynamic here which matters to me and which I think about, all the time.[12] When I write, I am constantly gauging the speed and power distribution between the sentences. Now, I also work — and I think this is principally my hallmark — on the signifier. It's here that the unconscious comes to my rescue. Because it unfolds. Very often, I'm on the track of a signifier which appears suddenly, and which I think will be followed by countless "effects of meaning". When I write, I also alter the way I write, submitting French to alteration, letting in the other continuously, the strangeness in language — it's essential. Cultivating it — it's natural, but I also cultivate all the indecidability, amphibology of language. It's the only way to avoid fixity, to ensure that a movement always opens itself up and that the unconscious can also speak: that which escapes me, that which I do not control.

In times past, I wrote texts which were structured: and I . . . do it all the time for the theatre, where such structural work is absolutely crucial, but I think that I work in the depths more and more, which demands all my concentration, and all the experience I have collected not only from the process of writing, but also from living, from reading.

BL Rather than bringing you back to Joyce, to whom you devoted your doctoral thesis, it would be wonderful to write you into a literary genealogy that would run from Kafka, through to Rimbaud or William Blake, a stream of visionaries.

CIXOUS I'm primarily on the side of the poets. Joyce is a constructor. I start out from dream, which is vision by definition. I give vision words. But it's a blind person's vision, which is very important. I write blindly: what I see is voice. That which speaks. I love the visionary poets, and I love Milton whom nobody knows, and who's blind, and who wrote after becoming blind, which is the main thing. There, I feel completely at home. Joyce is a great storyteller, inspired, but there has always been something missing in his world for me, which meant that I could distance myself from it, an idea. There is a powerful mythology in place in his work, but Joyce has never been quoted the way Kafka is. Having said that, what he did with language was indispensable — we owe him a great deal.

BL At heart, what interests you is what resists, what survives, in language, on that side or this, in the most tragic conditions in history. This was already the central subject matter in your book, *Manne aux Mandelstams aux Mandelas.*[13]

CIXOUS It's a vital subject. My language is my only refuge, knowing that everything can be lost, even countries. And I have always had a terrible fear that language itself won't last. Kafka was my last resort: he still wrote, even when nothing was left of him, even when ravaged by tuberculosis, but if tuberculosis is the enemy, death . . . it's not this dehumanization that means no more writing, because there are no more humans left to write. That absolutely terrified me. I have always followed that route, cherished the people who saved language, particularly in the concentration camps. Hence Mandelstam.

BL In search of what you call the human, in the final analysis.

CIXOUS Yes, but — the human becoming human. I cherish these examples. The *Marranos*,[14] with whom Jacques Derrida strongly identifies, move me deeply, these people who, cut off from the source, shut away in oblivion, stammering a language they don't understand, which no longer means anything, who are passed down stories orally, altered, strange. That, however, is supreme faith, continuing to pass on, from mouth to mouth, the spoken word, and what a word it is: highly poetic, borne by the spirit, by an aspiration.

BL She is blind but she can see.

HC And she hears what she cannot understand.[15]

NOTES

1. It is prefaced with the following introduction: "It is in the most individual that one encounters the universal, in the underground depths of the self which blindly seeks its own becoming. With amazing ease, laying out the development of the personal and historical in her most recent books as well as in the theatre (in particular, in her collaborations with the *Théâtre du Soleil*), Hélène Cixous follows this with *Le Jour où je n'étais pas là* [The Day I Wasn't There], which sees a re-emergence of buried grief for a mongol child, a work which will prove to be of great significance." The references are to *Le Jour où je n'étais pas là*, (Paris: Galilée, 2000).

Cixous's use of the term "mongolien" to refer to Down's syndrome presents a problem to the contemporary translator. However, in light of the plea in *Le Jour où je n'étais pas là* for its retention, particularly in the *Chœur de Mongoliens* [Mongols' Choir] and the link made between the sanitization of language and the refusal to accept disability and difference, this translation has chosen to retain the term.

2. In English, the paronomasia is lost between the homophones of "*lettre* caché" (the hidden *letter*) and "*l'être* caché" (the hidden *self*).

3. In fact, the word Cixous uses is "ensainte", which is a neologistic combination of the phrase "en sainte" (meaning an inner sanctum, which includes in the word "sainte" the English "Saint" or "saintly", "holy") together with a play on the homophonic "enceinte", meaning pregnant.

4. Cixous's recurring theme of relation between History, personal histories and stories is arguably more inherently intuitive in the original French, as they are all subsumed under the umbrella of "histoire".

5. The seamless transition of the original from the identically-pronounced "nez" (nose) to "né" (born) is unavoidably lost here, which makes the final connection to *La Jeune Née* [The Newly Born Woman] less self-evident.

6. *Osnabrück* (Paris: Éditions des femmes, 1999).

7. *Or, les lettres de mon père* [Gold, My Father's Letters] (Paris: Éditions des femmes, 1997).

8. *Neutre* [Neuter/Neutral] (Paris: Grasset, 1972).

9. The French wording (*je la traduirais, donc [...] je la trahirais*) evokes the same phonic juxtaposition as the well-known aphorism: "traduttore traditore".

10. See also p. 180, below. See also Frédéric-Yves Jeannet, "The Book That You Will Not Write: An Interview with Hélène Cixous", *New Literary History* **37**(1), 2006, for further instances where Cixous interweaves the textual with textile, texture.

11. Parenthesis in original French.

12. The original French, which is "les phrases parlent, elles s'entreparlent, elles se disent, elles s'intredisent", plays with multiple reflexivity, antiquated lexis and phonic similarity and repetition, much of which is unavoidably lost in translation.

13. *Manne aux Mandelstams aux Mandelas* [Manna for the Mandelstams for the Mandelas] (Éditions des femmes, 1988).

14. The Marranos [*Les Maranes*] were Jews who were forced to convert to Christianity in order to escape the persecution which followed the Spanish inquisition, and who, while ostensibly practising Christianity, secretly practised Judaism in all the countries to which they scattered. See the dialogue with Jacques Derrida, below.

15. "Et elle entend ce qu'elle n'entend pas".

134

11. Being a Jewish woman is the ideal place

Interview with Jacqueline Sudaka. Translated by Carol Gilogley.

This interview appeared as "Être femme juive, situation idéale", in *Les Nouveaux Cahiers* **46** (Autumn), 92–5, 1976.

JS Did you have a Jewish consciousness linked to history, to anti-Semitism?

CIXOUS In biographical, personal terms, one of the determining features of my childhood and my youth was the fact of being in a melting pot[1] in which the question of anti-Semitism was always there, in an atmosphere that was truly poisoned by it: no matter how far I go back in my childhood, it was there. Becoming conscious of this and hearing myself being called Jewish must have happened almost simultaneously. From that perspective, and from my account of what aggression can etch upon the Jewish unconscious, of course I bear its marks.

In my earliest childhood, when I was in Oran, I lived in a wholly Jewish environment for the simple reason that Jews were not allowed to attend educational establishments. So I was, without knowing it, in a sort of private school at which there can't have been any non-Jews, but I didn't know that: I was too little to know that this was a result of an historic situation. But, later, when my family settled in Algiers, which was not their home town, it was in a *lycée* where I realized once and for all, where there was an unacknowledged, "tacit" *numerus clausus*, and I spent my secondary education without any other Jews around me, and I missed that a great deal.[2] I felt my difference fiercely, my strangeness, and I had no co-conspirators in this strangeness [*étrangeté*]. Looking back, I'm not sorry about it — I am more than happy to have been in the desert wilderness of opposition. But my friends were non-Jews. Their families were anti-Semitic. The world of children is both infinitely more anti-Semitic and infinitely less — a child is able to make different compromises to those of an adult, and I was always aware of this. It was always there. Once I arrived in France in 1955, the problem no longer presented itself in the same way, because the situation in France was such that, in fact, being Jewish was not the first thing people noticed from the first moment you appeared, as was the case in Algeria, where you were picked out immediately as belonging to such and such an ethnic or racial community. France, when I arrived, was a foreign country to me. My close relationship with this problem immediately disintegrated because there was no place for it to exist. It shifted focus somehow or other. When I realized that a certain aunt had died in a concentration camp, and that this was part of my history, I didn't feel un-involved — how could I not have been, given that, since my earliest childhood, I thought the opposite: that is to say, I thought it was through extraordinary happenstance that my mother, who came from Germany, was one of the few people in my family to find themselves alive. I was born in a place where people took part in that war. I identified with the German-Jewish community, never with the Jewish-Algerian community. As for my own historical and political consciousness, it has remained on a par with that of my generation. The conflict I remember from that time is the Algerian one. I found monstrous the fate of the Jews during the war; I found monstrous the fate of the Arabs in front of me. The war — I thought it was a date which carved itself into a collective history to which I belonged, which would determine all of history to come.

JS Did you observe traditional Jewish practices in your family?

CIXOUS It was peaceful on my father's side: these were people with very humble origins. They would always tell the story of my ancestor who had been bought a pair of shoes on her wedding day and who had not been able to put them on: she was never able to wear them, they hurt too much. Or the story of the only pair of shoes, which took turns being worn by the children, so that in the end only the shoe-wearer of the day could go to school. These were very poor people, who had not been formally educated. It was my father and his brother who were the first to benefit from the tremendous work of this family, all of whose children had to try and earn a living from the age of eight or nine. My grandfather worked tirelessly, had under-the-counter relationships with the Jewish and the Arab communities, and spoke both their languages. There was no Talmudic tradition (that was the real Algeria), but these were very religious people. The women, although well treated and loved, nonetheless occupied the position of servant-mother. They were really deprived of everything. They never complained because, just as they were supposed to, they loved their fathers and their brothers deeply.

What I have come away with from this was their love, their devotion, without limits or ambition. A life which had its beauty. What I took from that world was the simple ritual, the Friday cleaning days, the fact that the door was always open on Fridays, and, at my paternal grandmother's house, beggars would come inside. All these practices were spontaneous, not thought-out. And as what remains of that community continues to be like this, I loved them and have always loved them. It was a gift without asking [*un don sans demande*]. But, as soon as I arrived in Algiers, I learned to uncover the social scene, the hate and the horror. That's why I was never with the Algerian French — and justifiably so — nor with the Arabs, who were still brother-enemies. Then, I felt like I was in a world of delirium, unaware of what was happening in Europe.

Festivals were still held, emptied of all religious content. I remember, one day, having asked my German grandmother: "Do you believe in God?". She had never asked herself the question, so meaningless was it for her. She had answered that she believed in the faith of her parents, out of loyalty [*fidelité*] to her father.

At our house, when we celebrated feast days, Hanukkah or Rosh Hashanah, I was vaguely aware of what it signified, but it always gave rise to festivities, and I treated them like family birthdays. That's why it is, at the same time, childlike, childish and legendary.

I have never thought in terms of loyalty to my parents. It was my grandmother who decided herself in that way: it really was a line of passing on, of transmission. I have to say that I cut it off — that transmission contained meaning. To me, she stopped transmitting something. I think, for example, that if I hadn't respected my family's behaviour, I would have stopped loving them. While my family would have loved me anyway, even without respect.

JS Being a Jewish woman — does this sentence hold meaning for you?

CIXOUS None at all. Throughout my entire life, I have never thought of myself in those terms. I don't like hearing that phrase, because it can be the root of all kinds of misunderstanding, of falsification. For me, being a woman, that has a meaning; it's even the primary meaning. That determines me absolutely, and among the many determinations which constitute "me", there is also that I am of Jewish origin. It is not a privileged distinction.

JS In *La Jeune Née*,[3] you write about identifying with Achilles and Penthesilea, with Greek heroes and heroines. Are there any Jewish figures, masculine or feminine, with whom you perhaps identify?

CIXOUS It largely stems from the fact that I don't know Jewish history all that well. I have read the Bible; that's where it ends. I know nothing apart from that. In the Bible, I have never found any subjects with whom to identify. I have a great deal of admiration for the events it recounts. Somehow, I have always felt that it makes no room for women. Esther is a woman who seems terrifying to me, caught between an uncle and a father-king. There is too much subordination to the law. As far as men are concerned, it is very disturbing [*bouleversant*], but it seemed to me to be one long political narrative, like a kind of logos on power in the process of its transformation. That led me to my interest in figures who, like David, for instance, are the epitome of strength, of joy, and who, when they reach the summit, are beset by contradiction; it is this Shakespearian quality to the Bible that I admire, and which distances me as a woman. I don't know if, as a man, I wouldn't have had the same reaction. But it is certain that as this constantly passes through a representation of power — in any case, that is how I read it — and the way in which this power is described in its truth, and the decomposition which that entails, I have always found the Bible to be a lesson in humility and humiliation.

I think that the internal contradictions of women's position had to be presented much more violently in Greek mythology — in which there are numerous feminine figures, not triumphal figures, let it be said — who are figures of opposition, never of submission. So, at least, on this level, I understand — it means something to me. The fate of women in Greco-Roman mythology is not a fate I would envy, but it always leads to decisions, to oppositions, to tragic situations.

JS You say that, when you write, you surround yourself in books, some permanently, like the different versions of the Bible, and the works of Kafka. Is it possible to find a path through these readings to a Jewish-text?

CIXOUS For me, there is not only *the* Bible: there are many bibles, books which serve in the same way, like Shakespeare — these great collections of writing which are almost complete books, whose pages chronicle both human passion, everything at stake in life and death, and a vast development of political thought, with issues concerning the absolute. It is never a question of minor ambition, but rather of the knot of contradiction which results when the pleasure principle finds itself having to negotiate with the reality principle. And when the pleasure principle has the absolute to contend with, what will the outcome be? That's really what the Bible is about. When I desire the absolute, and the real denies me it, what do I do? That is what's in play in the Bible, always, and that's what matters to me.

As for Kafka — I certainly have some identificatory affects towards Kafka which are very involved, disordered, a simultaneous attraction to and rejection of everything which Kafka represents, that is to say, not just his work, but the inter-twining of his work and his reflection, of his history and the fact that his universe looks remarkably like the fantastical universe which was mine when I was a child, and which is brought about by the logos of the German language which weighed heavily on me, and which I rediscover just as it was in his text. The fact that he is someone who is completely at one with writing, just as I am. Maybe that is some-how a Jewish thing, I don't know, but, in any case, the total life or death investment in writing which I have is perhaps made possible by what is passed on in a Jewish environment: sharing interest [*intéressement*] in writing. This is one of the first things a child learns in the Jewish community, to consider the relationship with books, with language [*la parole*], and in particular, language which had already been passed on, written, as essential, no less so than food.

What bothers me about Kafka is not his being a man, as his way of being a man is, somehow, deeply feminine, but that so as to achieve his objective, which is really himself in writing, he was driven to murder. He couldn't not kill, particularly women, more precisely woman. He looked upon her, when it was not his woman, which was not specifically cruel, but to save himself, he had to kill what it was in woman that could get close to him. That has always been distressing for me.[4]

JS Is there a Jewish image which surfaces — unconsciously or otherwise — in your writing?

CIXOUS It takes the form of identificatory affects, such as the fact that I familialize, for example, my relationship with Freud. It always makes me laugh. I know that I systematically write about my Uncle Freud. On an unconscious level, I think this history sets down a certain relationship to the threat of death as permanent, as always there, a threat both personal and historic. I've also always thought the oppo-site, that you cannot escape the fact of having been Jewish, but having been a Jewish woman, now that's a different story. An ideal situation — it allows me to be nowhere, or somewhere else entirely, all the time — that's to say, having points of reference without being tied to those points of reference. The passion which I have in relation to the text makes me feel completely textual, I don't feel divided in relation to it. This can be combined with the fact that my memory was imme-diately flooded with (hi)stories, by the recounting of a past endlessly told and retold by Jews, for reasons of self-defence. Moreover, the issue of anti-Semitism, which was real in Algeria, could not help but bring about a separation in my subjectivity which fosters writing, like a constant gesture of reparation.

I don't know if this is a Jewish tendency, but the dialogue which was established with the other in me might be compared — it's a poor metaphor — to the dialogue between the prophet and God, that is to say the never-ending struggle with the call to take "one more step". But when I say that, it's a poor metaphor, as it means I think of the inner scene as taking place between the prophet and God, which is stupid because I never think in those kind of terms. It is, shall we say, the separation contemplating itself, the work of a relation to self which does not relate to self closing up once more, which does not follow the Hegelian model — finding myself again through repression, in fact — but, quite the opposite, through expression. I imagine that the ease with which I use God's name as a common noun is one way of naming this kind of force which I don't want to name "the superego". Jacob's Ladder is something which remains very vivid for me, I don't know why.

In my texts, I have cast Moses as a classically masculine character, that is to say, limited power, phallus threatened by castration. Castration . . . the Bible, in fact, abounds in it. It's a world of such threat that it's not by chance that Freud found his way there: psychoanalysis is the Bible of the phallus. I have also used the character of Samson because there, the issue of castration presents itself again. Samson remained a very compelling figure for me as an example of a mix of gentleness and strength. Samson appeared to me as the gentleness which can emerge from strength. Through a series of twists and turns, what I consider to be positive in Samson is his capacity for giving, for excessive trust, which I believe is a good.

What comes to my mind as a Biblical love story is that of David and Jonathan, a homosexual story. Nothing at all like the love of Penthesilea and Achilles, or Anthony and Cleopatra.

JS What is your relationship to the law, as it is conceived in the Bible?

CIXOUS The whole point of my activism is to have increased oppositional gestures to the law, and to have attempted to encourage gestures of freedom with respect to all kinds of expressions of the law, all forms of despotism at the level of relations of political power, to be an integral part of the history of women who have been under the law's power, beginning simply by thinking it. I'm always working on the forbidden so as to shift it, on transgression to crush it and laugh about it. And this, not from a kind of anarchic romanticism, but from a desire to see every living *individual* made flesh. When I write, I never find myself transported by the Jewish idea. There are signifiers which spring up, here and there, originating from different cultural horizons.

NOTES

1. The French uses the term "bain", which literally means "bath" or "pool", but there is also the sense here of "être dans le bain", meaning "to be in the know" or "to be implicated in", which is lost in the English.
2. Cixous' juxtaposition of *numerus clausus* (a "restricted number" in Latin, used to determine limited quotas of students to study) with "*tacite*" (tacit) is perhaps not unintentional, given that it was *Tacite* (Tacitus) who is best known for chronicling religious persecution by the Romans, albeit directed at the early Christians in his time.
3. *La Jeune Née* [The Newly Born Woman], Union Générale d'Éditions, Collection 10/18, 1975.
4. This is possibly a reference to Kafka's short story "A Hunger Artist" (1924), about a man whose distaste for food first of all draws morbid audiences to observe his fasting, but who eventually, uncelebrated, dies alone: "And he looked up into the eyes of the ladies [*Damen*] who were apparently so friendly but in reality so cruel, and shook his head [...]". See Franz Kafka, "A Hunger Artist", in *The Complete Short Stories*, Edwin and Willa Muir (trans.), 271 (London: Vintage, 2005).

Part VI: On painting, music and nature

12. You race towards that secret, which escapes

Interview with Martin McQuillan.

This extract is taken from a much longer public interview with Martin McQuillan at the University of St Andrews on 24 June 1999. The interview was conducted in English and was published as "'You race towards that secret, which escapes': An interview with Hélène Cixous", in *The Oxford Literary Review*, "Reading Cixous Writing" **24**, 185–201, 2002. After questions from Martin McQuillan the interview was opened up to include the audience, and it is a member of the audience who asks the questions in this extract.

QUESTION I am struggling with the relationship between painting and writing, I would like to ask something about that area, which might lead back to why Hélène Cixous thinks that perhaps writing is more important than painting? And I think that in one piece of her writing, she says that painting is more sensuous and immediate than writing, but there is a lovely bit where she says that when offered an apple or an orange (that was painted), she would like to eat it. In a sense writing can eat the apple. So, I would like to know about that, and the last point of the question is whether painting has more space for women to transform and transgress than writing does, or whether it is the other way around?

CIXOUS Well, thank you. These are huge questions — and beautiful questions.

You know when we started, I should have said one thing regarding "Cixous", which is something very difficult to say, because I think that while one should read, unfortunately one should in the original, but it is not given to us. We mostly read in translation. So, what do we do with that? It is a huge question of translation. So, let me just linger on that for a few minutes.

I, myself, read in translation. I've learned to read Brazilian in order to read Clarice Lispector because I know that the secrets are in the skin and flesh of the original language. So, what happens when we are cursed by (or blessed by) the fact that we encounter through different languages. Usually I try to come to terms with the situation by reminding myself that all languages are translations. The moment I write, I translate. I translate what I feel in this or that language, which I am going to destabilize. The encounters of my emotions in my thought with the French language, for instance, is going to de-French French and re-French French — to free French. I think it's the same, well, it's not exactly the same, but it's in this direction that we read works in translation. But then of course the responsibility of the translator becomes huge, which is also one of the problems that, we, literary people meet all the time. All those who teach literature here know about the problem with translation. Of course the translator has to be a great poet and also a kind of mathematician of an equivalent order to displace the original to its next of kin, and maybe one might think of painting and writing in different terms of translation, except that, of course, I am fascinated by painting. I also realize that I have a wider scope in reading than in looking at painting. That is, I read painting in a way that is much more selective. I don't know why it's something in me that is less open. I think I read painting when I am touched because I only read paintings that touch me and there are not so many. I read books instead, except in a book I go throughout the pages and actually the book might be unfolded as a long surface of paper. Painting is on the contrary along the lines of depth. What I do with a painting is to start climbing up or down the pages of the painting. Because I was born a writer, and not a painter, I privilege writing. It is quite unfair. Part of writing, I am sure, is analogous to a certain type of painting. It's an analogy or metaphor. I am sure that now and then, when I try to write, I am doing exactly what a painter does with colours, brushes, and so forth. When I write, I start painting (because it is a good metaphor), a very small incident which presents itself at first as quite innocuous, instantaneous, something very rapid, and the moment I start describing and analysing it will take twenty or fifty pages because it is as if the words are doing the work that a brush would do on a limited surface. What also touches me in painting, and what I have been writing about in several essays on painting — I don't know whether it is apparent — is the unendingness of painting. A great painting is as unending as a real book or poem. It will yield effects of meaning endlessly, which doesn't mean that it has been painted or written as if it should be "unended". Monet is exemplary of this because you have all the stages of his painting. It's as if you were starting on a race, towards something that is far away, which is a secret. What you want to reach is a secret because you don't know what it is, except that it emits signs that appeal to you in a way that is vital. So, you race towards that secret, which escapes. You approach it, and it escapes, and the painting, or the writing (what will be the painting or the writing, or the work of art) happens in the chase. It's the chasing — every way you move in the direction of the secret. And I feel that in the pictures, in the paintings that attract me.

Do you know that painting of Goya, which is in Madrid? It's almost nothing. It's almost Japanese in its making. It's entitled, "Dog head buried in Sand". Do you know that painting? Have you seen it? It's incredible. It's vertical, and it's as if it were the epitome of all of the spirit of painting. So, just part of a dog, and you can't interpret it. You don't know whether the dog is coming out of the sand, or on the contrary being buried in the sand. It is the most incredible picture you can see, and it's so nothing because it's really only infinites. The sky exchanges with the beach, but the beach . . . we usually think of beaches as long, wide and extending, whereas here, the beach is vertical. And for me, I could write a book on that. It is a transposition of life, death — all the big motives that are the rhythm of our thinking, of our fate, are summarized in this epiphany, in this vision. Besides, the dog is an individual. You want to adopt him, or her (because of course you don't know whether it is a him or a her and that is also very important), and you don't know either whether it's sky or sand — again you have the difference, which merges — and you don't know whether it's life or death, whether it's beginning or end — but it touches you. You just cannot take your eyes off this picture of human life — you feel that this is exactly how you are inside and how you relate to time and space, it's incredible. I do not feel as moved or struck by painting as much as I am by writing. Maybe it's because I am not sensitive enough — I don't know — it's a question of ear as for music. So, I do not resound as much for painting, as for writing, where I can say that each hue in the signifiers is a light for me — I have a wealth of possibilities within language, but this of course has to be cultivated. For instance, practising diction is most important for writers. Even in my seminars, we have decided that we would always have dictionaries, not only to learn dictionaries by heart, which is absolutely essential, not only for their definitions and wealth of vocabulary but to refresh or trigger our knowledge of etymology. I think that one of the mysteries of writing, of language, is really the fact that when we write at a surface level (while we write or weave something on the surface) — underneath the ground where the half of the body, where the dog is hidden, is where language goes on weaving kinds of effects of meaning, of music, and so forth which we don't know of. The question whether it is easier for women to transgress in painting: I don't know. Really, I don't know. I would say, yes: it is a temptation to say yes because I have met so many women painters who enjoy their paintings immensely, and who are wonderful artists. But then after the moment of creation they come upon the same obstacles as women will find in publishing etc., so, I don't know. It's probably a mirror. You don't create without transgressing. But I couldn't give advice that I myself could really believe regarding that.

13. We must hand our inheritance on

Interview with Susan Sellers.

The questions for this interview were suggested by a wide range of Cixous scholars and readers (see "Acknowledgements"). The interview was conducted in English, at the same time as the one that opens this volume, on 4 September 2007.

SS First, a question about influences. You have written — and spoken — a great deal about your literary influences, and about the profound and abiding dialogue you have with Jacques Derrida, but you have written — and spoken — less about the influence of philosophy more generally. Could you take a few moments to reflect on the importance of philosophy to your work? Which philosophers would you distinguish as being of particular importance in the evolution of your thinking?

CIXOUS I belong to that species of writer who is philosophically structured. Shakespeare is a great philosopher. My dialogue with Derrida has developed over time. We started writing almost at the same time, and the back-and-forth of reading between us and exchanging — thinking, writing, analysing the world, textuality, philosophy, poetry — has been ceaseless all our writing lives. Regarding other philosophers, it all depends on what I'm writing. During the summer I've been writing a book where quite accidentally I came upon the necessity to include a dialogue with Plato — it was unexpected. I feel close in a way that is almost second nature to Derrida and Freud (although he opposed philosophy, he is an inspirer to philosophers). I have always read Heidegger with the utmost attention because he's interested in writing. And of course Montaigne. But which Montaigne? Is he a philosopher — or a writer? There again you see that you can't separate them. As for evolution, I'm not sure my thinking evolves in the sense of changing — if you read my first book you'll find everything there that I think today. But it's a long journey and you discover new forms, new ways of applying the nuclei of your thought to new situations.

SS In an essay accompanying your play *L'Indiade* you describe theatre as "the place of crime but also of forgiveness".[1] Your ideal theatre includes Shakespeare, Verdi, Schoenberg, Sophocles and Rossini, whose theatrical works tell stories "legendarily and yet straight in the eye".[2] Are there other writers and composers you would include in this list? Your phrase reminds me of Wagner's music dramas . . .

CIXOUS I would add Bartok — and Aeschylus is missing: for me he's most important. And then I would add Ibsen — some of Ibsen's plays — or Strindberg, who is an admirable playwright, and Chekhov here and there. So it's not closed — and nor am I — although of course my hero is Shakespeare. I adore him. I know I share this opinion with the whole world. I don't think anyone has gone further than Shakespeare, because he's not only an artist in writing, he's a painter, a sculptor, a musician, a psychoanalyst — he's everything, really. So, as regards "crime and forgiveness", yes, it's true that theatre is there to allow us to illustrate in a way that is limited in its effects our death. We kill on stage — I mean of course that we are dream killers; in dreams we kill, we commit suicide, etc. There are corpses everywhere — and then we forget our dreams. When you go to the theatre, it's exactly what the Greeks thought: there is catharsis, you shed blood — which is a good thing. You enact what is repressed. This is the kernel of Dostoevsky's *Crime and Punishment*. It's vital.

As for Wagner: he has built his operas on the canvas he borrowed from the Eddas[3] — they are like Homer, like *Crime and Punishment*, except more fantastic because it's the northern mythology, which I adore. It's the most extraordinary, the craziest. I do love Wagner, but I don't for reasons which I can't account for include Wagner in my writing. Perhaps I will. I am certainly touched by a number of his themes, his arias.

SS Could you say something about the place music has in your work?

CIXOUS It has the place my ignorance allows it. Among gardens it's my secret garden. I'm totally ignorant of musical composition; I'm a lay person in music, though I'm never without music. It's why I wrote *Beethoven à jamais*.[4] Beethoven has left so many written traces that give you an inkling or at least an instinct of his relation to music. I feel very close to Beethoven. I admire his versatility enormously. I love the sudden interruption — the tempest of Beethoven. I acknowledge Monteverdi, Purcell. None of this means I am in any way competent.

SS You've written a great deal about painting, but could you say more about how we might apply a practice — or poetics — of *écriture féminine* to the visual arts? For instance, how might an artist working in a medium which depends on representing its subject as an object — on "taking" its picture as we say in the case of photography — evolve a corresponding *"peinture féminine"* that might bring self and other into a relation of equality?

CIXOUS This is a most interesting question but I think its bias is too feminist, because you cannot separate sexes or genres: they exchange, they communicate. Still, I would like to say a few words about all my women friends who are artists — great, talented artists; though I also have many artist friends who are men. There is something I observe though it isn't a law — I certainly can't theorize it, I just notice it. I'm talking about artists like Roni Horn, Alexandra Grant, Nancy Spero or Maria Chevska. I realize that something in my writing echoes what they are searching for in their *enacting* — because it's not painting they do, it's everything. They produce all kinds of visual art, they paint, they have installations, they make pictures, they draw, etc. They *write*. Roni writes, she even uses fragments of writing — real writing. So there is certainly something in common which is probably a way of over-vaulting borders: they're not captive or static — either their medium or their representation. Feminist invention — a way of escaping, of doing away with definitions that are closed — this is what we have in common. And yet all of them have transposed so differently that they don't relate at all. There's a common root — which may be the vulnerability of what they do, and the audacity of permanent freedom: they apply to the whole world. For instance, Roni is becoming the artist of the weather in all its shapes and forms, all its expressions. She has an immense ambition which doesn't obey the limits, it doesn't even obey the restrictions of the frame — particularly the institutional frame. This makes them out-institutionalize what they do and look for new institutions, even invent or create them. Is it "feminine"? The way I see it, it is — it's rebellion.

SS Nature and a sense of place is an important component in your work — in your novel *Manne aux Mandelstams aux Mandelas*,[5] for instance, the South African landscape is a central, vibrant thread in the narration, and you have repeatedly incorporated animals into your texts. How important is the green debate and consideration for the other of the environment in your work?

CIXOUS I think nature is human nature. Whatever is "nature" is human: we are its products as well as its managers. Of course it's important. I've never felt apart from the garden. As you know, it's a central trope in my writing. It's the real garden and all the other gardens — the metaphorical gardens etc. If I can say on the one hand that all the world is a stage, then I can also say that all the world is a garden — except that we're destroying it. So of course I feel committed, although I'm not militant. It's there, originally. I'm not without animals, I'm not without plants — you can see that even on my balcony.[6] It's the uninterruptedness of life, from the mineral to the so-called "human". We should be the guardians, the keepers of the environment. I don't read ecocriticism but of course I'm aware of the debates — and of the paradoxes.

SS You've often written in your work about the dangers of the media — how the media does our thinking for us, and presents events in the most banal and dehumanized way. How do you feel about the internet? Do you see it as enabling and egalitarian, or do you see it as yet another "screen"?

CIXOUS I have to say I don't use it, although I know what it is of course. Why don't I use it myself? Because there is a trend of persecution which is multiplied a million times by the internet. I need to retire, I need silence in order to write — and yes, I need information, but selected information, and for that I prefer the pace of books, which are at my body's speed. I don't want to be outrun. Regarding democracy, I think it's a good thing. The medias — particularly the paper medias — have sold out to governments. You see that in France, it's a revolution, but a counter-revolution — they belong to the political powers. So you have to have clandestine or other types of incorruptible medias, and the internet provides that. The internet is also a new kind of culture. For instance, blogging is good because it allows everybody to express whatever they want to express. On the other hand, it's also a way of tyrannizing because everybody blogs, and particularly the political people. So the net is everywhere. You are caught in the net. You can cut the meshes, but the net is there.

SS In your 1997 interview with Bernadette Fort you describe how as a member of the Left, following the election of François Mitterand in 1981: "I was beside myself with joy [...]. But I at once perceived that if I had childish dreams of 'the perfect government' I would have to give them up because, at the level of day-to-day politics, there would be compromise in every way, although I couldn't measure the depth, the length, the degree, or the forms of the compromise."[7] You go on to explain that this was due to "Realpolitik", which is a common phenomenon. However, since that time we've also witnessed a number of other European parties of the Left drift towards the so-called "centre-ground", or even the Right — Blair and Brown's "New Labour" in Britain (first elected in 1997) is an example but there are others. As "a militant of '68" (in Fort's words), do you think much is left of the impact made by the events of May '68? And, bearing in mind the 2002

Chirac/Le Pen presidential run-off, and the more recent election of Nicolas Sarkozy, what are your thoughts about the present state of the Left, the Socialists, in France?

CIXOUS I think the impact made by the events of May '68 is on the verge of disappearance. The remains are all in the writing and thinking of those it helped — those who breathe freely thanks to the opening of May '68. It's as if history has strange cycles corresponding to those of memory. There is rebellion — then after forty years that's it, it's over. I think you realize this once you reach a certain age. You live through the rebellion, but after forty years — two generations — it no longer has meaning. It's like an old photograph. For the young it's the remote past — not two generations but two centuries. It's not only true for May '68. When I went back to Algeria a year or so ago I realized that their war of independence has become the remote past. It's something you have to accept. We live in a day-to-day history. Now, with technology and globalization, with militarization and the globalization of militarization, things reach the past even faster. They last a season.

As for the last part of the question, I think that we are crossing the desert now and will be for a long time to come. The Left is falling to pieces and they're not about to recover. They will, because parties have disappeared too. The spirit of the Left — the desire for ethical values, for the respect of the rights of peoples — is not there. The half of France who thirst for enlightenment is alive. But they have no representatives.

SS Several of your more recent poetic texts might be categorized as "poetic memoir" rather than "poetic fiction". Yet — as Derrida notes in your dual interview with him in 2004[8] — this terrain, while localized, is nevertheless part of the larger mythic terrain we share as human beings. How conscious are you of this larger dimension when you are writing, say, about your mother or father? How important is family, race and place to us as human beings and how far do you think it is the task of literature to explore these?

CIXOUS I don't think the human being exists as a skeleton without determinations. I used to consider the metaphor Shakespeare uses for England — an emerald set in a silver sea — is a metaphor you can apply to the human being. It's an emerald set in the silver seas of the scenes of the world. It's a tiny precious stone, but it sends and it receives — its extensions and depths are the whole world. The human being is a world — and a world of words. Take my mother for instance, who I call "my mother" — she would be the centre, decentred, of two centuries at least of human experience. You can draw lines from her life to different continents, to Australia, or Buenos Aires — wherever she has acquaintances. If I were a painter

I would draw the portrait of my mother as an immense . . . I don't want to use the word "net", but something woven, a text, but a world-text. I could say the same of myself or you. You cannot reduce a human being to the ideal picture in their passport. Even that, if you start looking at it, will give you a number of messages that far outreach what you seem to see.

Did you know that in France now we have to justify that we're French? We have a reactionary political programme and we've all become "foreigners". Every day there are infamous moments where people who have been French for a hundred years have to prove their ancestors are French. They are hunting people in the streets, whereas the street is one street, the huge body of the world's citizens. It's the same in the States. How can you shrink people in this way? People are *huge*. As for race, we now belong to a world that is hybridized — and the phantasm of purity defends itself like mad against this mix.

SS You've consistently left a space for God in your writing — a decision that has sometimes met with opposition, particularly where your writing has overlapped with feminist or postmodern debates. And yet, as we face the challenges of a new century, one of the elements we must renegotiate is precisely our relationship with the divine — I'm thinking of new ethical debates as advances are made in science, as well as the difficulties created by religious fundamentalisms. Do you think it is possible for human beings to relate to each other without the intermediary of a god? Can you say more about your vision of the divine?

CIXOUS I'm very suspicious of this question! First of all let me separate "religion" and "faith". "Religion" is a government, a political institution; even if it pretends not to be, it is (except in certain religious practices which are more philosophical, like Buddhism). But the main religions in the world, from Islamism to Christianity, are governments and I'm not interested in that at all. They vie with one another; I think they are the enemies of mankind. So this is something I try to be wary of. "Faith" is different. We all have faith. To remain alive is to believe that one has to live — otherwise one has so many reasons not to live. There is something stronger than ourselves that keeps us surviving what is unsurviveable. This is what I call "faith". And I also use a word which is current in different religions, which is the word "grace". And what is grace? It's not the grace of God, or a god; but the feeling that you have escaped. It's a moment of blessing when you realize that somebody who might have died hasn't died. That is what I call "God". But of course God has so many names . . . You know, what is interesting in God is that His name is written in three letters — it's as short as possible. It's a shout: "God" is a shout. And everybody uses "God" because when you want to shout, you say this word, it's something that grows out of itself; perhaps it helps you, perhaps it doesn't. Now, of course, when you relate to somebody and you feel that something has been saved, it's more than yourself, and it's in the more-than-myself that I may equate with "God". Or I may call my friend "God": "you are 'God' ", "no *you* are 'God' ". It's the in-between-us that keeps us open to the other, to otherness. But then of course you have to cope with the fact that we are all inheritors. We are inheritors of cultures. For instance I am the inheritor of a little (not much) Jewish culture. We are all responsible for something that has been transmitted — an inheritance — which is a treasure of good and bad memories, of memoirs or archives as you've said — of which you have to take care. We must hand our inheritance on. If I had been born in Islam, I would be responsible for what happens with Islamic culture; if I had been born a Christian, same thing. So, we are responsible for the house, for the family: for the archives. We are in charge of this body of traces that we will hand over to the next generation. Not because they will believe in the body of thinking — they can change sides — but because they have to make their nests, as birds do, with all the bits and pieces of different cultures. It's an apprenticeship of the values of fidelity. But it's a fidelity to mankind.

SS Many of your interviewers begin their interviews with a preamble about the difficulty of categorizing your *oeuvre*. If you could decide how future generations would categorize your work, what would it be?

CIXOUS I can't answer that! The fact that it's wide-ranging is something I'm happy about. I'm an inheritor, as I've said, of writers like Shakespeare and Montaigne, who were interested in human nature. I'm just in the genealogy. I can't decide about the future . . .

NOTES

1. *L'Indiade, ou l'Inde de leurs rêves, et quelques écrits sur le théâtre* [Indiada, Or the India of Their Dreams], 253 (Paris: Théâtre du Soleil, 1987).
2. *Ibid.*
3. A collection of poems in Old Norse relating mythological tales.
4. *Beethoven à jamais ou l'existence de Dieu* [Forever Beethoven or the Existence of God] (Paris: Éditions des femmes, 1993).
5. *Manne aux Mandelstams aux Mandelas* [Manna for the Mandelstams for the Mandelas] (Paris: Éditions des femmes, 1988).
6. The interview took place at Hélène Cixous's home.
7. Interview with Bernadette Fort Greenblatt, "Theater, History, Ethics: An Interview with Hélène Cixous on the Perjured City, or the Awakening of the Furies", *New Literary History* **28**(3), 1997, 425–56.
8. See pp. 166–79.

Part VII: Dialogues

14. On Marguerite Duras, *with Michel Foucault*

Translated by Suzanne Dow.

This interview appeared as "'À propos de Marguerite Duras', par Michel Foucault et Hélène Cixous", in *Cahiers Renaud-Barrault* **89**, 8–22, 1975.

FOUCAULT I've been a little nervous about the idea of talking about Marguerite Duras since this morning. Whenever I've read her books or seen her films, they've always left — always leave — a very strong impression on me. However long it's been since I've read her, the presence of Marguerite Duras's work remains very intense — and yet, now that I come to talk about her I feel as if it's all gone. It's a kind of naked force that one just slides off, that slips through the fingers. The presence of this same shifting, slippery force, of this presence that at the same time runs away from you, is what keeps me from being able to talk about her, and no doubt also so attached to her.

CIXOUS I felt much the same earlier on. I got out all of Marguerite Duras's texts that I've read several times and that I naively thought I knew so well. But one can't know Marguerite Duras; she won't be grasped [*on ne peut pas la saisir*]. I think that I know her, that I've read her, and then I realize that I've not "retained" anything. Perhaps that's what it is: there's a Duras effect, and this Duras effect is that something very powerful drains away. Maybe that's what her text is for — so as to drain away, so as not to be retained, like her characters who are forever draining away out of themselves. If I "retain" anything, it's that impression. That was a real lesson for me. She taught me something that almost exceeds [*dépasse*] the text, even as it is an effect of writing — something about a certain effusion.

I'd been thinking about the mystery of what it is about her texts that creates the attachment. There are moments in these texts that touch the reader and which — for me in any case — are bound up with [*rattachent à*] Seduction. You become very attached, caught up, carried away. What had stayed with me, for example, about a book, was an image. The book was *Moderato Cantabile*,[1] and the image that of the edge of a woman's neckline. I projected the image of a breast — though I don't know whether that was in the text — with a flower emerging from it. My whole gaze is transplanted there and you reach [*atteins*] the woman, and you are held there in her [*retenu en elle*] by that flower and that breast. And then it occurred to me that the whole book will end up having been written so as to end up as that image that you get so caught up in. And so the space of the book, which is at one and the same time the desert, sand, beach, life broken up into bits, leads us to something so tiny, which is nonetheless valorized, which is so searingly set out in that form as body or flesh. What Marguerite Duras creates is what I'd call the art of poverty. The further you get into her work, the more monuments and wealth she strips away. I think she's aware of it too, meaning that she whittles away more and more decoration, furnishings, ornaments until it's so impoverished that something remains lodged there and then gathers up, gathers together everything that refuses to die. It is as if our every desire were being reinvested in something very small indeed that at the same time becomes as big as love. And I don't mean the universe — I mean love. And this love is this nothing at all that is everything. Don't you think that's how it works?

FOUCAULT Yes. I think you're absolutely right. That's a really beautiful analysis. You can really see what has underpinned an *oeuvre* like that since Blanchot — whom I think was very significant for her — and through Beckett. It's this art of poverty, or what one might also call memory without recollection [*la mémoire sans souvenir*]. The whole discourse, with Blanchot as with Duras, is concerned with memory, but memory utterly purged of all recollection, such that it's no more than a kind of fog constantly referencing memory. It's memory about memory, with each memory effacing all recollection *ad infinitum*.

That's how an *oeuvre* like that managed suddenly to write its way [*s'inscrire*] into cinema, to generate a cinematic *oeuvre*, which is, I think, equally as important as the literary works . . . to use images and characters to achieve this art of poverty, this memory without recollection, this space outside and which is ultimately crystallized in a single movement or gaze.

CIXOUS The other real power [*puissance*] that she exudes is her relationship to the gaze. That was what would block my reading of her initially. I didn't find it easy to read Marguerite Duras at first. I used to read her with resistance because I didn't like the position she put me in. I've always found it somewhat unpleasant, coming around to the idea of occupying the position that she draws people into, or "puts" them in. I had to get over that. I think it has to do with the gaze. You called it memory without recollection. That's it. The work she does is a work of loss, as if loss were something that could never be fully achieved. It's a real paradox. As if loss were never lost enough, as if there were always more losing to be done. Her work is always moving in that direction.

So this memory without recollection of hers, yes, it's as if the memory were always failing to present itself, as if the past were so past that you'd have to go into the past in order for there to be any recollection. *Being* past. The past is gone for good. It's monstrous, unthinkable, and yet I think that's what it is. So what do we get when that gets put into images? What we get is a gaze of extreme intensity because what gets looked at is never got-back.[2] It's gaze that never gets.[3] You've got those characters everywhere being looked at, and that was one of the things that bothered me until I accepted what she asks of me — namely, the utmost passivity. These characters just keep coming, coming at each other with this gaze upon the other as a demand that demands nothing. She has such beautiful formulations that are always passive formulations, as in "someone is being looked at". "She" is being looked at, she does not know she is being looked at. On the one hand the gaze settles upon a subject who doesn't receive the gaze, who in her or himself is so lacking in images that they have no means of returning the gaze. And on the other hand, the one looking is equally so impoverished, so cut-off, that they want to be able to get hold [*attraper*], as one does with a look — they want to catch [*capter*]. As ever, it's that sand running out . . .

FOUCAULT Would you say it runs out in the same way in the films and books? In the books it's a perpetual cancellation. As soon as anything — a presence, say — starts being sketched out, the presence hides behind its own gestures, gazes, and dissolves. There's nothing left but a kind of glimmer that refers to another glimmer, and the slightest appeal to recollection gets cancelled out. But in the films I think, quite the opposite, that there are apparitions [*des surgisse-ments*]. There are these apparitions without there ever being any presence, but there's the apparition of a movement, of an eye, a character that looms up out of the fog. I'm thinking of Francis Bacon. I have a sense that her films are related to Bacon just as her books are to Blanchot — cancellation on the one hand, apparition on the other.

CIXOUS The two go together. I've only seen two of the films, though. I've seen *Destroy, She Said* [*Détruire, dit-elle*] and *India Song*,[4] which are very different.

FOUCAULT Tell me about *India Song*. I've never seen it.

CIXOUS I loved that film and yet I feel as though it went straight through me. What's left of *India Song* for me? *India Song* is a film with a very strange dimension to it, even for Marguerite Duras, because it's a film in which there's an utterly intense *jouissance*. Marguerite Duras has managed to do something marvellous for any human being — namely to stage what I consider to be her fundamental fantasy. She has presented herself with the vision of what she has kept on looking at all her life without ever managing to keep it.[5] There's something we haven't talked about but which is very important to me, and it's that everything Marguerite Duras writes that is so much whittling down, so much, precisely, loss, is at the same time fantastically erotic — because Marguerite Duras is someone who is fascinated. I can't help saying "she" because she's the one pushing. Fascination goes with poverty. She is fascinated, she is absolutely caught up by something — or in someone — so absolutely enigmatic that all else in the world just falls away. There's absolutely nothing left.

It could be a religious fascination. There is in any case a religious dimension to her. But what fascinates her, as we gradually discover — and, I think, she herself discovers, has us discover — is a mixture of eroticism bound up with female flesh (it really functions through what can be so overwhelming and beautiful in something indefinable in woman) and death. And it all blends into one. And so it gets lost once again. As if death enveloped life, beauty, with the terrible tenderness of love. As if death *loved* life.

In *India Song* it's as if she were seeing herself something, as one gives oneself something [*c'est comme si elle se voyait, comme on se donne*]. It's as if she were finally (herself) seeing her — the woman who has always fascinated her [*c'est comme si elle se "la" voyait enfin celle qui l'a toujours fascinée*]. And it's a kind of very black sun, with this woman in the centre — the one who saps all the desires in all the books. In text after text there's an engulfing [*ça s'engouffre*], a gulf, an abyss. It's the body of a woman that doesn't know itself, but that knows something there in the darkness, that knows darkness, that knows death. She's there, she's embodied and then once again there's this inside-out sun since all its rays are male and they come to graft themselves onto this abyss that she is, shine towards her. Of course film shifts the impact of the books because in film there are the faces. You can't but see them. Whereas in the books they're always written in as not visible, as dispersed.

FOUCAULT Yes, that's right. Although, the visibility of the films is not that of a presence. I don't know whether Londsale [sic] is in that film. I expect so because as an actor he's really made for Marguerite Duras. He has a kind of fog-like solidity to him. You can't say what shape he is. You can't say what kind of face he has.

Has Londsale got a nose, has Londsale got a chin? Has he got a smile? I honestly couldn't say. He's thick-set and broad like a formless fog. And then from there there are these throbbings that come from nowhere and which are his voice or his movements that don't seem to be attached to anything, that travel across the screen towards you. It's like a kind of third dimension, but where there is only the third dimension left without the other two to support it, such that it's always between the screen and you — never on or in the screen. That's Londsale. To me, Londsale is one and the same thing as Duras's text — or rather as this blend of text and image.

CIXOUS He really is (himself) nobody personified [*Il est en effet lui-même (en) personne*]. He's uncertainty itself, or at least uncertainty personified. He's much less than uncertainty. He really is there. He's wonderful as lost, as he is lost [*Il est admirable comme perdu, comme il est perdu*].

FOUCAULT He's at once cotton and lead.

CIXOUS And he has his voice. He is gifted for voice [*doué de voix*]. That's very important, a shift in stress [*un déplacement d'accent*]. What you have in the book is gaze, but gaze always cut-off, gaze that doesn't make it [*qui n'arrive pas*]. In the film it's voice because ultimately *India Song* is song.

When you see *India Song* you realize that the visual — which is very beautiful, very erotic and at the same time very blurred, and which is precisely very seductive because it's there without being there — is entirely caught up in a permanent network of voice.

She did some amazing work on the voices and they are those famous wandering voices, disembodied voices. There are bodies without voices and voices without bodies. The voices are like birds that are constantly there around you, which are very beautiful, very stylized, very soft voices. They're women's voices like a chorus, but like an anti-chorus — I mean that they are voices that flit about, that come from elsewhere. The elsewhere is of course time. But time that's irreparable, such that if you don't listen carefully there's a kind of confusion between the voices that takes place. A voice is sounding now, and so it seems to be present, and in reality it's a voice from the past — a voice telling a story, taking you back. The voices take up what you are seeing and project it back into a past that itself remains indeterminate.

FOUCAULT That's another instance of something that came out very strongly in Duras's novels — what is traditionally called dialogue. But in Marguerite Duras's novels they don't at all have the same position, the same stature, the same place as in the traditional novel, because dialogue isn't bound up with plot. It doesn't break the narrative flow. It's always in a very uncertain position, traversing it, undermining it . . . it comes from somewhere beside [*d'en-deçà*] or beyond [*d'au-delà*]. It isn't at all at the same level as the text and it produces an effect of blurring or floating around the non-dialogue and what seems as if it were said by the author.

CIXOUS That's absolutely true. It stems from what's at stake in, or the affects of, her texts, because ultimately whatever gets emitted, sighed, across her texts, is because speech comes from somewhere . . . From this problem of time, memory, the past etc, and also from, out of, an absolutely infinite, horrifying despair. At the same time, it's a cut-off despair — a despair that can't even be called despair because then it would already be being recuperated, there would already be a work of mourning there. There isn't even any possibility or will there for the work of mourning to take place. So where one would find dialogues in any other novel, there are exchanges. And that's what love is anyway — the fact that they manage to exchange something. And these exchanges take place out of their shared unhappiness. And also out of their relationship to death which, it always seems, is calling to them — in almost all the texts, because there's one that escapes that. I'd go so far as to say that I have a sense that there's one text that doesn't lead to the beach of the endless, where everyone comes to ruin, and that's *Détruire dit-elle*.[6] What comes across there is a kind of joyfulness [*gaîté*]. It's joyfulness with an underlying violence of course, but between those three strange people who always manage to remain above the others — who are active whereas the others are passive or overtaken by events — namely, Stein and Thor and Alissa — there's something that communicates, that circulates all the time, and that triumphs. There is laughter, and it ends with the phrase "dit-elle" — "she said". It ends with laughter and music.

FOUCAULT You feel as though that's something unique in Marguerite Duras's work. This sort of laughter can't really be called joyfulness as such. How can one describe that sort of bubbling that runs through the text? You were just talking about exchange, and the word "exchange" bothered me a bit because there is no reciprocity — something circulates. It's more like a parlour game where you have to guess which hand the ball is in, only where the ball could move of its own accord . . . the object gets passed on, and that person has to take it, only in Marguerite Duras's version the object spontaneously jumps from one hand to another, without either person being responsible. In any case, it circulates. The object itself has its ruses, as do the players with it. There's a perpetual irony, an oddness [*drôlerie*] which, against the backdrop of what I think you're right to call despair, nonetheless makes the texts glisten. All the smiles, the movements . . . sparkle a little, like a sea.

CIXOUS That would apply to *Détruire dit-elle*, where there's a terrible irony. I don't read oddness into the others, but perhaps I'm missing something. I read them as a kind of melancholic song — the song of death. If there's anything odd about it it's in the subplots, but it's a peripheral thing. It would be in all the social scenes, all the socio-cultural passages — those extraordinary scenes that are just sketches of embassies, cocktail parties, where the whole thing is captured by one word: fake. But everything that has to do with people, to do with what's left of people has nothing odd about it to me. I see something that isn't closed, a sort of infinite generosity. Infinite because everyone is admitted as paupers. Anything that's lost everything is admitted. It never shuts down. It's infinitely open, but infinitely painfully so [*ça s'ouvre à l'infini, mais à l'infini de la douleur*].

FOUCAULT You know I had my doubts about the word "odd". I don't mean to defend it. For me it's not incompatible with "pain", nor even with history, and certainly not with "suffering". There's an oddness to suffering, an oddness to death. I mean "odd" in the sense of something strange, immediate, unfathomable. "That's odd" as in "disturbing".

CIXOUS It's something particular to you that makes you pick up on that. I see it more as horror. It's maybe because I feel profoundly threatened by Marguerite Duras's texts. "I don't want anything to do with that" is what I think to myself. I don't want there to be people like that. To me, all that is about impotence. Impotence that's only redeemed — although it's not really anything to do with redemption — that only becomes bearable to me because it is humble. It gives out an extraordinary amount of love. That's what's beautiful about it.

A moment ago you were saying that the word "exchange" is wrong. That's true. It's that in the poverty of language as well they *touch one another*. Who? They? These human beings, these wanderers who, across this truly vast earth, touch one another, caress one another, brush against one another. It's incredibly moving. What I like about her is that the relationship of touch is always there.

That's what I see in *India Song*. I seem to recall that Anne-Marie Stretter played the piano when she was young, or at least that she was musical. And then by now she's given it up and at the same time she's surrounded by all these men. I can't remember how many there are, but there are several of them. And they all find themselves engulfed by her, although not fatally because she herself wills them no harm, because she wants nothing from them. And even as she doesn't call to them she does, because she's precisely the woman who has renounced her claim on everything, whereas they haven't because they want. They want *her*. They have this attachment to her and she's attached to nothing. And so through her they touch the nothing. What I mean by its being open, what passes and what that means, is that she is *someone who has given up music*. Meaning that she no longer gives herself what music gives you, no longer gives herself the pleasure of music, no longer gives herself voice. She has made silence [*elle a fait silence*] and because she made silence she is someone who can listen to others. She has inside her the space, the openness that means that she can hear others either being silent or yelling [*qui hurlent*], as the vice-consul yells. There are those who yell, and those who say nothing. She can hear speech [*la parole*], she can hear others' desire, she can hear the unhappiness of others. And in the end that's her love force [*force d'amour*].

She has the ability to listen (obviously I don't mean the way a psychoanalyst listens, the kind of listening that acts as a wall and which reflects back so that you hear yourself. There you aren't being listened to, you are hearing yourself. I might be wrong about that).

She is like the sea in which she comes to be lost — the infinite. Something is uttered [*on lance quelque chose*]. She receives. Her body is like the threshold to the infinite. You sense that the something is received because it passes through flesh that one can touch, and then it passes on to the infinite. That's what despair is: you get there via love and fall into death [*tu passes par l'amour et tu tombes dans la mort*]. Marguerite Duras is someone whose unconscious has an extreme force to it. She's "blind". That has always really fascinated me and I believe I see. I believe Marguerite Duras as she appears to me. She "sees" nothing and I also think that when she doesn't see the faces that it's because she can't see. And at the same time there is someone within her who does see. You have to see how she sees. I can't separate the conscious from the unconscious with Duras. I don't know where it's happening. What I admire about her is precisely the fact that she is so blind that it all gets suddenly revealed. All of a sudden she *sees*, although whatever it is has always been there. And it's that "all of a sudden" that allows her to write.

FOUCAULT Something appears in her books, because she has seen it, or because she's touching it? I think it's undecidable. That's where she managed to define a kind of crossover between the visible and the tactile which is quite astounding.

CIXOUS I think it's precisely at that cut-off point that it all takes place. Because it's always cut off. The gaze's cut-off is the point at which the gaze, if you like, gets interrupted by touch.

164

FOUCAULT A moment ago you were saying that she was blind. I think that that has a profound truth to it. She's blind — almost in the technical sense of the term — in the sense that touch really is positioned as a kind of possible visibility, or else it's that the ways of looking available to her are touch. When I say "blind", I don't mean that a blind person substitutes touch for gaze — it's more that they see with their sense of touch, and what they touch produces the visible. I'm wondering whether it's not this profound blindness that's at work in what she is doing.

CIXOUS And which is really her incalculable.

FOUCAULT That perhaps cuts across what one might say about the outside. It's true that on the one hand we never get inside either the characters or what's going on between them. And yet there's always another outside in relation to them — as with the beggar woman, for example. This other outside is made up of the screams, the things that occur which are really given as things that come from the outside and which have as a result a certain effect upon the characters. That's what goes on between them, such that there are three outsides: the one you find yourself in; the one defined as being the characters' place; and finally this third outside with their interference. And yet a blind person is someone who is always outside it all. They don't have their eyes closed — on the contrary, they are someone who has no inside.

CIXOUS And so the entry point, and the place where it all starts from too (because she somehow has an astonishing level of control over it, in such a way that you can't tell where the control comes from. Where is the control?) is voice. The place you hear from — because she has a real ear, even though her gaze is cut off, she does have an ear — that's where it returns. What I mean is that which is outside comes back in; voice is precisely that which penetrates.

NOTES

1. M. Duras, *Moderato Cantabile* (Paris: Editions de Minuit, 1958).
2. "Ça donne un regard d'une intensité extrême parce qu'il n'arrive pas à re-garder."
3. "C'est un regard qui n'arrive pas à garder."
4. *Détruire, dit-elle* [Destroy, She Said] (1969) and *India Song* (1975) were both directed by Duras.
5. "Elle s'est donné à elle-même à voir ce qu'elle a toujours regardé sans arriver à le garder."
6. *Détruire, dit-elle* was first published by Éditions de Minuit in 1969.

15. From the word of life, *with Jacques Derrida*

Interview with Aliette Armel. Translated by Ashley Thompson.

This interview first appeared as "Du mot à la vie: un dialogue entre Jacques Derrida et Hélène Cixous", in *Magazine Littéraire* **430** (April), 22–9, 2004. This translation was published as "From the Word of Life: A Dialogue Between Jacques Derrida and Hélène Cixous", *New Literary History* **37**(1), 1–13, 2006.

AA You have agreed to participate in an oral interview: Hélène Cixous has written about the danger of the "spoken word" with regards to "thinking". The voice also plays a role here: it has an important place in both of your texts.

DERRIDA Those who do not read me reproach me at times for playing writing against the voice, as if to reduce it to silence. In truth, I proposed a re-elaboration and a generalization of the concept of writing, of text or of trace. Orality is also the inscription [*frayage*] of a trace. But the serious treatment of these problems requires time, patience, retreat, writing in the narrow sense. I have difficulty improvising about the questions which count the most for me. Our three voices are setting out on a formidable and singular exercise here: to give each other the floor [*la parole*], to let each other speak in order to trace out an unpredictable path. Our words should form more than one angle, they should triangulate, play at interrupting each other even while they are articulated together. Yes, for Hélène and for me, despite an abyssal difference, writing models itself on voice. Interior or not, the voice always stages itself, or is always staged. I write "out loud" or "in a low voice" [*à voix haute, à voix basse*]. For my seminars as well as for texts which are not meant to be pronounced. For more than forty years I have written what I teach from the first word to the last; I try out in advance the rhythm and the tonality of what, pretending to improvise, I will "vocalize" in the lecture theatre. I never write in silence, I listen to myself, or I listen to the dictation of another voice, of more than one voice: staging, therefore, dance, scenography of terms, of breath and of "changes in tone". The preparation of a seminar is like a path of freedom:

I can let myself speak, take all the time which is given to me in writing. For publication, as it involves texts of very different genres, each time the register of the voice changes.

CIXOUS We both have several writing practices. One that uses what is called the speaking voice [*la voix qu' on dit haute*], but which for me is meagre and unequivocal, which is on the order of teaching; another that silently gets deeper and deeper with the degrees of writing, which seems to be without voice, whereas in a single voice it makes a chorus of voices be heard. When you write your seminars you foresee [*pré-voix*], your voice is a pre-voice, you write a text in order to respeak it. This respeaking is a theatricalization of what is already a staging. You double the theatrical stakes. You are the actor performing what you write as an author. You double yourself — in all ways. I don't write my seminars. For days I travel through a region of multiple texts by ramifications crossings grafts until I can think them through by heart. Then I improvise for four or five hours with two pages of notes serving as a seedbed. I have this need to let myself be haunted by voices coming from my elsewheres that resonate through me. I want to have voices. As a result I am at the mercy of their inspiration [*insufflement*]. They can fail me. I master nothing, I submit to the oracles. This risk is the condition of my creative energy and of my discoveries. It can happen that I run out of breath [*souffle*], that something loses steam [*s'essouffle*]. I saw myself clearly in your incredible text on Artaud [*"La Parole soufflée"*], in this bivalence of the soufflé: a word whispered/given by someone else, and a word stolen, whisked away.[1] We both let the word take its flight:[2] this release of the word like the release of a bird or a breath: let go something that will have made a crossing. Choreographilosopher, coryphaeus, choir, you make the text dance, waltz, turn, go out of control, even rap [*déraper même rapper*] along with your supremely precise and improvisational thought. A flight of texts. I have rather the feeling of song, of music. Where does it come to me from? Beautiful ancient voices lead me, those of my ancestors?

DERRIDA The *parole soufflée* is also the dictation of more than one voice (masculine and feminine). They weave together, intertwine, replace each other. Always more than one voice that I let resonate with differences in pitch, timbre, and tone: so many others, men or women, who speak in me. Who speak (to) me. As if I ventured to take responsibility for a sort of choir to which I should nonetheless render justice. In countersigning, to confirm, going with or against the other, that which comes to me from more than one other (masculine or feminine). Other unconsciouses also intervene, or the silhouettes of known or unknown addressees, for whom I speak and who let me speak, who give me their word.[3]

First encounter

AA This dialogue between the two of you has lasted for forty years. Did your first meeting at the brasserie *Le Balzar*, in 1963, leave traces, sediments of voice?

DERRIDA It would be difficult for me to evoke here, in improvising, the concrete and living traces of my encounter with Hélène. There was her first card after reading "Force and Signification", the first face-to-face at the Balzar, yes. But I am not sure that the effect of these experiences survives intact. I remember the first manuscript Hélène confided in me (*Le Prénom de Dieu*[4]). It arrived like a meteor in my garden. The cultural or socio-editorial field, the "readership" of the time was not ready, it seemed to me (was I mistaken?), to receive and to measure what was beginning there. So I feared for her in the course of the reading, with this double feeling: dazzlement and anxiety.

CIXOUS Around the same scenes, my feelings were slightly different. Everything was put in place for me when I nonsaw him the first of the first times. What was inscribed in what came to be a sort of legend for me — that is, something legible — is that I nonsaw him: I only heard him. It was an extraordinary accident. I was eighteen years old. It was at the Sorbonne, he was taking his agrégation,[5] I was way in the back of the lecture theatre, I "saw" only his back. I saw only his voice. He was speaking of that which has eternally interested me: the question of death. I was seized by nothing other than his absolutely other language, so powerfully alive, thinking the question of death. It was for me the opening of thought and literature. Years later I wrote to him after having read his first texts. Thereafter, each time it was the same: I nonsaw him. It was a sort of prophetic phantasm where he was the prophet. I wrote this in "Quelle heure est-il?".[6] I saw not his person but his being walking on the crest of a mountain. At our first encounter, at the *Balzar*, we spoke for a long time and about Joyce. We progressed step-by-step around a limit-work, we were at the limit, each coming from our own edge trying to think "the thing". My way of nonseeing was visionary: one nonsees what one has to see otherwise. In describing in *Spectres of Marx*[7] the visor effect, he makes his own self-portrait. He has a helmet [*heaume*] (what word of words: home homme heaume, om), a natural visor, he looks without being seen. *Unheimlich*. The being, this man, stays back and looks at you. All you have is the letter. From the beginning, what I have seen is his language, in which I knew my thought could wander. I have never stopped reading him meticulously and each time it is as if I was seeing what he thinks. The person that he is, which has an appearance and is part of my life, is the incarnation of his thought in his language, "Derridian". He is the speech of this language. This Derridianized French language, he ransoms it, unmakes it, scours it, plays out its idiomatic potential, awakens the words buried under forgetfulness. He resuscitates it. When I heard him I found the liberty I needed: of course this liberty existed in Rimbaud, but with Jacques Derrida poetry began to gallop philosophy.

DERRIDA From a certain point of view, that of writing itself if I may put it that way, Hélène reads me in an incomparable manner. She immediately finds the best access, the most secret, to the forge and to the form, to the meaning and unconscious body of what I write. My gratitude for this is boundless.

Writers, Jews, from Algeria

AA In *Monolingualism of the Other*,[8] Jacques Derrida explains that this language that unites you was forged in shared origins. You are both "Writers, Jews, from Algeria".

DERRIDA In the beginning (it was however just after the "Algerian War"), our shared origins were not very present in our exchanges. Later, in an increasingly acute manner, we became aware of this. I began to write on "my" Algeria, on my childhood, Judaism, etc., with *The Post Card*,[9] *Monolingualism of the Other*, "Circumfession",[10] etc. Beyond all that we share in this sense, it is only too obvious that we write texts as dissimilar as could be. Our altercations with the French language are also different. We don't have the same training. Although my taste for literature came first, I am a "philosopher". I began by trying to have my philosophical work legitimized by the academic institution. Before taking a certain number of liberties with writing, it was necessary that I first be accorded a certain amount of credit. Before this, I betrayed the norms only in a prudent, cunning, and quasi-clandestine manner. Though this didn't escape everyone. My strange and stormy passion for the French language freed itself bit by bit. I remain obstinately monolingual, without any natural access to another language. I read German, I can teach in English, but my attachment to French is absolute. Inflexible. Whereas through her origins, which are not only Sephardic but also, by her mother, Ashkenazi, Hélène has a native relationship to German. And reads many other languages.

CIXOUS When we met, we were each in our own way busy trying to approach the shimmering heart of the French language, to speak to it intimately [*à la tutoyer*].

For me, also coming from my other languages. We are each foreign otherwise. And this foreignness also presided over our first encounter: he perceived me as foreign, even to his world, for this part of me which he calls Ashkenazi and which for me is German. What brings together our dissimilarities is a thematized experience of the inside of the outside. My imagination was marked by the first experience of my childhood, the event he would say. I was two-and-a-half years old and suddenly my father was a lieutenant-doctor, in 1939: I had the right to enter this place of admission and exclusion that in Oran was called the *Cercle Militaire*.[11] I enter into this garden: and I was not inside. I had the Experience: one can be inside without being inside, there is an inside in the inside, an outside in the inside and this goes on infinitely. In this place which had appeared to me like paradise, hell gaped: I was not able to enter into that into which I had been admitted; I was excluded because of my Jewish origins. And everything is inextricable. I did not understand it until the other children spat the message of rejection on me. I have never stopped living the exclusion, without it bothering me or becoming a home. The passage between the inside and the outside is found in everything I write, as in all of Jacques Derrida's thought. I did not know that he had in the beginning been concerned with legitimizing his presence in philosophy. The secret alien that he is inscribed something else in his texts. In any case, I had the impression of slipping into *The Origin of Geometry*,[12] *The Voice and the Phenomenon*[13] through secret cracks, through literature, benefiting from explosions that were illuminations and destinies for me. One of these books was placed under the epigraph of Edgar Allen Poe. In the other, Jacques Derrida slipped Joyce into the middle of Husserl. Through literature he gave me access to philosophy, showing me its arrow slits and draw-bridges; I slipped through underground passages. The question of the presence of the present, of the present of presence, of survival, was already at work. And even of the henceforth. We had experienced expulsion by Vichy. I was three years old when I watched my father unscrew his doctor's signboard. We share what I have called *nosblessures*, "ournoblewounds": wounds [*blessures*], but ours [*nos*] and they become our tide to nobility [*noblesse*]. We have been able to understand each other to the tenth of a word, because the work of stigmatization, of the scar, was originally inscribed in the life-book of both of us.

AA When Hélène Cixous writes, in *Photos de Racine*,[14] "We are from the same garden", are you alluding to the garden of the *Cercle Militaire*?

DERRIDA "We are from the same garden" could open onto all the world's gardens. But the literal reference is first the *Jardin d'Essai*, a botanical park, in Algiers, with tropical trees, next to a soccer stadium where I often played This Garden still exists. We have never been there together, but it represents a sort of paradise lost. In *H.C. for Life*,[15] the word "essai" (trial, attempt, essay) overwrites itself, imposing its letters and its syntax at a crossroads of sentences and "logics".

CIXOUS French literature begins with the *Essais*. It is a book of *c'est*, "it is". It's extraordinary — a garden called *d'Essai*. The Latin *Esse*: to be.

In the beginning, there is the word

AA For both of you, writing draws on words, takes off from a word play, an expression that nourishes the progression of thought and even, at times, the progression of the narrative.

CIXOUS One could make a poem with nothing but the titles of his books. While *Writing and Difference*[16] was grammatically proper, as time goes on, the words start playing more and more, causing zeugmas, and a certain number of texts are engendered by a brilliant word in the French language brilliantly replayed in Derridian. *Fichus!*[17] Who would have thought? And *Demeure!*[18] *Béliers!*[19] I envy his titles. His hypersensibility to what French words conceal both follitterally and philosophonically.

DERRIDA Yes, in the beginning there is the word. Both the nomination and the term. As if I think nothing before writing: surprised by some resource of the French language that I did not invent, I make of it something that was not programmed but already rendered possible by the lexical and syntactic treasure trove. Hence this overloaded feeling: jubilation, mission accomplished in the service of the language — and a certain irresponsibility. It is all mine, but it comes to me from the language — which does without me in passing through me. During a recent interview the expression *jurer avec* came to me by surprise: it meant exactly what I was looking for: "to clash with", but at the same time "to countersign", "to swear with", "to speak under oath with" . . . And then "to swear with" this conspiracy [*conjuration*] itself. Miracle: I was not thinking of this a second before. I then exploited the resources of this untranslatable expression. *Jurer avec* cannot be translated into another language while preserving the multiplicity and the contradiction that a certain use of the expression can have. Untranslatability is always what guides me: that the sentence is eternally indebted to idiom. The body of the word should be inseparable from the meaning to such an extent that translation can only lose it. In an apparent paradox, translators have been much more interested in my texts than the French themselves, in trying to reinvent in their language the experience I have just described. For example, once I retained *H.C. for Life* as the most just title, I organized my text in such a way as to philosophically exploit the resources of the idiom on different registers: the minute analysis of texts by Hélène, by Freud, of an affirmative thought of life, etc. It is the contingent chance of her name and initials: Hélène Cixous.[20] *C'est pour la vie* means at once faithful and unfailing friendship, "forever", "for life", but also the *pour la vie* which is for her an affirmation, a taking sides with life which I have never been able to share. I am not "against life", but neither am I "for life" like her. This discord is at the heart of the book — and of life.

CIXOUS You are against death and fiercely for life. But otherwise. Dis/quietedly. As for titles, I had to do my mourning in the translation of *Portrait de Jacques Derrida en jeune saint juif.*[21] In *en jeune saint juif* ("as a young saint") can be heard *en jeune singe*, "as a young monkey". I would have liked for the monkey to have survived, but that didn't work.

DERRIDA Hélène's texts are translated across the world, but they remain untranslatable. We are two French writers who cultivate a strange relationship, or a strangely familiar, familiarly strange (*unheimlich*, uncanny) relationship with the French language — at once more translated and more untranslatable than many a French author. We are more rooted in the French language than those with ancestral roots in this culture and this land.

From the word to life

AA The process that you describe beginning with the word can appear very abstract. To the contrary, both of you write books that are marked by autobiography, therefore by life itself: words bring back to life.

DERRIDA Since *Le Prénom de Dieu*, Hélène's books have been fictional and fantastical, fantasmatic, certainly, but also enriched by her singular, even familial, history. For me it is very different! In my first books, there are no biographical hints or signals. They are autobiographical — if they are at all — in another manner. It is very late, with "Circumfession", *Monolingualism of the Other*, etc., that, in a more or less fictive style, I made references to what is called "my life". The "I" has a fictive status there, of course, but which is different from that which it had in my first texts where I said "I" or "we" in the abstract fashion of the philosopher or classical theoretician. Our trajectories are thus very different, with regard to the relationship between the "word" and "life", and to the life of the word.

CIXOUS Nonetheless, even if everything I have written is thought through from experiences I have had, I find myself relatively absent from my texts considered to be autobiographical. The essential part of what I have been is completely secret. I write from this tension between what is hidden and what comes about, that is, the book. The book comes to me, it has a power superior to that of the person who believes she is writing the book. My books are stronger than I am, they escape me. They submit me to translation.

DERRIDA But ever since your first books, the so-called "autobiographical" vein irrigates an underground stratum that is absolute, even if it gives birth to an immense familial mythology: the dead father is always there, the "true" father! And the brother. Later there is the mother.

CIXOUS I don't deny that the family is there, but my family is not all me. In addition it is my invention, as my mother says. And it is the primitive structure of every human being. It is that which causes Greek tragedy, it is a mythical construction from which I reflect on the destinies of all human beings. As for you, your philosophical problematics are sorts of self-portraits. It has to do, always already, with your soul, your psyche, your body in passion, your dislocations. The being behind your letters is you otherwise and more naked than Rousseau, your philosophy is a transparent veil. All your books constitute an autobiography of an unknown genre written "interiorly and on the skin".

DERRIDA I would hope so, but if it were true, it will have been so above all after the fact, retrospectively.

AA Is what Hélène Cixous describes as the presence of the body in Jacques Derrida's texts an element of this autobiography of an unknown genre?

CIXOUS In all of his texts a naivete is manifest, something native. He writes the autobiography of his body as a stigmatized body, a body of blood and of signs. He had the extraordinary audacity to show that the philosopher writes with all his body, that philosophy can only be brought into this world by a being in flesh in blood in sex in sweat, in sperm and in tears, with all his physical and psychic circumcisions and scarifications. It is unique, and unprecedented. This stranjewish body which fears trembles climaxes and triumphs reveals what it hides. He cannot lie.

The values of truth

DERRIDA You see what Hélène's friendship gives me: she is undoubtedly the only person who thinks I never lie. Even when I lie (which I have to do sometimes, like everyone, perhaps a bit less), I remain (according to her) innocent. I am taken to be someone who questions the value of truth, who thinks twice about it at least, and always submits it to questions of history (there is a history of "values of truth"), so much so that my enemies consider me, wrongly of course, to be a sceptic or nihilist. However, when something appears to me to be "true" (but I am now giving this word an altogether different meaning that I cannot explain here), no power in the world, no torture could keep me from saying so. It's not about courage or defiance, it is an irresistible impulse. If I have to interrogate in a critical manner the work of a respected author, I am conscious of the risk I take but I can't keep myself from doing it: when something should be said, it is said. And when it passes through me, no dam can contain it.

CIXOUS This procedure [*démarche*] of truth is for me the gift you give to humanity. In reading you we learn that the truth is always a bit further on. From the place where you arrive, you set off again, you take yourself back up, you relaunch yourself, you do not sit the truth on your knees. Truth makes you tick[22] in all the senses of the word. It's also the law of writing: one can only write in the direction of that which does not let itself be written and which one must try to write. What I can write is already written, it is no longer of interest. I always head towards the most frightening. This is what makes writing thrilling but painful. I write towards what I flee. I dream about it. It is always a *Jardin d'Essai*, but it is an infernal, expelling garden.

Between possible and impossible

DERRIDA We come again to the theme of the impossible. Pardoning is possible only when one pardons what is *impossible* to pardon. If one pardons what is pardonable, in exchange for repentance or a request for pardon, one does not pardon. Pardoning is only possible for the impardonable. Therefore the possibility depends on the impossible. This goes also for the gift, hospitality. Unconditional hospitality is impossible. But it is the only hospitality possible and worthy of the name. I could give any number of concepts obeying the same logic, where the only possibility of the thing is the experience of impossibility. If one does only what one can do, what is within one's power, one only develops the possibilities which are within oneself, one follows a programme. To do something it is necessary to do more than what one can do. To decide, one must cross through the impossibility of the decision. If I know what to decide, there is no more responsibility to take. This is true of experience in general. For something or someone to arrive, it must be absolutely unanticipateable. An event is possible only as impossible, beyond "I can [*je peux*]". I often write "impossible" with a hyphen between im- and possible, to suggest that this word is not negative in the way I use it. The im-possible is the condition of possibility of the event, of hospitality, of the gift, of the pardon, of writing. When something is foreseen, on the horizon, it is already over. Therefore it does not happen. This is also a political reflection: only what the available schemas fail to foresee happens.

CIXOUS Responsibility, where you situate it and as you evoke it, is an absolute and blind responsibility.

DERRIDA It is the responsibility of the other,[23] but of the other in me before me. Of the other as me.

CIXOUS It is an absolute yes to the other, and totally blind. You take on something of which you cannot measure the development, the effects, the destiny. You cannot do otherwise.

AA How is power exercised with regard to the impossible?

DERRIDA It is a certain powerlessness [*im-puissance*], exposure to what is irreducibly other, as heterogeneous or as someone else. Exposure to the other can only take the form of powerlessness. The other is he or she before whom I am vulnerable, whom I cannot even deny. I cannot access the alterity of the other, who will always remain on the other side, nor can I deny his or her alterity. I cannot say that I open the doors, that I invite the other: the other is already there. That is unconditional hospitality (foreign to politics and law, even to the ethical in the narrow sense). Hospitality of visitation and not invitation. The other has already entered, even if he is not invited. Between the conditional and the unconditional in general, there is at once radical heterogeneity and indissociability. This is what we have to deal with.

CIXOUS For me, this exposure to the other takes the form of acquiescence: what translates, for you, in terms of powerlessness, is, for me, a power that accepts submission, infinite acceptation.

DERRIDA It's not a powerlessness of simple resignation, of weakness, but rather an abandonment.

CIXOUS You arrive (to yourself) where you were not expecting (yourself).

AA How is the *"puisse"*, this verb used by Hélène in a sentence you analyse at length in *H.C. for Life*, conjugated with the impossible?

DERRIDA *"Puisse"* is one of these precious possibilities of the French language which are given to me, which I transform and put into play: I tried to elaborate a logic of the efficacy of such a *"puisse"*. A subjunctive operates here, bringing something about through the simple utterance of the vow. *"Puisse cela arriver"*. "May that happen" — and that happens in the text. The singularity of this *"puisse"* is, in its *"puissance"*, its power, more and other than performative. For there to be performative language, one must anticipate, master the conditions, agree upon the codes and conventions, which neutralizes, to a certain degree, the irruptivity of the event. The pure event defies performativity. The *"puisse"* at work in Hélène's texts, this strange subjunctive, which is thus neither an imperative nor an indicative, is situated on this tangential line which I follow between the possible and the impossible. I try to think otherwise what the philosophical tradition, from Aristotle to Hegel, bequeathed us with regard to the possible. It is necessary to think otherwise the possibility of the impossible. This looks like a sort of verbal facility or playful paradox; it is for me the most serious issue in the world.

The right to the secret

AA The theme of the secret occupies both of you: if one must let texts come, how then can the secret be protected?

CIXOUS There are many secrets. The word secret is full of secrets. There is the secret about which I know nothing, so secret and secreted away that I have no trace of it, except maybe in the form of dreams. There is a secret that is something known and hidden, impossible to reveal because the revelation would bring about the destruction of the secret thing, and also of life. The unknown of this secret is buried in night and silence: we will never know the face it would have if it could appear. The thing Aboutwhichiknownothing [*dontjenesaisrien*] remains secret, this gift [*don*] which makes me who I am. One writes like a rescue effort to oneself in the dark: an act of despair because we know there is a treasure to which we will never have access. How ignorant we are about ourselves! And yet we sign.

DERRIDA   This is an inexhaustible theme. I am the inheritor, the depository of a very grave secret to which I do not myself have access. The word or the writing that I send into the world transports a secret that remains inaccessible to me but that leaves its traces in all my texts, in what I do or live. I have often presented myself, barely playing, like a marrano, one of those Jews converted by force, in Spain and Portugal, who cultivated their Judaism in secret, at times to the extent of not knowing what it consisted in. This theme has also interested me from a political point of view. When a State does not respect the right to the secret, it becomes threatening: police violence, inquisition, totalitarianism. I take the right to the secret to be an ethical and political right. Now, literature opens this privileged place where one can say everything and avow everything without the secret having been betrayed: due to the fictional status of the literary work, even if I reveal to you the truth of my secret, I can always claim, by right, without being refuted, that "it is not I who speaks in my name". This poses again the question of the "proper name". Who speaks? Literature has this political right to say everything. It's there, it's published, but nobody can trust it, because it is fiction: I may have lied, invented, deformed, as is the case in all so-called autobiographical texts. A truth is deformed and transformed. Sometimes in order to access an even more powerful, more "true" truth. We can never prove — what is called proving — that someone lied. This right — to say everything without avowing anything — weaves a link of principle between literature and democracy. One can certainly object that, consciously or unconsciously, someone exploits literature which would not be this thing in itself, but a strategic function, a ruse to be able to deny, to avow without avowing. But if literature is only an immense weave of symptoms, what singular symptomatology! It fascinates psychoanalysts. From Freud to Lacan, this symptomatology overpowers them, it is stronger than them. Freud avowed: "It is the poets who teach me."

CIXOUS   In front of the book there is a door. The inspired reader opens it, we think we enter. But the text works to dissimulate the thing in its folds and the author can do nothing about it. He would give his life to discover it. Literature is tragic, panicked by the necessity of pursuing the secret but in vain. In the end the book escapes, there is no end. The book is a letter on the run [*lettre defuite*]. Literature owes its life to the secret, its mission surpasses it. As soon as one writes to exhume one secretes secrets.

DERRIDA The secret is tied to what we said of the truth — and of the impossible. It is not only that which one hides. It is existence itself. However close I am to the other, even in fusioning "communion" or erotic ecstasy, the secret is not revealed. The other is separated. We speak French, therefore Latin: "secernere" is to separate. This interruption is not negative. It makes possible [*donne sa chance à*] the encounter, the event, love itself. But we must not forget, the secret is told from other roots and according to other semantics in Greek or German.

CIXOUS We could add secretion: the secret is not a diamond, it is in a state of continual secretion, it constantly augments itself: never can an author reach its heights.

DERRIDA In "Un ver à soie", which I published in *Veils*,[24] face to face [*en regard*], if I may say so, with Hélène's text ("Savoir"), which I had just read, the figures of the secret and of secretion command a trajectory wholly "autobiographical": the journal of a trip to South America, my "history of truth", childhood, religion, Judaism, the tallith (the shawl that Jewish men, and not Jewish women, must wear). This is just a recent example of all the sharing and separating [*partages*] that we can only evoke here.

NOTES

1. Souffler means to breathe, to whisper, including when one whispers a secret, but also to steal, such that the expression "la parole soufflé" can mean either to whisper or to tell (someone) the word (the secret word, the forgotten word) or to take or steal the word.
2. Cixous is working here on the bivalence of the word "vol", which means both "flight" and "theft".
3. "Me donnent la parole, me donnent leur parole."
4. *Le Prénom de Dieu* [First Name of God] (Paris: Grasset, 1967).
5. The agrégation is the highest level French national academic exam; Cixous is referring to the oral part, which is traditionally open to the public [translator's note].
6. "Quelle heure est-il ou la porte (celle qu'on ne passe pas)" [What Time Is It or The Door (The One We Cannot Enter)], was first read at a conference on Jacques Derrida at Cerisy-la-Salle in 1992; it is published in *Le Passage des frontières: Autour du travail de Jacques Derrida* [The Crossing of Borders: On the Work of Jacques Derrida], M. L. Mallet (ed.), 83–98 (Paris: Galilée, 1994).
7. J. Derrida, *Spectres de Marx* [Spectres of Marx] (Paris: Galilée, 1993).
8. J. Derrida, *Monolinguisme de l'autre ou la prothèse d'origine* [Monolingualism of the Other: or The Prosthesis of Origin] (Paris: Galilée, 1996).

9. J. Derrida, *La Carte Postale: De Socrate à Freud et au-delà* [The Post Card: From Socrates to Freud and Beyond] (Paris: Flammarion, 1980).

10. "Circonfession" [Circumfession], in *Jacques Derrida par Geoffrey Bennington et Jacques Derrida* (Paris: Seuil, 1991).

11. Military Circle.

12. *L'Origine de la géomètrie* [The Origin of Geometry] (Paris: Presses Universitaires de France, 1974).

13. *La Voix et le phénoméne* [The Voice and the Phenomenon] (Paris: Presses Universitaires de France, 1967).

14. *Hélène Cixous: Photos de Racine* [Rootprints], with Mireille Calle-Gruber (Paris: Éditions des femmes, 1994).

15. J. Derrida, *H.C. pour la vie, c'est à dire . . .* [H.C. for Life, That is to Say] (Paris: Galilée, 2003).

16. J. Derrida, *L'Ecriture et la différence* [Writing and Difference] (Paris: Seuil, 1967).

17. J. Derrida, *Fichus* (Paris: Galilée, 2002). "Fichu" has various meanings in French, the most usual, perhaps, being that of the expletive "rotten" or "lousy".

18. J. Derrida, *Demeure* [Residence] (Paris: Galilée, 1998).

19. J. Derrida, *Beliers — le dialogue interrompu: entre deux infinis, le poéme* [Rams — The Interrupted Dialogue: Between Two Infinites, The Poem] (Paris: Galilée, 2003).

20. The letter "C" in French is a homophone of "c'est", "it is", such that the book title, published under the translation *H.C. for Life* could also be rendered *H, it is for life* [translator's note].

21. *Portrait de Jacques Derrida en jeune saint juif* [Portrait of Jacques Derrida as a Young Jewish Saint] (Paris: Galilée, 2001).

22. "La vérité te fait marcher". "Faire marcher" means to make tick, to make walk, to give orders, but also to pull (one's) leg [translator's note].

23. This expression, "la responsabilité de l'autre", plays on the double genitive to signify both "the other's responsibility" and "the responsibility for the other". In French this latter sense is reinforced by the common expression "être responsable de", meaning "to be responsible for" [translator's note].

24. *Voiles (avec Hélène Cixous)* [Veils] (Paris: Galilée, 1998). A "ver à soie" is literally a silk worm. Derrida's usage also plays on the idea of belonging — the French "à soi" (one's own). Cixous's text "Savoir" (included in *Voiles*) means literally "knowledge", but also includes the idea of seeing (the verb "voir" means to see) [editor's note].

Envoi: But the Earth still turns, and not as badly as all that

Interview with Frédéric-Yves Jeannet. Translated by Amaleena Damlé.

This extract is taken from a book of verbal and written interviews with Frédéric-Yves Jeannet, *Rencontre terrestre: Arcachon, Roosevelt Island, Paris Montsouris, Manhattan, Cuernavaca* (Paris: Galilée, 2005). The exchange is headed "New York, 24 janvier-Paris, 25 janvier 2002" and is given the heading "Mais La Terre tourne, pas si mal".

F-YJ I am emerging from a period of great mourning. This explains my recent silence. Since our last interviews the wheel has continued to turn and here we are, embarked on the second year of this new century that has certainly begun rather badly, despite all the hopes we might have had for it, above all that it might have been different to this century "stitched of camps"[1] which has been the twentieth century as you defined it. What do you say to the present state of the world?

CIXOUS But the Earth still turns — and not as badly as all that — I tell myself, feeling pleased to see once again the print of the planet that you stamp upon your fine pages (where the crossings-out are also beautiful, just like writing), and to find once again your "hand" — I can see, in the sections that cross it out, the text that I'm unable to regard without a pang, the eternal hollow spaces like dog-kennels,[2] and this page, then, which comes to me as a new sign of life, or a sign of new life, is also plunged in commemorative mourning for dogs (all animals are like family to me) and for grandmothers — mine as well, both of mine are evoked, the first scenes where one starts to lose the mother's body.

I have a touch of flu, I can see it in the wandering of my handwriting, please excuse me — yesterday evening then, upon discovering your lines and your voice, I had that kind of pleasure that comes from the heart, and this despite and despite — despite the farewells, the spirals the desolation. For, and to respond to your question already, I am guided by the "despites" in my vision of the world: despite the ill will[3] of almost the whole world, I continue to be able to feel the benefits that chance and miracle incarnated in certain people have in store even for people as nauseated as me. I don't stop counting my luck, wondrous that it might exist, and admiring the recourse of the human universe, my always unexpected "heritage", without measurement, without an expected form, yet which arrives, just as one day you arrived.

The state of the world — I don't think it will ever be better. It's been a long time since I have found myself at the point of acquiescing to its tragic structure. When I was small, I must have believed (before the age of ten) that Good was destined to conquer. I think that the [hi]story (History)[4] is afflicted by the demon of repetition, of repetition with differences. Evil (and its evil spirits — who have the power and the majority) is invincible at the root and inevitable. The source of one plague is extinguished. So evil invents another plague. Yes, the twentieth century was stitched of camps (I used to see it as an immense skin sewn up with threads of barbed wire), and the twenty-first century will be lacerated, wounded, stabbed with other technologies. All that happens is a changeover of instruments of blackmail, of subjugation and of torture. And of scapegoats, once again the throats of one people are cut in place of another. That's how it works.

Can one stop repetition, or unexpectedly jar the machine? That's the question which to me represents "hope". Hope, that I don't have, that is at most an incessant search for lines of flight.[5] What I'm certain of, regrettably, is that "the world" will always be "world", *mundus*, "exclusive" [*propre*], appropriating, eliminating, devouring, purifying, excluding — that there will always be "two worlds" as proclaimed, naively prophetic, the sign on my grandfather's tobacconist shop in the Place d'Armes in Oran — one then, dominant, which is now the worldwide propagator, or the globalizer; the other the *unworldly*, the banished, the marginalized, the "dirty" in the particularity of the clean,[6] and composed of people or classes considered to be the damned of that era, on the political plane; but — and this is what matters a lot to me too — is also composed on the cultural plane, of the "wealthy" of mind, the intolerables, poets, philosophers, seekers of the absolute, all those who find ecstasy in barely reachable heights, who live on languages that have found the second innocence Kleist speaks of, who would not desire power but the poem, and who are hated and feared for not being in alignment and conformity with the spirit of imitation and predation.

Well, there are few of those — and so, few poems. But this scarcity is immense, infinite, and I have nothing more to ask of it. No need to hope. On the other hand, one should resist the temptation of weariness and discouragement (the fact that we are writing this "book", upon the swell, with breaks and reprises, under the trade wind, is a modest form of resistance. It requires an adhesion, *which exceeds us*, to literary love).

NOTES

1. See p. 130.
2. In French "les niches éternelles pour les chiens". "Niche" can mean both "dog-kennel" and "recess" in the sense of a hollow space.
3. In French "malgré le mauvais gré". Cixous's formulation draws attention to the "gré" ("will") implicit in "malgré" ("despite" or "against one's will").
4. The word "histoire" in French signifies both "story" and "history". Cixous's adoption of a capital to distinguish the two is relatively common in her work.
5. Cixous is perhaps evoking Deleuze's notion of "lines of flight" here. See Gilles Deleuze and Felix Guattari, *A Thousand Plateaus: Capitalism and Schizophrenia* (Minneapolis, MN: University of Minnesota Press, 1987), 3–25.
6. In French "le 'sale' du propre". The noun "propre" implies exclusivity and particularity ("être le propre de" meaning "to be peculiar or unique to"), recalling the exclusivity of the "*mundus*". However the adjective "propre" (clean) is also recalled here in opposition to "sale" (dirty).

Bibliography of the works of Hélène Cixous

Books and plays in French

1967   *Le Prénom de Dieu* (Paris: Grasset).

1969   *Dedans* (Paris: Grasset) [repr. Paris: Éditions des femmes, 1986].

———   *L'Exil de James Joyce ou l'art du remplacement* (Paris: Publications de la Faculté des lettres et sciences de Paris-Sorbonne) [repr. Paris: Grasset, 1985].

1970   *Les Commencements* (Paris: Grasset) [repr. Paris: Éditions des femmes, 1999].

———   *Le Troisième Corps* (Paris: Grasset) [repr. Paris: Éditions des femmes, 1999].

1971   *Un Vrai Jardin* (Paris: L'Herne) [repr. Paris: Éditions des femmes, 1998].

1972   *Neutre* (Paris: Grasset) [repr. Paris: Éditions des femmes, 1998].

———   *La Pupille, Cahiers Renaud-Barrault*, 78 (Paris: Gallimard).

1973   *Tombe* (Paris: Seuil).

———   *Portrait du soleil* (Paris: Denoël) [repr. Paris: Éditions des femmes, 1999].

1974   *Prénoms de personne* (Paris: Seuil).

1975   and Catherine Clément, *La Jeune Née* (Paris: Union Générale d'Éditions, Collection 10/18).

———   *Un K. incompréhensible: Pierre Goldman* (Paris: Bourgois).

———   *Révolutions pour plus d'un Faust* (Paris: Seuil).

———   *Souffles* (Paris: Éditions des femmes) [repr. 1998].

1976   *La* (Paris: Gallimard) [repr. Paris: Éditions des femmes, 1979].

———   *Partie* (Paris: Éditions des femmes).

———   *Portrait de Dora* (Paris: Éditions des femmes) [repr. in *Hélène Cixous: Théâtre* (1986)].

1977   *Angst* (Paris: Éditions des femmes) [repr. 1998].

———   with Madeleine Gagnon and Annie Leclerc, *La Venue à l'écriture* (Paris: Union Générale d'Éditions, Collection 10/18) [Title essay repr. in *Entre l'écriture* (1986)].

1978   *Le Nom d'Oedipe: Chant du corps interdit* (Paris: Éditions des femmes).

———   *Préparatifs de noces au-delà de l'abîme* (Paris: Éditions des femmes).

1979   *Anankè,* (Paris: Éditions des femmes).

——   *Vivre l'orange/To Live the Orange* (Paris: Éditions des femmes) [Bilingual, translation by Hélène Cixous, Sarah Cornell & Ann Liddle] [repr. in *L'Heure de Clarice Lispector* (1989)].

1980   *Illa* (Paris: Éditions des femmes).

1981   *(With) Ou l'art de l'innocence* (Paris: Éditions des femmes).

1982   *Limonade tout était si infini* (Paris: Éditions des femmes).

1983   *Le Livre de Promethea* (Paris: Gallimard).

1984   *La Prise de l'école de Madhubaï, Avant-Scène du Théâtre* **745** (March), 6–22 [repr. in *Hélène Cixous: Théâtre* (1986)].

1985   *L'Histoire terrible mais inachevée de Norodom Sihanouk, roi du Cambodge* (Paris: Théâtre du Soleil).

1986   *La Bataille d'Arcachon* (Laval, Quebec: Trois).

——   *Entre l'écriture* (Paris: Éditions des femmes).

——   *Hélène Cixous: Théâtre* (Paris: Éditions des femmes) [*Portrait de Dora* and *La Prise de l'école de Madhubaï*].

1987   *L'Indiade, ou l'Inde de leurs rêves, et quelques écrits sur le théâtre* (Paris: Théâtre du Soleil).

1988   *Manne aux Mandelstams aux Mandelas* (Paris: Éditions des femmes).

1989   and Ariane Mnouchkine, *La Nuit miraculeuse* (Paris: Théâtre du Soleil).

——   *L'Heure de Clarice Lispector, précédé de Vivre l'orange* (Paris: Éditions des femmes).

1990   *Jours de l'an* (Paris: Éditions des femmes).

1991   *L'Ange au secret* (Paris: Éditions des femmes).

——   *On ne part pas, on ne revient pas* (Paris: Éditions des femmes).

1992   *Déluge* (Paris: Éditions des femmes).

——   *Les Euménides* (Paris: Théâtre du Soleil).

1993   *Beethoven à jamais ou l'existence de Dieu* (Paris: Éditions des femmes).

1994   and Mireille Calle-Gruber, *Hélène Cixous: Photos de Racine* (Paris: Éditions des femmes).

——   *L'Histoire (qu'on ne connaîtra jamais)* (Paris: Éditions des femmes).

——   *La Ville parjure ou le réveil des Erinyes* (Paris: Théâtre du Soleil).

——   *Voile Noire Voile Blanche/Black Sail White Sail, New Literary History* **25**(2), 219–354 [Bilingual, translation by Catherine A. F. MacGillivray].

1995   *La Fiancée juive de la tentation* (Paris: Éditions des femmes).

1996   *Messie* (Paris: Éditions des femmes).

1997   *Or, les lettres de mon père* (Paris: Éditions des femmes).

1998   and Jacques Derrida, *Voiles* (Paris: Galilée).

1999   *Osnabrück* (Paris: Éditions des femmes).

——   *Tambours sur la digue: Sous forme de pièce ancienne pour marionnettes jouée par des acteurs* (Paris: Théâtre du Soleil).

2000   *Le Jour où je n'étais pas là* (Paris: Galilée).

—— *Les Rêveries de la femme sauvage: Scènes primitives* (Paris: Galilée).

2001 *Benjamin à Montaigne: Il ne faut pas le dire* (Paris: Galilée).

—— *Portrait de Jacques Derrida en jeune saint juif* (Paris: Galilée).

—— *Rouen, la Trentième Nuit de Mai '31* (Paris: Galilée).

—— and Mireille Calle-Gruber (eds), *Au théâtre, au cinéma, au féminin* (Paris: L'Harmattan).

2002 *Manhattan: Lettres de la préhistoire* (Paris: Galilée).

2003 *Rêve, je te dis* (Paris: Galilée).

—— *L'Amour du loup et autres remords* (Paris: Galilée).

2004 *Tours Promises* (Paris: Galilée).

—— and Rachid Koraïchi, John Berger, Michel Butor, *Les Sept Dormants* (Arles: Actes Sud).

2005 *Le Tablier de Simon Hantaï: Annagrammes, suivi de H.C. S.H.: Lettres* (Paris: Galilée).

—— and Frédéric-Yves Jeannet, *Rencontre terrestre: Arcachon, Roosevelt Island, Paris Montsouris, Manhattan, Cuernavaca* (Paris: Galilée).

—— *L'Amour même: Dans la boite aux lettres* (Paris: Galilée).

—— and Jean-Pierre Lefebvre, Jean-Louis Backès, *Vingt et unièmes assises de la traduction littéraire* (Arles: Actes Sud).

2006 *Insister: À Jacques Derrida* (Paris: Galilée).

—— *Hyperrêve* (Paris: Galilée).

2007 *Le Voisin de zero: Sam Beckett* (Paris: Galilée).

—— *Si près* (Paris: Galilée).

Books and plays in English

1972 *The Exile of James Joyce*, Sally A. J. Purcell (trans.) (New York: David Lewis) [repr. London: John Calder, 1976; repr. New York: Riverrun, 1980] [See *L'Exil de James Joyce ou l'art du remplacement* (1969)].

1977 *Portrait of Dora*, Anita Barrows (trans.), *Gambit International Theatre Review* **8**(30), 27–67 [repr. in *Benmussa Directs* (London: John Calder/Dallas: Riverrun, 1979)] [See *Portrait de Dora* (1976)].

1979 *Vivre l'orange/To Live the Orange*, Hélène Cixous, Sarah Cornell & Ann Liddle (trans.) (Paris: Éditions des femmes) [Bilingual].

1983 *Portrait of Dora*, Sarah Burd (trans.), *Diacritics* (Spring), 2–32 [See *Portrait de Dora* (1976)].

1985 *Angst*, Jo Levy (trans.) (London: John Calder/New York: Riverrun) [See *Angst* (1977)].

1986 *The Conquest of the School at Madhubaï*, Deborah Carpenter (trans.), *Women and Performance* **3**, 59–95 [See *La Prise de l'école de Madhubaï* (1984)].

—— *Inside*, Carol Barko (trans.) (New York: Schocken) [See *Dedans* (1969)].

—— and Catherine Clément, *The Newly Born Woman*, Betsy Wing (trans.) (Minneapolis. MN: University of Minnesota Press) [See *La Jeune Née* (1975)].

1988 "Neutre", Lorene M. Birden (trans.), in "Making English Clairielle: An Introduction and Translation for Hélène Cixous' 'Neutre'", unpublished MA thesis (University of Massachusetts at Amherst) [See *Neutre* (1972)].

1990 *Reading with Clarice Lispector*, Verena Andermatt Conley (ed. & trans.) (Minneapolis, MN: University of Minnesota Press) [Abridged transcripts of Hélène Cixous's seminars at the Centre de Recherches en Études Féminines, Université de Paris VIII, 1980–5].

1991 *The Book of Promethea*, Betsy Wing (trans.) (Lincoln, NE: University of Nebraska Press) [See *Le Livre de Promethea* (1983)].

—— *Coming to Writing and Other Essays*, Deborah Jenson (ed.), Sarah Cornell, Deborah Jenson, Ann Liddle & Susan Sellers (trans.) (Cambridge, MA: Harvard University Press) [Selections from *La Venue à l'écriture* (1977), *Entre l'écriture* (1986) and *L'Heure de Clarice Lispector* (1989)].

—— *Readings: The Poetics of Blanchot, Joyce, Kafka, Kleist, Lispector, and Tsvetaeva*, Verena Andermatt Conley (ed. & trans.) (Minneapolis, MN: University of Minnesota Press) [Abridged transcripts of Hélène Cixous's seminars at the Centre de Recherches en Études Féminines, Université de Paris VIII, 1982–4].

1993 *Three Steps on the Ladder of Writing*, Sarah Cornell & Susan Sellers (trans.) (New York: Columbia University Press) [The Welleck Library Lectures, Irvine, CA, 1990].

1994 *The Hélène Cixous Reader*, Susan Sellers (ed.), Susan Sellers & others (trans.) (London: Routledge) [Includes excerpts from *Dedans* (1969), *Neutre* (1972), *Prénoms de personne* (1974), *La Jeune Née* (1975), *Souffles* (1975), *La* (1976), *Angst* (1977), *Vivre l'orange/To Live the Orange* (1979), *(With) Ou l'art de l'innocence* (1981), *Limonade tout était si infini* (1982), *Le Livre de Promethea* (1983), "Extrême Fidélité" (1987), *L'Histoire terrible mais inachevée de Norodom Sihanouk, roi du Cambodge* (1985), *L'Indiade, ou l'Inde de leurs rêves* (1987), *Manne aux Mandelstams aux Mandelas* (1988), *Jours de l'an* (1990), *Déluge* (1992) and *Three Steps on the Ladder of Writing* (1993)].

—— *Manna for the Mandelstams for the Mandelas*, Catherine A. F. MacGillivray (trans.) (Minneapolis, MN: University of Minnesota Press) [See *Manne aux Mandelstams aux Mandelas* (1988)].

—— *The Name of Oedipus*, Christiane Makward & Judith G. Miller (trans.), in *Plays by French and Francophone Women: A Critical Anthology*, Christiane Makward & Judith G. Miller (eds) (Ann Arbor, MI: University of Michigan Press) [See *Le Nom d'Oedipe* (1978)].

—— *The Terrible but Unfinished Story of Norodom Sihanouk, King of Cambodia*, Juliet Flower MacCannell, Judith Pike & Lollie Groth (trans.) (Lincoln, NE: University of Nebraska Press) [See *L'Histoire terrible mais inachevée de Norodom Sihanouk, roi du Cambodge* (1985)].

—— *Voile Noir Voile Blanche/Black Sail White Sail*, Catherine A. F. MacGillivray (trans.), *New Literary History* **25**(2), 219–354 [Bilingual].

1996 with Marilyn French & Mario Vargas Llosa, *Bloom* (Dublin: Kingstown Press).

1997 and Mireille Calle-Gruber, *Hélène Cixous Rootprints: Memory and Life Writing*, Eric Prenowitz (trans.) (London: Routledge) [See *Hélène Cixous: Photos de Racine* (1994)].

1998 *First Days of the Year*, Catherine A. F. MacGillivray (trans.) (Minneapolis, MN: University of Minnesota Press) [See *Jours de l'an* (1990)].

—— *Stigmata: Escaping Texts*, Keith Cohen, Catherine A. F. MacGillivray & Eric Prenowitz (trans.) (London: Routledge) [rev. 2005].

1999 *The Third Body*, Keith Cohen (trans.) (Evanston, IL: Northwestern University Press) [See *Le Troisième Corps* (1970)].

2000 *A True Garden*, Claudine G. Fisher (trans.), *Paragraph* **23**(3), 252–7 [See *Un Vrai Jardin* (1971)].

2001 and Jacques Derrida, *Veils*, Geoffrey Bennington (trans.) (Stanford, CA: Stanford University Press) [See *Voiles* (1998)].

2004 *The Selected Plays of Hélène Cixous*, Eric Prenowitz (ed.) (London: Routledge) ["Portrait of Dora", Ann Liddle (trans.), "Black Sail White Sail", Donald Watson (trans.), "The Perjured City", Bernadetee Fort (trans.) and "Drums on the Dam", Judith G. Miller & Brian G. Mallet (trans.)].

—— *Portrait of Jacques Derrida as a Young Jewish Saint*, Beverley Bie Brahic (trans.) (New York: Columbia University Press) [See *Portrait de Jacques Derrida en jeune saint juif* (2001)].

—— *The Writing Notebooks*, Susan Sellers (ed. & trans.) (London: Continuum).

—— *Neuter*, Lorene M. Birden (trans.) (Lewisburg, PA: Bucknell University Press) [See *Neutre* (1972)].

2005 and Tony Godfrey, *Vera's Room: The Art of Maria Chevska*, Susan Sellers (trans.) (London: Black Dog).

2006 *The Day I Wasn't There*, Beverley Bie Brahic (trans.) (Edinburgh: Edinburgh University Press; Evanston, IL: Northwestern University Press) [repr. New York: Columbia University Press, 2008] [See *Le Jour où je n'étais pas là* (2000)].

—— *Dream I Tell You*, Beverley Bie Brahic (trans.) (Edinburgh: Edinburgh University Press) [See *Rêve, je te dis* (2003)].

—— *Reveries of the Wild Woman: Primal Scenes*, Beverley Bie Brahic (trans.) (Evanston, IL: Northwestern University Press) [See *Les Rêveries de la femme sauvage: Scènes primitives* (2000)].

2008 *Insister of Jacques Derrida*, Peggy Kamuf (trans.) (Stanford, CA: Stanford University Press) [See *Insister À Jacques Derrida* (2005)].

—— *Manhattan: Letters from Prehistory*, Beverley Bie Brahic (trans.) (New York: Fordham University Press) [See *Manhattan: Lettres de la préhistoire* (2002)].

Interviews in French

1969   with Gilles Lapouge, "L'exil de Joyce: Entretien", *La Quinzaine Littéraire* (1–15 March), 6 – 8.

   —   with Ginette Guitard-Auviste, "Hélène Cixous, une grande fille pas simple: Le Prix Médicis", *Les Nouvelles Littéraires* (27 November), 1, 7.

   —   with Guy Le Clec'h, "Hélène Cixous ou l'illusion cosmique", *Le Figaro* (1–7 December, "Le Figaro Littéraire"), 19.

1973   with Claudine Jardin, "Dans *Tombe* de Cixous c'est la culture qui est enfouie", *Le Figaro* (2 June, "Le Figaro Littéraire"), 16.

   —   with Gilles Deleuze, "Littérasophie et Philosofiture" [Radio broadcast, 3 November, "Emission Dialogues, 30, with Roger Pillaudin", France Culture].

1975   " 'À propos de Marguerite Duras', par Michel Foucault et Hélène Cixous", *Cahiers Renaud-Barrault* **89**, 8 –22.

1976   with Claire Devarrieux, "Hélène Cixous et le *Portrait de Dora*", *Le Monde* (26 February), 15.

   —   with Anne Surgers & Nicole Casanova, "Hélène Cixous: Voyage autour du mythe de Dora", *Le Quotidien de Paris* (9 March), 12.

   —   with Nicole Casanova, "Le Grand JE au féminin: Un entretien avec Hélène Cixous", *Les Nouvelles Littéraires* (8 April), 6.

   —   with Jean-Louis de Rambures, "Hélène Cixous: Lorsque je n'écris pas, c'est comme si j'étais morte", *Le Monde* (9 April, "Le Monde des Livres"), 20 [revised version (with additions made in October 1977) in *Comment travaillent les écrivains*, Jean-Louis de Rambures (Paris: Flammarion, 1978), 56 – 63].

   —   "Textes de l'imprévisible: Grâce à la différence", *Les Nouvelles Littéraires* (26 May, "Le Dossier 'Éditions des femmes en écriture' "), 18 – 19.

   —   "Le Sexe ou la tête?", *Les Cahiers du GRIF* **13** (October), 5 –15.

   —   " 'Quelques questions posées à Hélène Cixous': Entretien avec Françoise Collin", *Les Cahiers du GRIF* **13** (October), 16 –21.

   —   with Jacqueline Sudaka, "Être femme juive, situation idéale", *Les Nouveaux Cahiers* **46** (Autumn), 92 –5.

1977   "Entretien avec Madeleine Gagnon, Philippe Haeck et Patrick Straramn, sur le *Portrait de Dora*", *Chroniques* (Montreal) **1**(2), 16 –25.

   —   with Lucette Finas, "L'étrange traversée d'Hélène Cixous", *Le Monde* (13 May, "Le Monde des Livres"), 21.

   —   with Nicole Casanova, "Le Quitte ou double de la pensée féminine: Un entretien avec Hélène Cixous", *Les Nouvelles Littéraires* (22 –9 September), 8.

   —   "Entretien avec Françoise van Rossum-Guyon", *Revue des Sciences Humaines* (Lille) **44**(168) (October–December), 479 –93 [see "Poésie e(s)t politique: Entretien avec Hélène Cixous", *Éditions des femmes en Mouvements Hebdo* **4** (30 November–7 December 1979), 28 –33; also *Le Cœur critique: Butor, Simon, Kristeva, Cixous*, Françoise van Rossum-Guyon, 197 –216 (Amsterdam: Rodopi)].

1978   with Colette Godard, "Entretien avec Hélène Cixous: Un destin révolu", *Le Monde* (28 July), 16.

1981   "'Biographie de l'écriture': Entretien avec Alain Poirson", *Révolution Magazine* (31 July), 18–20.

——   "Hélène Cixous: Dossier Jean Genet", *Masques* **12** (Winter), 59–63.

1982   "'Hélène Cixous ou le rêve de l'écriture': Entretien avec François Coupry", *Libération* (22 December), 27.

1983   with Anne Laurent, "Hélène Cixous a rencontré la reine des Dacoïts", *Libération* (30 December), 23.

1984   with Henri Quéré, "Le Roman d'aujourd'hui: Entretien: Hélène Cixous", *Fabula* (Lille) **3** (March), 147–58.

1986   with Véronique Hotte, "Une témérité tremblante", *Théâtre/Public* **68** (March–April), 22–5.

——   with Gisèle Barret, "Petit essai sur la dramaturgie de *L'Histoire terrible mais inachevée de Norodom Sihanouk, roi du Cambodge*", *Les Cahiers de Théâtre: Jeu* (Montreal) **39**, 131–41.

1987   with Gilles Costaz, "*L'Indiade*: Un troupeau d'animaux furieux. Un double entrtien avec Hélène Cixous et Ariane Mnouchkine", *Le Matin* (28 September), 18.

1988   with Bernard Golfier, "'Le tragique de la partition': Entretien avec Hélène Cixous", *Théâtre/Public* **82–3** (July–October), 81–4.

——   with Dominique Lecoq, "Les Motions contre l'émotion de l'Histoire", *Politis* (7 July), 46–8.

——   with Pascale Hassoun, Chantal Maillet & Claude Rabant, "Entretien avec Hélène Cixous", *Patio* **10** ("L'Autre Sexe"), 61–76.

1989   "Je suis plutôt un être de bord", *La Quinzaine Littéraire* (16–30 May, "Où va la littérature française?"), 10.

1990   with Françoise van Rossum-Guyon, "A propos de *Manne*: entretien avec Hélène Cixous", in *Hélène Cixous, chemins d'une écriture*, Françoise van Rossum-Guyon & Myriam Díaz-Diocaretz (eds), 213–34 (Saint-Denis: Presses Universitaires de Vincennes/Amsterdam: Rodopi).

——   with Marie-Claire Ropars & Michèle Lagny, "L'auteur entre texte et théâtre", *Hors Cadre* (Presses Universitaires de Vincennes) **8** ("L'état d'auteur"), 33–65.

1992   with Frédéric Regard, "Le Lieu de l'autre", in *Logique des Traverses. De l'Influence* (CIEREC Travaux LXXVII), 11–26 (Université de Saint-Etienne).

1994   with Christa Stevens, "Questions à Hélène Cixous", in *(en)jeux de la communication romanesque*, Suzan van Dijk & Christa Stevens (eds), 321–2 (Amsterdam: Rodopi).

——   with Sabrina Weldman, "Hélène Cixous: Attention, la nouvelle peste arrive", *Globe Hebdo* (May), 37.

——   with Mireille Calle-Gruber, "On est déjà dans la gueule du livre: Entre tiens", in *Photos de Racine*, 11–121 (Paris: Éditions des femmes).

1995   with Lucien Attoun, "Derrière le miroir", *Théâtre/Public* (July–October), 90–1.

1997   with Mireille Calle-Gruber, "Aux commencements, il y eut pluriel . . .", *Genesis* (Spring), 131–41.

——   with Françoise van Rossum-Guyon, "En juin 1995", in *Le Cœur critique: Butor, Simon, Kristeva, Cixous*, 234–47 (Amsterdam: Rodopi).

——   with Jean-Louis Perrier, "Notre spectacle serait comme une descendance d'un film muet", *Le Monde* (30 December), 18.

1999   with Sylvie Nicolet, *Théâtre Magazine* 3 (October–December), 76–9.

2000   with Antoinette Fouque & Anne Berger, "Genèses", in *Hélène Cixous, croisées d'une œuvre*, Mireille Calle-Gruber (ed.), 407–18 (Paris: Galilée).

——   with Bertrand Leclair, "La Langue est le seul refuge", *La Quinzaine Littéraire* **793** (1–15 October), 10–12.

——   with Rosette Clémentine Lamont, "Conversation with Hélène Cixous", *Western European Stages* **12**(2) (Winter), 30–40.

2001   with Éric Loret, "Hélène Cixous en déplacement", *Libération* (4 October), 4.

——   with Daniel Ferrer, "Je suis d'abord une lisante", *Genesis* **17**, 45–55.

2002   with François Noudelmann, "Hélene Cixous, la voix étrangère la plus profonde, la plus antique", *Périphéries* **37**, 111–19.

——   with Mirelle Calle-Gruber, "Le Livre personage du livre", *Cahiers de la Villa Gillet* **16** (April), 16–26.

——   "Variations autour du moi", *Magazine Littéraire* **409** (May), 26.

2003   with Chantal Maillet, "Aller vers le plus effrayant", *Revue de Psychanalyse* **19**, 14–32.

——   "L'amour est peur", *Magazine Littéraire* **426** (September), 65–7.

2004   with Aliette Armel, "Du mot à la vie: Un dialogue entre Jacques Derrida et Hélène Cixous", *Magazine Littéraire* **430** (April), 22–9.

2005   with Frédéric-Yves Jeannet, *Rencontre terrestre: Arcachon, Roosevelt Island, Paris Montsouris, Manhattan, Cuernavaca*, (Paris: Galilée).

——   "Stendhal aujourd'hui avec le témoignage d'Hélène Cixous", *Magazine Littéraire* **44** (April), 62.

——   with René de Ceccatty, "La Littérature suspend la mort", *Le Monde* (16 December, "Le Monde des Livres"), 12.

Interviews in English

1976   with Christiane Makward, "Interview", Ann Liddle & Beatrice Cameron (trans.), *Substance* **13**, 19–37.

——   "The Fruits of Femininity", *Manchester Guardian Weekly* (16 May), 14 [See interview with Jean-Louis de Rambures, "Hélène Cixous: Quand je n'écris pas, c'est comme si j'étais morte" (1976)].

1979   "Rethinking Differences: An Interview", Isabelle de Courtrivon (trans.), in *Homosexualities and French Literature*, Elaine Marks & Georges Stambolian (eds), 78–88 (Ithaca, NY: Cornell University Press).

1984   with Verena Andermatt Conley, "An Exchange with Hélène Cixous", in *Hélène Cixous: Writing the Feminine*, Verena Andermatt Conley, 129–61 (Lincoln, NE: University of Nebraska Press) [repr. "Voice i . . . : Hélène Cixous & Verena Andermatt Conley", *Boundary 2* 12(2) (Winter), 51–67].

1985   with Susan Sellers, "Hélène Cixous", *The Women's Review* (7 May), 22–3.

1987   with Linda Brandon, "Impassive Resistance", *Independent* (11 November), 17.

1988   with members of the Centre d'Etudes Féminines, "Conversations", Susan Sellers (ed. & trans.), in *Writing Differences: Readings from the Seminar of Hélène Cixous*, Susan Sellers (ed.), 141–54 (Milton Keynes: Open University Press).

——   with Alice Jardine & Anne M. Menke, "Exploding the Issue: 'French' 'Women' 'Writers' and 'The Canon'", Deborah Carpenter (trans.), *Yale French Studies* 75, 235–6.

1989   "A Realm of Characters", "The Double World of Writing", "Listening to the Heart", "Writing as a Second Heart", in *Delighting the Heart: A Notebook by Women Writers*, Susan Sellers (ed.), 18, 69, 126–8, 198 (London: The Women's Press; repr. 1994).

——   with Catherine Franke & Roger Chazal, "Interview with Hélène Cixous", *Qui Parle* (Berkeley: University of California) 3(1) (Spring), 152–79.

1991   "Hélène Cixous", Deborah Jenson & Leyla Roubi (trans.), in *Shifting Scenes: Interviews on Women, Writing and Politics in Post-68 France*, Alice Jardine & Anne M. Menke (eds), 32–50 (New York: Columbia University Press).

1996   with Kathleen O'Grady, "Guardian of Language: An Interview with Hélène Cixous", Eric Prenowitz (trans.), *Women's Education des femmes* (Canadian Congress for Learning Opportunities for Women) 12(4) (Winter), 8–10.

1997   with Bernadette Fort Greenblatt, "Theater, History, Ethics: An Interview with Hélène Cixous on the Perjured City, or the Awakening of the Furies", *New Literary History* 28(3), 425–56.

——   with Mireille Calle-Gruber, "We Are Already in the Jaws of the Book: Inter Views", in *Hélène Cixous Rootprints: Memory and Life Writing*, 1–115 (London: Routledge) [See *Hélène Cixous: Photos de Racine* (1994)].

2000   "Hélène Cixous in Conversation with Sophia Phoca", *Wasafiri* (London) 31 (Spring), 9–13.

——   with Ian Blyth, "An Interview with Hélène Cixous", *Paragraph* 23(3) (November, "Hélène Cixous"), 338–43.

2002   with Martin McQuillan & others, " 'You race towards that secret, which escapes': An Interview with Hélène Cixous", in *The Oxford Literary Review*, "Reading Cixous Writing" 24, 185–201.

2004   with Eric Prenowitz, "On Theatre: An Interview with Hélène Cixous", in *Selected Plays of Hélène Cixous*, Eric Prenowitz (ed.), 1–24 (London: Routledge).

—— with Ian Blyth & Susan Sellers, "Cixous Live", in *Hélène Cixous Live Theory*, Ian Blyth with Susan Sellers, 99–112 (London: Continuum).

—— with Susan Sellers, "'Magnetizing the World': An Interview with Hélène Cixous", in *The Writing Notebooks of Hélène Cixous*, Susan Sellers (ed. & trans.), 116–22 (London: Continuum).

2006 with Aliette Armel, "From the Word of Life: A Dialogue between Jacques Derrida and Hélène Cixous", Ashley Thompson (trans.), *New Literary History* **37**(1), 1–13 [see "Du mot à la vie: un dialogue entre Jacques Derrida et Hélène Cixous", (2004)].

—— with Frédéric-Yves Jeannet, "The Book that You Will Not Write", Thomas Dutoit (trans.), *New Literary History* **37**(1) (Winter), 249–61.

Index

unconfessable and literature 28
unconscious and writing 23–4, 54, 67–8, 132, 167
    dreams 6, 28, 43–5, 55, 67, 68, 70–71, 130
understanding 12, 20–21, 68, 69
    misunderstanding and interviews xiii–xiv
Université de Paris VIII, Vincennes: women's studies course 52, 58–60, 85–6
untranslatability 171–2
USSR 89

Verdi, Giuseppe 149
Vincennes *see* Université de Paris VIII
violence and writing process 28, 55, 129
voice(s) 9–10, 86, 132, 161, 165, 166–7
    see also spoken word and written word

Wagner, Richard 149
"wandering" and writing 3–4
Wittig, Monique 64, 65
women
    repression 61–2, 63–4
    situation in Algeria 136
    situation in France 64, 86
    transgression in painting 147

see also femininity in writing; sexual difference
women's studies course 52, 58–60, 85–6
Woolf, Virginia 17
word play 171–2
world, state of the world 180–82
writing process 1–48
    effect of illness 28
    and emancipation of women 63
    fecundity of output 6–7, 51–2, 77
    and femininity 22, 49–78
    and language 35–6
    and painting 145–7
    physical demands 56
    practice and training 6
    and sexual difference 22, 36–7, 53–4
    and theatre 95–122
    and violence 28, 55, 129
    and voices 167
    and "wandering" 3–4
    writing/living conflict 16–17, 139
    see also unconscious and writing
written word and spoken word xii–xiv, 15–16, 27, 166–7

Zola, Émile 84

2407